The Road
to Mass
Democracy

The Road to Mass Democracy

Original Intent and the Seventeenth Amendment

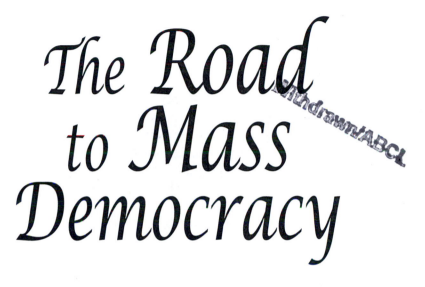

C. H. Hoebeke

With a new introductory essay and epilogue by the author

Transaction Publishers

New Brunswick (U.S.A.) and London (U.K.)

Library of Congress Catalog Number: 2014020897
ISBN: 978-1-56000-217-8 (cloth); 978-1-4128-5480-1 (paper)
Printed in the United States of America

Library of Congress Cataloging-in-Publication Data

Hoebeke, C. H. (Christopher Hyde), 1960-
   The road to mass democracy : original intent and the seventeenth amendment / C. H. Hoebeke.
      pages cm
   Includes bibliographical references and index.
   ISBN 978-1-4128-5480-1
   1. United States. Congress. Senate--History. 2. United States. Congress. Senate--Elections. 3. United States. Constitution. 17th Amendment. 4. Democracy--United States--History. 5. Representative government and representation--United States--History. 6. Legislative bodies--Upper chambers. I. Title.
JK1161.H55 2014
328.73'0734--dc23
                                                        2014020897

To all the king's horses, and all the king's men

Contents

An Introductory Essay

The Paradox of Popular Sovereignty

One of the perks of working in an international university is talking with students from around the world. Only days before the military coup in Cairo last summer, I asked one of our Egyptian students his opinion of the tumultuous events in his country. He had already earned his master's degree several months before and was auditing a second area of studies for as long as his father could afford to keep him safe in Sweden, or until civil conditions had stabilized at home. The young man was unabashed in expressing his hopes for the army to step in and take control from the elected government: "Democracy doesn't work in our country."

In the building where I live work two cleaning women from the Balkans. My wife occasionally talks with them about our respective homelands. One is a Macedonian whose family fled the ethnic violence that followed the breakup of Yugoslavia. The other is a Serb who grew up in Bosnia. Her father disappeared and is presumed dead and buried somewhere in a mass grave. Although they acknowledge that things have improved in recent years, they maintain that tensions still seethe, the infrastructure is a wreck, and there are no jobs. Neither woman is old enough to have lived under the iron rule of Marshal Tito, but both nostalgically remember a more authoritarian, yet more peaceful time, a time when "we were all Yugos."

These conversations do not conclusively prove anything other than that democracy is not the universal aspiration that US secretaries of state might assume it to be. Nevertheless, a categorical proposition is false, so the logicians tell us, if a single example to the contrary is true, and the modern world can furnish millions of such contrary examples, of men and woman for whom having an equal say in their country's political direction is not as high a priority as having public order, a means of livelihood, and a degree of certainty that the rules around which they plan their commerce and social transactions will be the same tomorrow as they are today and enforced equally for one as for all.

Indeed, judging from American political events in the two decades since *The Road to Mass Democracy* was originally published, these prerequisites of liberty do not seem to adhere merely from the universal right of suffrage. Despite the fact that practically any warm body not convicted of a felony may cast a vote for the highest office in the land, the government of the United States is more intrusive and more arbitrary than at any time in its history. The solicitation of votes by our increasingly poll-driven, image-conscious politicians, obliged at all times to appear in public as regular folk, coincides miraculously with government's runaway legislation, regulation, confiscations, violations, currency inflation, and war.

However widely accepted, or at least tolerated, by the mass electorate, the regular activities of the regime in Washington are not merely unconstitutional. They are *anti-constitutional*, opposed to the purposes for which the Constitution was created. Take, for example, the founders' concern about "mutability of legislation." An often expressed fear at the constitutional convention and in the ratification debates was that the proliferation of new laws, which were frequently repealed, superseded, or in conflict with other laws, made it impossible for the average citizen to know the rules or the consequences of not observing them. Two-and-a-quarter centuries after checks and balances were instituted to inhibit this "excess of lawmaking," it is the members of Congress, themselves, who can not keep pace, as they routinely ratify volumes of legislation they have not even read.

According to those checks and balances, "All legislative powers herein granted shall be vested in a Congress of the United States." It is simply no longer true. Our representatives in Washington could not churn out such a massive heap of enactments without the army of unelected staffers and lobbyists who in reality control the legislative process. Of course, without vetting and discussion by constituted authority, it is a lawless legislative process, adding new meaning to the Government Publication Office's *Statutes at Large*. And this colossal compendium of US legislation does not include the thousands of executive orders, judicial rulings, and regulatory agency decrees that have the force of law, blindsiding unwary citizens with forfeiture of property and freedom on a daily basis.

"The right of the people to be secure in their persons, their houses, their papers, and effects, against unreasonable searches and seizures" is as much imperiled by recent regimes as it was under King George III. Without so much as a knock on the door, the FBI, DEA, ATF, ICE (formerly INS), or any of the numerous federal agencies with a special weapons and tactics unit can come crashing into family dwellings, guns drawn, demanding submission and ready to open fire at the least show of resistance. The Fish and Wildlife Service has a paramilitary arm, and apparently so does the Department of Education.[1] With the advent of "civil forfeiture," compliments of the War on Drugs, property involved in an alleged crime is liable to be confiscated even if the owner of the property was not involved in or had no knowledge of the criminal activity in question. Captured cash and auction proceeds from property thusly acquired has become a growing source of revenue for governments at all levels.

Since the initiation of the War on Terror, government trespasses have taken an even darker turn. Not only are Americans liable to be detained without charges, trials or lawyers, but the executive branch claims the right to abduct anyone, anywhere to be rendered abroad for "enhanced interrogation," outsourcing in what less euphemistic times would have been called cruel and unusual punishment. And in what has to be the greatest abuse of authority to date, the president's men maintain a "kill list" from whom the Commander-in-Chief can select human beings, US citizens included, to be terminated on sight. Within hours, or minutes, of this death sentence imposed by the chief executive on the basis of secret evidence, unmanned flying machines drop fire from the sky, and any women, children, or wedding guests unfortunate enough to be in the vicinity of these sneak attack are written off as "collateral damage."[2] Two centuries ago, representatives of the British colonies in America declared their independence from an arbitrary monarch:

> For depriving us in many cases, of the benefits of Trial by Jury:
> For transporting us beyond Seas to be tried for pretended offences.

Today, public officials call for inquiries and the arrest of citizens who expose the same offenses and worse.

At least we are not forced to quarter troops, and as long as home construction continues to be fueled by Fed-sponsored bubbles, we might never have to. The low-interest lending and high-volume currency creation that encourages these housing booms are among the chief props supporting the debtor economy in general and the prodigal spending of the world's number-one debtor in particular. As with other activities of government, this inflationary policy is at odds with the purposes of the Constitution's authors. It is not by mere happenstance that the Constitution grants Congress the power to *coin* money, while no mention is made of the power to *print* it.

Respectable opinion might differ on the constitutionality of paper money. The consensus at the constitutional convention seemed to be that the expressed power to borrow implied the power to issue IOUs, which creditors could use as negotiable instruments in trade. But the delegates were only too familiar with the saying "not worth a Continental," a disparaging reference to the paper currency that had collapsed into worthlessness by the end of the Revolutionary War it was intended to finance. They wished to avoid drawing attention to a power which, combined with the power to regulate the value of money, could be construed as a license for the government to print away its debts with inflated paper. Hence, the Constitution's authors left the power to print money at best vaguely implied, striking out a clause expressly granting the power to "emit bills" of credit.[3]

In 1913, when Congress delegated its currency regulating responsibility to the Federal Reserve (critics would say abdicated its responsibility to a private banking cartel), the justification was that technical experts would expand and contract the money supply according to rational economic assessments rather than under the political pressures faced by elected officeholders. But the history of the Fed provides few examples of monetary contraction and a long, steady history of monetary expansion. However justified in the disquisitions of learned economists, the elastic money supply accommodates what appears to be an eternal extension of credit to the US government. It remains to be seen whether the debts will be paid and, if so, whether the dollars returned will approximate their worth at the time of the loan or the worth of a Continental.

Throughout history, the most popular pretext for public debt and paper money has been for the support of war. Although the modern welfare state advances numerous social problems to be redressed with similar fervor and commitment of public resources, expenditures for defending the nation against enemies real and imagined traditionally elicit support from both sides of the trough. Since Congress no longer declares war, its main role now is to make appropriations, even for weapons and equipment that the generals and admirals insist they do not need but that provide lucrative contracts to campaign donors and jobs to constituents. This explains why the human horror that was visited upon the United States with mere box cutters on 9/11 was met with requisitions for submarines, fighter jets, bombers, and missile defense systems. The spending of the United States on the upkeep of its hundreds of bases in scores of countries, on maintaining state-of-the-art weaponry, and supporting its extensive combat operations exceeds the military expenditures of the next several highest military budgets in the world combined. It comprises half of the "discretionary spending" requested of the US government for fiscal year 2014. The Pentagon's budget does not include the scores of billions annually associated with nuclear weapons research, veteran's benefits, pensions to retirees and widows, military aid to foreign countries, or the counter-terrorism and snooping activities of the Homeland-affiliated agencies. Truly, as General Smedley Butler stated, "War is a Racket."[4] Fortunately for the cause, we have the elastic money supply to support these critical needs.

The last Congressional declaration of war came three quarters of a century ago. Since then Congress has issued authorizations for the commander-in-chief to do as he intended, with or without its authorization, or to provide a fig leaf of constitutional cover for a war in which he had already involved the nation's forces. The executive prerogative to initiate war has waxed, the expectation of prior deliberation by the legislature has waned, and military adventures have become unsurprisingly routine. A Congress disposed to deliberate might have granted Letters of Marque and Reprisal[5] to apprehend and punish the conspirators who attacked the World Trade Center and Pentagon. Instead, our Congress acquiesced in the president's open-ended crusade to rid the world of evildoers, a cause being fought on even more fronts with the change of administrations.

A country founded in suspicion of standing armies and entangling alliances, in the belief that war was the greatest destroyer of liberty that could befall a people, has sacrificed the blessings of two oceans and militarily weaker neighbors in exchange for the self-appointed responsibility of garrisoning the world. It is a posture that prompts foreign lobbies to intrigue over American military deployment and makes every outpost a tripwire, every provincial quarrel a matter of national honor, a sacrifice of blood and wealth which is sold to the voters as an existential struggle. It has failed to achieve the peace and security for which it has ostensibly been waged, and there seems to be no end of it in sight before we are too bankrupt to continue.

War, debt, and arbitrary power: such is the state of the union twenty years after the first publication of *The Road to Mass Democracy: Original*

Intent and the Seventeenth Amendment. The amendment, which transferred the election of United States Senators from state legislatures to the people directly, is not exclusively—or even primarily—responsible for the ravages of American officialdom in the twenty-first century. But as much as the book is a history of the Seventeenth Amendment, it is also a philosophical criticism of mass democracy, which I continue to believe is at the root of the current troubles. Unlike other studies which interpret the amendment in the context of machine politics in the Gilded Age or the regulatory reforms of the Progressive Era, mine has taken, as has been pointed out, an "external" view[6] in which the direct election of senators is seen within a broader—and in my thesis, an ongoing—movement to democratize the American political system.

The fact that the amendment has not been followed by constitutional amendments enabling the recall of elected federal officials or establishing popular initiatives and referenda at the national level has been offered as a refutation of this thesis. In answer, I have refined some of my conclusions in the Epilogue and pruned the phrasing elsewhere, but the core argument stands. The point of the book was to illustrate, through the events that brought about the direct election of senators, a historical disregard for constitutional restraints. The fact that the federal Constitution did not become pockmarked with amendments, as the state constitutions became in the decades before the popular election of senators, is less significant than the surrender of the Senate's role in restraining the excesses of popular government. With senators elected directly, it turned out to be easier to ignore, bypass, or misinterpret the Constitution than to amend it. (But it should also be noted that whenever a portion of the population is sufficiently disaffected, there is rarely a shortage of proposals for constitutional change).

The "internal" explanations for the Seventeenth Amendment have not been slighted or overlooked and are in fact integral to the story. Chapter 5 summarizes the pre-amendment performance of the senators in the bicameral legislative process and in executive matters requiring their Advice and Consent. Their role in refining federal legislation, deliberating foreign policy, and protecting the interests of the states which sent them, particularly in matters of appointments and appropriations, tended to be one of delay, which, even if by constitutional design, made the Senate unpopular with the muckraking press as well as with special interests impatient for quicker results from government. Chapter 6 narrates the role of the "Progressive bosses" in effecting a directly elected Senate, cutting out state legislators as middlemen and inaugurating a Senate lobbying process that now starts directly in the halls of Congress without first having to persuade or purchase a majority of legislators in a majority of state capitols.

But the two preceding chapters take a broader view in which is narrated the deterioration of representative processes in the states under the pressures of populism, followed by repercussions to the intended federal procedures. These repercussions manifest themselves in the popularly sanctioned collapse of the Electoral College completed in the Jacksonian Era and the all-but-popular election of senators brought about by party primary nominations in the decades immediately preceding the Seventeenth Amendment.

The Road to Mass Democracy has been criticized for discounting states' rights as the primary reason for electing senators by state legislatures. One reviewer took me to task for thinking it "absurd" that the founders had arranged this manner of representation in the upper house of Congress.[7] James Madison came close to saying that very thing in the Convention but fell in line with the unanimous consensus when the issue was put to vote, and he defended the arrangement in *The Federalist.* Among the reasons he gave, the first was that it was an easy sell to the people, who were accustomed to having representatives to the Continental Congress appointed by state legislatures. Continuing this method of Senate appointments gave the states a vital role in the federal system, a role I have neither denied nor minimized.[8]

It overstates the case, however, to claim that senators were intended merely to serve as ambassadors from the states. Were that the case, they would have served at the pleasure of whoever appointed them rather than for six years without a provision for recall, removable only by a two-thirds majority of their Senate colleagues. They would have been expected to act exclusively on the instructions of the governments which sent them. Certainly, some in the Senate might have viewed themselves as ambassadors, but there were ample instances of senators acting with the deliberative independence for which the chamber had been uniquely constituted. We will not belabor the argument already made in Chapter 2, but in representing the states and not the people directly, the Senate was intended to approximate Montesquieu's idealized version of the British House of Lords[9]—without hereditary distinction, of course, but distinction of some kind—something refined and aloof, giving the Senate the inclination as well as the authority to resist political interests intent on swinging the stick of government without full consideration for the consequences. It would be representative of the people at heart but not elected in the same way or by the same criteria as the popularly elected House. The appointment would be more select, the tenure more secure, the rotation of its membership more gradual.

As the popularly elected House had the power to hold the Senate in check until the next election and the state legislatures that elected senators were themselves chosen by popular vote, the theory was that no legislation desired by the people would fail to be enacted as long as the desire was widespread and sustained. The founders, however, were more concerned with thwarting proposals for which there was only regional or temporary enthusiasm. Their diaries, correspondence, speeches, and published tracks demonstrate a profound distrust of simple democracy, where demagogues pulled strings behind a facade of popular support and profiteering middle men reaped unearned harvests from the chaos of fluctuating laws and policy. The framers' discussions were suffused with references to the balancing of monarchy, aristocracy, and democracy in a "mixed constitution," a concept originating with Greek and Roman political thinkers and evolving over the centuries. The idea was to enable the best of all three forms of government while avoiding the perversion of each: tyranny, oligarchy, and mob rule. Under a constitutional monarchy, the King, Lords, and Commons represented different social elements, but of course there was no question of instituting hereditary offices and titles in the American republic.

The challenge in the Convention was to appoint the monarchical president and aristocratic Senate in a manner different from that of the democratic House, so that each answered to a different type of constituency, supplying natural rivalry to check the interests in the other branches. In looking for the proper "complication of principles," the framers turned to the states as a constituency distinct from "the people." The states, after all, preexisted the union, and their jealousy and suspicion had already proven to be effective checks on the Continental Congress under the Articles of Confederation. The founders hoped that state legislatures would promote a higher caliber of statesman to the Senate, statesmen who would not have to curry favor with the masses in popular elections, but in more factious times they expected that the representatives of the states would act as a counterforce to the representatives of the people as well as to the executive branch. To complete the mix, the president was to be chosen by a college of electors, who were originally appointed at the discretion of the legislatures. All three elements had to act in concert for any proposal to become law at the national level, and none answered, in the immediate sense, to the same constituency.

The critic who discounts the founders' adherence to the classical notion of balancing "the one, the few, and the many," who sees the rationale for the original method of Senate elections solely in terms of states' rights, would assume that all was well until 1913, when the amendment took away the representation of state legislatures in favor of mass elections. Mass elections proved to be expensive, which necessitated today's alignment with moneyed interests, which, ironically, was among the chief complaints of reformers *before* the amendment. The interpretation is valid as far as it goes but does not explain why two-thirds of the Senate and three-fourths of the state legislatures (which are needed to pass a constitutional amendment) approved a resolution requiring the legislatures to abdicate their role in electing senators. Surely, significant populist groundwork had been laid in the states before they surrendered their corporate representation in the national government. As for the progressive's insistence that corrupt Senate elections demanded constitutional change, an amendment predicated on the malfeasance of the very agents who affected it invites skeptical inquiry.

As investigation revealed, the egalitarian folly of the states immediately after independence was the primary inducement for calling the convention to begin with. In that light, the framers' reliance on state legislatures to check the national democracy would seem to have been ill founded. I therefore presented it as almost inevitable that the states would collapse as distinctly represented agencies in the federal system, but in pointing out the chink in the constitutional armor, I never used the word "absurd." I have no idea what could have been done differently to establish the representational balance and governmental restraint that the founders were trying to achieve. The method they adopted lasted 125 years. The ill effects of its erosion are felt a century later. Had I summed up the original manner of Senate elections in a single word, it would have been "tragic."

The Seventeenth Amendment can not be described as a national encroachment on the representation of states when to all appearances the people of the states no longer believed in the importance of such representation. Indeed, among the highly mobile and rootless individuals of our modern world, Americans participate much less in local elections than in national elections and are likely to have stronger opinions about who should be president than who should be city councilman, if indeed they even know the names of anyone running for local office. With a hindsight not available to the founders, who could not have foreseen the loss of the local attachments upon which their system depended, we can see the limits of relying on state legislatures as a check on the national government.

Unlike some admirers of my work, as well as some of the critics, I am not an advocate of repealing the amendment, notwithstanding the urgent need to bind government to constitutional limits. This is not because I prefer the popular election of senators but because state legislatures proved themselves inadequate to the task when they ratified the Seventeenth Amendment in the first place. But neither do I oppose repeal, inasmuch as it would signify that a healthy majority of the American people, enough to pass a constitutional amendment, had accepted the need of an institutional check upon its political will.

The history of the Seventeenth Amendment underscores an essential paradox of popular sovereignty, which is that a people who respect their constitution have little need of one. It is a redundancy, a written testament to what is already etched in their character, whereas a people most in need of constitutional restraints is also the most intolerant of them and will not be bound by them for long.

Appreciating this paradox presupposes an understanding of constitutionalism different from that which prevails today. Modern constitutionalism focuses on individual rights that supposedly have been secured and protected through the power of government. The focus of the Convention, however, was on the powers to be delegated to the government and on the procedural rules that safeguarded the legitimate exercise of those powers. The original, unamended Constitution was not concerned with defining what private citizens had the right to do but with what the federal government had the right to do and under what circumstances. Indeed, the unamended Constitution, properly applied, made a Bill of Rights unnecessary, which is why its authors submitted it to the states for ratification without one.

In exchange for ratification, however, the states insisted on a list of popular rights that Congress could not abridge. For example, a state could establish a religion at taxpayer expense, as Connecticut and Massachusetts did for several decades after the First Amendment was ratified, and Congress could make no law concerning that establishment. Each state had its own bill of rights, but in so far as its relationship to the federal government was concerned, a state without a bill of rights could presumably administer cruel and usual punishment, insist on self-incrimination, and commandeer whatever muskets could be pried from the hands of its citizens. Or it could form its armed populace into a militia and secede from the union. Just to be safe, the Ninth Amendment stipulated that the proposed list of rights "shall not be construed to deny or disparage others retained by the people," while the Tenth Amendment provided that any powers not granted to the federal government, nor prohibited to the states, belonged to the states, or to the people, in that order.

Without the eight amendments that preceded them, the Ninth and Tenth were superfluous, for it is in enumerating the inalienable rights that the rights not mentioned become imperiled. The Ninth and Tenth Amendment catch-all clauses technically addressed Noah Webster's mock concern for the right to go fishing in good weather, but the very concept of a bill of rights contained the seeds for a radical shift in constitutionalism. The original emphasis on how government was constituted, how powers were defined and apportioned, and under what conditions they could be employed would in time give way to the preoccupation with discovering and protecting rights. In the aftermath of the Civil War, the Fourteenth Amendment's so-called "incorporation clause" was said to have applied the federal Constitution's Bill of Rights to the states, as in *neither Congress nor any state shall abridge* . . ., but after nearly a century and a half of usage, the rights incorporated are no longer limited to those plainly listed in the first ten amendments, and the strictures against violating them seem to apply to municipalities, county school boards, private businesses, volunteer organizations, and even families. In direct contrast to the intentions of those who insisted on a constitutional list of rights that the federal government could not abridge, the federal government became the actual arbiter of the list, which is another way of saying the arbiter of its own powers.

Both the Bill of Rights and the checks and balances of the unamended Constitution were intended to prevent arbitrary rule, but omitting a list of rights in the original version did not necessarily minimize the constitutional protection of freedom. Certainly, free speech, free press, free assemblage, and the evolutionary liberties that accord citizens due process before the law are rights worth defending, even with life. But carving them on sacred tablets does nothing to secure them for posterity. The globe is littered with dictatorships that have written bills of rights. The French guillotine and the Bolshevik firing squad both found service in regimes with popular privileges proclaimed in print, and no one in a position of power in the United States is going to jail for violating them now.

The genius of checks and balances is that they do not assume the benevolence of those who rule. The powers to make, enforce, and apply the law are in separate hands, which is the first defense against capricious government. In the case of the federal government the separation of powers was reinforced by a labyrinthine system of elections in which each branch was appointed in a different manner and for different tenures in office. A law could hardly be criticized as arbitrary, for example, if passage required a majority in two houses, one of which was chosen directly by the people, the other by state legislatures, and was also subject to the veto of a president who was chosen by an electoral college—a veto that could only be overridden by a two-third majority in both houses. Even then, having run the constitutional gauntlet to become law, if it should turn out that it in some way imposed *ex post facto* punishment, impaired the obligation of an existing contract, or enacted what was prohibited or unauthorized for the federal government to enact, citizens, states, and corporations had a remedy in court. Federal judges, nominated by the president and confirmed by the Senate, could be removed after impeachment by the House and a two-thirds vote in the Senate, but otherwise, their life tenures were intended to protect their scholarly, independent judgment without consideration for political interests, even of those who put them in office.

In the view of those Federalists who voted down a bill of rights in the original Constitution, it was the restraints imposed by checks and balances—the due process of lawmaking and law enforcement—that were the bulwark of liberty, not a catalog of rights declared on paper. But as a fortification against arbitrary rule, the system of checks and balances turned out to be hardly stronger than a bill of rights. To recall the paradox of popular sovereignty, without respect for the representative process, the fixed rules of constitutionalism are ignored and eventually discarded. We will not here retrace the history of the populist triumph over what in the book is termed the "representative hierarchy," but after several waves of reform intended to make government more responsive to the popular will, after the Electoral College had been stripped of its pretensions as a conclave of independent deliberation and representative government in the states had been sufficiently weakened by the direct legislation movement, state legislators surrendered their responsibility for electing US Senators in 1913.

A generation after the Seventeenth Amendment, and not before, Bill of Rights cases came to the forefront of constitutional issues. The timing suggests a possible corollary between the overthrow of the representative hierarchy and the rise of the rights industry determined to legislate through the courts. In any case, without the original hierarchy empowered to ensure governmental observance of constitutional processes, the system of checks and balances that depended on it collapsed. This resulted in the current free for all in which the executive and judiciary make law, Congress makes laws in areas beyond its authority, and rogue bureaucrats make confiscations and serve as judge, jury, and executioner in their own pet causes. The United States government had originally been fenced in by representative procedures for determining the reasoned expression of popular will at the national level, but under the banner of democracy and rights, it was set free to gallop anywhere inspired by the "living, breathing" Constitution.

Once government has escaped the fold, it is difficult to return it to its confines. Yet in an age when we have the power to obliterate ourselves and most other life in our dominion, whether by government or by the lack of it, the restoration of deliberation and restraint is worth consideration. To achieve that restoration, we should recognize the value of separating powers and ensuring their separation via checks and balances. I am open to suggestions about the best way of doing that, but I can only think of two: hereditary hierarchy or elective hierarchy. My preference for the latter is probably an inherited prejudice, for as is true of most Americans, my ancestors were not aristocrats. But I would also like to see elective hierarchy succeed because I like a challenge, and historically, the odds are against natural aristocracy and the republic of reason.

I can hear minds closing at the suggestion of rebuilding a political elite on the prejudices of the slave-owning patriarchs who wrote the Constitution. Before defending those patriarchs and their political assumptions, let us stipulate that America is better for having ended slavery and given women and minorities the right to vote. This does not mean that everything about the present is better than the past, or that the present is more-clear eyed and less prejudiced in every respect with regard to politics. If the founding generation, for example, based the right to vote on qualifications we find objectionable today, it does not follow that the vote should be accorded to everyone without any consideration of merit whatsoever. If poll taxes and literacy tests were unfairly administered in the past to exclude voters on account of race in some states, it is not necessarily the case that they are incapable of being administered fairly to exclude the poorly informed, or the transient passerby with no real stake in the community, or the incorrigible drain on the public purse.

And just because property qualifications existed when only white men could vote, it does not mean women and minorities would have to be excluded from the suffrage if property qualifications were in effect today. The ideal of the freehold property requirement premised that votes were less corruptible if every voter had a clear title to enough land to provide for his (or her) family. To modern ears, if such a notion does not sound racist or sexist, it sounds *classist*, or at best quaint and impracticable. After all, there is little chance of restricting the vote to freeholders when it already extends to the vast majority of landless tenants and heavily mortgaged "owners." Nevertheless, it is interesting to speculate on the contractual terms for agribusinesses, waste disposers, drillers, miners, and frackers if today's mega-corporations had to negotiate their land use rights with a regime of independent family farmers and homesteading commuters.

Dismissing the founders out of hand because some of them had slaves and because women did not vote is a form of ideological prudery that overlooks a great deal of history and judges from a very selective slice of it. Taking a sufficiently broader view, we can appreciate that conquered whites were slaves in Greece when Aristotle wrote his *Politics*. European mariners and coastal villagers were being sold in the Barbary markets when the constitutional convention met in 1787. The majority of delegates in Philadelphia did not own slaves. Those who did were aware of the moral dilemma and hopeful that the institution would die out under economic forces (instead, it gained new life with the advent of the cotton gin, geographic expansion, and the insistence of the upwardly mobile to have the same property rights as the old families had).

Had the states that were already emancipated from this inherited dilemma formed a free state confederation in 1787, rather than agreeing to the Three-fifths Compromise to keep the slave states in the union, the union might have been more morally consistent. To have allowed the original seven states to secede from the Union in 1861, not readmitting them until they had abolished slavery, might have been more *constitutionally* consistent. Aside from possibly keeping the four border states from joining the secession and sparing the nation the greatest loss of life in its history, it would have spared both sides the fate of mass conscription, paper money, and the precedent-setting damage to the separation of powers brought about by the Civil War.

As for patriarchy, it is easy to dismiss the less enlightened past before the right of female suffrage. In the long view, however, the women's vote followed rather swiftly after that of the men, for in the greater part of recorded history, most men have been subjects without political rights, sometimes even subjects of women with hereditary titles. In the early days of the republic, after the American revolutionaries rejected hereditary distinctions, suffrage did not extend to all men, but it did extend briefly to propertied single women in New Jersey. As the suffrage movement gained momentum, women in many states had the right to vote in national elections before the Finns, Norwegians, and Swedes. Throughout the nineteenth and early twentieth centuries, women wielded increasing political clout, until two-thirds of each house in Congress concurred in a resolution to amend the Constitution, a resolution ratified by three-fourths of the state legislatures, thereby binding the remaining minority of the country to grant voting privileges to women throughout the land. Whether or not the Nineteenth Amendment was a victory over the supposed misogyny of the founders, it was definitely a victory for the several generations of women and men who followed the Constitution and prevailed in the deliberative process which the founders had established.

Detractors who measure women's equality against a standard of perfection that has historically never existed are free to repudiate what the founders thought about government. The same for those who do not wish to look past the centuries of struggle between Europeans, Africans, and indigenous North Americans—as if slavery and race conflict were not prehistoric problems that affected other parts of the world and continue to do so even today. But for those with an interest in prudent statecraft and self-government, *The Federalist*, like Aristotle's *Politics*, will continue to be read in other times and other lands, even if it ceases to be regarded in the land of its origin.

Certainly, a constitutional restoration need not be based on the suffrage opinions of the caucasian gentlemen of the eighteenth century. The standards for voting should be subject to review by every generation, but the point is that there be standards. Currently, the main defense against freeloaders and illiterates would seem to be voter apathy, which celebrity do-gooders are trying to overcome using get-out-the-vote campaigns that insist it doesn't matter whom you vote for "as long as you vote." They have obviously not pondered the consequences. As technology improves the means of registering mass opinion and politics continues its downward slide into entertainment for the lowest common denominator, we shall likely have the chance to verify if lack of universal participation was the fundamental problem after all or if, having finally perfected the "voter app,"[10] we have resurrected and improved upon the age of free bread and circuses. The Roman world was laughing when it died, according to the fifth-century monk Salvian of Marseille.[11] The modern refusal to take seriously the basic prerequisites for participating in politics will not likely end well for the polity.

Defining qualifications is but the beginning. We must also share an understanding of government's inherent limits. The objective of politics is to affect policy, to get government moving in a desired direction. But government, or at least government as administered by the state, is in its essence an instrument of coercion. Democratic governments are no different. In almost every vote there is a winner and loser. Every appropriation approved by the majority is a confiscation in the view of those in the minority. The losers do not get to take their belongings and go home. They must comply or apply counterforce to overthrow or secede. If victorious, they will sooner or later face a minority or an individual within their association who feels an injustice in the common course. There is no inherent unanimity to be expressed simply because everyone has an equal vote on every issue at every level.

Homo sapiens are free-willed individuals in an uncharted universe of possibilities. There is no end to their ingenuity in improving their condition. Their ability to work together in common enterprises, to trade talents and resources for mutual benefit, seems to advance the entire species, if not equally at once, at least for all incrementally. But freedom also sows division. Each member of any association must continually accommodate or overcome the will of others. The more extensive the realm of cooperation and commerce, the greater the opportunity for increasing the general welfare, but also the greater chance of conflict among the increased aggregation of interests.

To acknowledge this potential of free-willed beings in free association is to appreciate the limits of politics. The sense of personal regard radiates outwardly to family, neighbors, colleagues, members of social groups, and so forth. Nobody has yet expressed it better than Burke reflecting on the revolution in France:

> To be attached to the subdivision, to love the little platoon we belong to in society, is the first principle (the germ as it were) of public affections. It is the first link in the series by which we proceed towards a love to our country, and to mankind.[12]

These smaller associations require "government" in the sense that their members must observe expected rules of behavior, but the rules are socially rather than legally prescribed. The more extensive the association and remote from personal familiarity, the less likely that its government will rest on social consent than on formal legislation and mandatory enforcement. This corollary explains why classical writers on the subject of small-"r" republicanism could not envision a popular government over an area larger than the city-state.

Whatever the size of the realm, having equal participation in its political process is not synonymous with the government of one's self. Self-government is a separate realm, encompassing the responsibility we bear for our own well-being as well as the goodwill we share with those in our association. The decisions we make for ourselves, the uses we make of our possessions, and the persons with whom we choose to keep company are by definition preferable to those that are forced on us. As soon as we appeal to the state, we invoke a restriction on someone's ability to act, an appropriation of someone's property, or an intrusion into someone's choice of affiliation. Whether or not the decree is arrived at democratically, we are ultimately resorting to force, and we should remember that the same force is available to any faction having interests in conflict with ours.

If we preferred governing ourselves to being governed, we would invoke the state sparingly. If Father Zossima is correct that the urge to make great gestures for humanity tends to go hand in hand with a tendency to treat individual human beings with contempt,[13] we need to bear in mind that the wider the realm being governed, the larger the force to be potentially wielded—whether on our behalf or against us. We should therefore wish to deploy state power at the level of government that is as close to our personal association as circumstances permit. The smaller the association, the greater our ability to deliberate within it, to hear out the opposition personally and present our case in detail. It would make more sense to reason with our neighbors in the town hall before lobbying for national legislation.

Also, the smaller the association, the greater the weight of our individual vote. In national decisions, our direct vote would be diluted among hundreds of millions. Deliberation among so large a mass is categorically impossible, which is one of the chief reasons for preferring representatives. But when those elected rely on focus groups, opinion polls, and media consultants, rather than on their own sense of the common good, the election of representatives merely preserves the outward form of republicanism. The animating spirit is closer to that of mass democracy.

The passion for equality is destructive to the representative process, for representation itself is a form of inequality, wherein the elected have the prerogative to propose, discuss, and cast votes on matters that the rest of us do not. We can only appeal to counterforces in the representative system or wait it out and elect new representatives. But modern democracy rests on an assumption that it is technologically possible to rule by the plebiscite, or by what amounts to nearly the same thing, the browbeating of representatives with polling data and electronic media blitzes, as if, even at the level of the continental nation state, the decision-making process requires no hierarchy. The *Road to Mass Democracy* argues otherwise: In any large political sphere there is always a hierarchy, a smaller elite to raise the issues and promote the cause, and in the case of democracy, to return favors to the supporting interests that fund the campaign machinery.

If representatives were promoted to *represent* constituencies in the national deliberations rather than to divine and register popular decrees, the hierarchy would at least be openly visible. The democratic facade we have applied to the original structure, by contrast, is buttressed by two party hierarchies operating largely outside the constitutional procedures, an overwhelmingly successful duopoly that has managed in almost every election throughout the 50 states to limit the choice to either Republican or Democrat. Considering how ardently the founding generation hoped to prevent the formation of permanent political parties, the Constitution of the United States stands out in this regard as an epic failure. In fairness to the founders, the social bonds so critical to self-government have likely deteriorated to the point that most voters only care whether the candidate for local sheriff or county clerk belongs to the party that supports or opposes the president of the United States. Casting a ballot demands no more deliberation than exercising an ideological reflex.

This convenience comes at a cost. We have noted that, as merely one among millions, the direct vote of an individual would carry no weight whatsoever in national decisions. Participation at all is limited to ratifying or rejecting what the party leaders have proposed, while the information about those proposals is watered down for mass consumption, the details and motives being known only to a few. Ironically, plebiscitary government proves not to be particularly accountable to the people. Every so often the injustices of insider politics and corporate graft provoke a grassroots movement of protest—a Tea Party on the right, a Wall Street occupation on the left, a Populist Party, a Reform Party, and so forth—but the oligarchs adapt and survive for they are operationally necessary to maintain the myth of democratic government on the scale of the nation state.

The cost of mass democracy is greater still in that providing the individual an equal share in the highest decisions of state, however illusory it proves to be in practice, coincides with the highest levels of the state deciding on the smallest decisions of communities and individuals. As De Tocqueville explained, "The principle of equality suggests to men the notion of a sole, uniform, and strong government" and "imparts to them a taste for it."[14] In equality's ruthless logic, what is right for one must be right for all. Affairs that could be settled between ladies and gentlemen become concerns for the civil authority, and any solution is an injustice that it is not nationally uniform. As democracy subordinates the government of self to the desire to govern everyone else, and governing everyone else requires consolidating power, we end up with a federal government popularly expected to settle matters pertaining to marriage, child rearing, education, housing, insurance, retirement and inheritance—the whole progress of private life.

Such matters are not only beyond its authority but often beyond its competence. Within the sovereign realm of over 300 million people disbursed across a continent, the federal government, when compared to levels of government closer to home, is the least visible to constituent oversight and the least amenable to personal persuasion. Of course, self-governing individuals would prefer to resolve their issues socially. When that can not be achieved, however, the preferred level of government intervention would, as we have stated, be the lowest possible. A national referendum would not settle the moral and philosophical disagreements Americans have over the subjects of unwanted pregnancies, same-sex unions, reciting the Pledge of Allegiance in school, or smoking pot, even if every eligible voter of the nation had an equal ballot in the decision. On the contrary, without changing a single opinion, it would simply become a target for the opposition to overturn in the next plebiscitary skirmish, providing fodder for the media warfare that keeps the political parties and talking heads in business.

Local variation on such issues might offend righteous sensibilities, but it allows for resolution on a level closer to that of self-government. To recall, self-government is a realm wherein politically irreconcilable differences might be reconciled without politics, where the "little platoons" of friendship and kinship hold more sway than the written law. In this realm, promoting "family values" on a national political platform seems grossly superfluous, and proposing constitutional amendments either to prevent or protect abortions and homosexual marriages reflects a poor understanding of what a federal constitution is meant to accomplish, as well as a naive, or perhaps cynical, expectation of what it *can* accomplish.

The urge to make law is not a characteristic of law abiding people, no more than an increased presence of police indicates more peaceful streets or a battery of medical regulations reflects a healthy population. On the contrary, the lawmaking regime seems to thrive best where the responsibility for self is least in evidence. To appreciate fully the link between undisciplined individuals and the unrestrained exercise of state power in democratic governments, I commend the writings of Claes Ryn, and before him, Irving Babbitt,[15] but for our purposes, it is sufficient to recall our opening observations on the current state of the republic. America's proliferating legislation and endemic lawsuit culture are contemporaneous with its unpayable public debts, its unwinnable wars, and its growing police-state tendencies.

The paradox of popular sovereignty holds that constitutional restraints on government have no force beyond the respect they are given by the sovereign people. A constitution imposes procedural impediments to the deployment of state power in order to protect self-government, by which we mean the voluntary undertakings and free associations sustained by individual conscience and social norms rather than by statute and government enforcement. When self-government is widely understood as fulfilling one's personal and social obligations, the impediments are hardly necessary. When it is confused with equality of political participation, the impediments are removed or circumvented to make government more responsive.

There is no telling what happens once the constitutional discipline has departed. Plebiscitary rule tends to vote for more of everything at state expense. Generally there is less accountability and greater fluctuation in the law. That could bring us to the point where the stability of authoritarianism is popularly preferred to the alternative of anarchy, or what the founders called "licentiousness." Or it could bring secession and dissolution, perhaps over the very social issues that can not be resolved nationally. Whatever the direction of America's future, it is hubris to forget that all empires have perished, some of the greatest of which began as republics.

On the other hand, some nations have managed, even if briefly, to rekindle an awareness of their original principles. The constitutional structure of the founders is basically intact, minus the manner of Senate elections, but the states would likely require constitutional repairs of their own before being re-entrusted with the role they abandoned a century ago. Perhaps, instead of states, the Senate could represent guilds or professions—distinct communities of some kind. Or perhaps, with a simplified, no-loopholes tax code, it could represent those contributing the most to the public treasury (which would at least make representation of the wealthy more transparent than it is now). At all events, merely to recognize that an upper house should represent something other than the undifferentiated mass brings us a step closer toward deliberative governance.

Restoration or not, we can always govern ourselves, whatever the form of government embodied by the state, so long as we are willing to face the consequences when Caesar is offended. My student friend from Egypt understandably prefers his exile and managed to obtain another educational deferment. Sadly, he was summoned home anyway. We have a mutual friend from Eritrea, which, to my knowledge, has not had a national election in its history, allows freedom of worship to only a handful of Christian denominations and Sunni Islam, and has no freedom of speech or press. Nevertheless, he was eager to return home after his studies and warmly extended an invitation for me to visit. He is living proof that government is not the wellspring of human happiness.

When last we spoke, he confessed how much he admires America, particularly its economic freedom with its fabled rags-to-riches possibilities. His Eritrean countrymen, so he said, believe, like Americans, that "self-reliance is the key to success." He clapped his hand to his heart, bowed his head slightly in my direction, and exclaimed, "I am pro-USA, very pro-USA."

Far be it from me to disagree.

Malmö, Sweden

January 2014

Notes

1. Elizabeth Flock, "Education Department Agents Raids California Home." *Washington Post* (June 13, 2011), http://goo.gl/4xe1tf.
2. Chris McGreal, "Military given Go-ahead to Detain US Terrorist Suspects without Trial." *The Guardian* (December 16, 2011), http://goo.gl/LFUOE9,

Globalising Torture: CIA Secret Detention and Extraordinary Rendition.
Open Society Justice Initiative (February 2013), http://goo.gl/CtjrHn; Glenn
Greenwald, "Three Myths about the Detention Bill." *Salon* (December 16,
2011), Politics, http://goo.gl/Ttv2mj; Jo Becker and Scott Shane, "Secret
'Kill List' Proves a Test of Obama's Principles and Will." *The New York Times*
(May 29, 2012), http://goo.gl/dlBzbb.

3.   James Madison and E. H. Scott, *Journal of the Federal Convention* (Lawbook
      Exchange, 1898), p. 543, http://goo.gl/mfY9dO.

4.   Scheer, Robert. "Indefensible Spending." *Latimes.com.* June 1, 2008. http://
      goo.gl/VzqAl6; "Federal Spending: Where Does the Money Go?" *National
      Priorities Project.* Accessed December 09, 2013. http://goo.gl/FnsKAf;
      Smedley D. Butler, *War Is a Racket: The Antiwar Classic by America's Most
      Decorated Soldier* (Skyhorse Publishing Company, Incorporated, 2013).
      http://goo.gl/ipGMv0.

5.   H.R. 3076, 107th Cong. (October 10, 2001), http://goo.gl/NbNhI4.

6.   Todd J. Zywicki, review of *The Road to Mass Democracy*, *The Independent
      Review: A Journal of Political Economy* 1, no. 3 (Winter 1997), http://goo.gl/
      FTEJSN.

7.   *Ibid.*

8.   Madison, p. 129, http://goo.gl/VhbV97; Alexander Hamilton, James Madison,
      and John Jay, "The Federalist Papers. No 62.," - THOMAS (Library of Con-
      gress), http://thomas.loc.gov/home/histdox/fed_62.html.

9.   Charles De Secondat Baron De Montesquieu, *The Spirit of the Laws*, trans.
      Anne M. Cohler, Basia C. Miller, and Harold S. Stone, *Cambridge Texts in
      the History of Political Thought* (Cambridge University Press, 1989), p.160,
      http://goo.gl/R5WxVE.

10.   "Internet Voting Systems Too Insecure, Researcher Warns," *Computerworld*
      (March 1, 2012): http://goo.gl/QZClsJ.

11.   Salvian, the Presbyter. *The Writings of Salvian, the Presbyter.* Translated by
      Jeremiah F. O'Sullivan. Fathers of the Church Vol. 3. Catholic University of
      America Press, 2008, p. 187, http://goo.gl/reAc1L.

12.   Edmund Burke, *Reflections on the Revolution in France: And on the Pro-
      ceedings in Certain Societies in London Relative to That Event. In a Letter
      Intended to Have Been Sent to a Gentleman in Paris* (London: J. Dodsley,
      1791), pp. 68–69, http://goo.gl/CR8T0e.

13.   Fyodor Dostoyevsky, *The Brothers Karamazov*, trans. Constance Garnett, ed.
      Max Bollinger (London: World Classics, 2012), p. 63, http://goo.gl/JYRsoE.

14.   Alexi De Tocqueville, *Democracy in America*, trans. Henry Reeve (Oxford
      University, 1862), v. II, p. 354, http://goo.gl/h5vmFS.

15.   e.g., Claes G. Ryn, *America the Virtuous: The Crisis of Democracy and the
      Quest for Empire* (New Brunswick, U.S.A.: Transaction Publishers, 2003);
      Irving Babbitt, *Democracy and Leadership* (Boston; New York: Houghton,
      Mifflin, 1924).

Introduction

No nation should be subject to the whims of its rulers. Impulsiveness and political power are always a dangerous pair, no matter if the responsibility for governing rests with a king, a representative assembly, or with the people directly. This is admittedly not a very sophisticated idea, nor an original one, but is a sound one nonetheless, and the guiding thought in my study of American constitutionalism. From it follows the secondary, equally obvious idea that self-restraint, while laudable, is a more dubious safeguard in the exercise of sovereign power than political institutions and constitutional proscriptions that force the sovereign to think twice before plunging the nation into action. In a popular government such as ours, the existence, let alone the exertion, of such a counter-force is by definition *unpopular*. But the power of negating, hindering, stalling or obstructing is by no means tantamount to the power of coercing, and if it is liberty that we seek to protect and perpetuate rather than the unreflective motions of the majority, then over the long road we should all be grateful for those negative forces which keep us from passing too many laws, installing too many regulatory bureaucracies, from trespassing upon the rights of property, and overtaxing the private economy.

Historically, however, the American sentiment toward such restraining agencies has not been gratitude. Anyone who suggests that the popular majority might make wiser decisions if it were prevented from making hasty decisions is likely to be assailed for "not trusting the people," while defending the necessity of institutions with power to counter majoritarian urges invariably elicits the rebuke of "elitism."

This book relates the history behind a constitutional amendment that, more than any act to date, symbolizes America's traditional resentment of political constraints, an act representative in and of itself, but also the culminating episode to a generation of reforms intended to make government more "responsive" to popular demands, in addition to being the logical and almost inevitable consequence of popular discontents that had been fermenting since the earliest days of our republic. This book also relates the disappointing results of both the amendment in particular, and of the attempts to abolish constitutional constraints in general. Although my intentions were historical, my efforts confined to the narration of what took place generations ago, the assumptions on which the amendment was advanced still prevail in the general consensus of American political opinion. They are indeed phenomenally resilient assumptions which have persisted in the face of all our contrary experience and against the documented intentions of the Constitution's framers. Accordingly, I have been asked to provide an introductory statement regarding what practical efficacy this book might have concerning current politics, and offer some insight as to where these assumptions, unchecked, are likely to lead as we enter the twenty-first century.

I should first concede that, other than the two wishful thoughts of spurring statesmen to sacrifice popularity for principle and of reminding the electorate that not all grievances must be redressed at the highest levels in Washington, I did not undertake this work with any agenda in view, least of all that of proposing that two-thirds of both houses of Congress and three-fourths of the state legislatures should repeal a constitutional amendment. As I hope to make clear in the narrative, the fact that the American people had managed to enact this particular amendment was itself an indictment on the original constitutional provision; a constraint removed by those it was supposed to constrain could not have been a very strong one.

Not politics, then, but a simple curiosity motivated my initial inquiry into the Seventeenth Amendment, which in 1913 transferred the election of United States senators from state legislatures directly to the people. Why, I wondered, did Americans of that time choose to elect senators by popular vote, en masse, in a constituency of millions, when, under the previous procedure, they had only to vote in a county or district for a state legislator, who would in turn elect a senator on their behalf? In theory, at least, the original method was a more personable arrangement. The average citizen would not have his vote swallowed up in a state-wide constituency. There would be no need for mass-marketing Senate candidates, and therefore no justification for the prodigal spending a typical campaign requires. This in turn would reduce the necessity for financial support, and whatever political obligations such support entailed. Yet in the place of this once collegial arrangement the people of 1913 substituted the methods of what I have termed "mass democracy."

Without venturing onto ground to be covered later, mass democracy can be roughly defined as a form of government in which decisions are made by attempting to apply the principles of the old New England Town Meeting on a far more impersonal scale. In 1913 those principles found application in state-wide initiatives, referenda, recall elections, party primaries, and the direct election of senators. In our times the spirit manifests itself in the constant resort to opinion polls and in the near total domination of public discussion by the forums of mass media instead of by the deliberations of representative assemblies. More recently we have seen the implementation of "National Town Halls," with the President of the United States attempting to engage in direct, televised dialogs with the assembled citizenry in studio audiences around the country. We even hear talk of "electronic democracy," whereby the American multitudes can govern directly via the so-called Information Superhighway.

The idea of direct popular rule is, of course, at least as old as ancient Athens, but only with the technological achievements of the last century has it become practicable to attempt it in political entities larger than the city-state. Yet to the degree that the means of mass democracy are brought to bear on the course of government there is a corresponding debilitation of our original representative institutions. With political figures and interested parties now able to "send a message to the American people," as they say on the talk shows, and with the near instantaneous means of obtaining the popular response, we have come to expect very little in the way of independent discussion among our elected representatives, who often rise on the floors of Congress or state legislatures with no larger purpose than to cite the latest polling data or the tally of pros and cons from constituent phone calls, faxes, and the ubiquitous e-mail. In most states we can decide questions of policy directly for ourselves in the form of initiatives and referenda. At the federal level we can flood our Congressman with telegrams. Many of them have been solicitous enough to mail us questionnaires regarding our positions on the issues. But whether by direct, plebiscitary decisions, as in the case of state-wide initiatives and referenda, or virtual plebiscites, whereby elected officials are expected to do little more than register the decrees of their constituents, the form of government to which we are tending belies an abdication, or at least a significant and I believe dangerous diminution, of the traditional role of representative institutions.

Why do I say dangerous? The premise underlying all these innovations in our form of government is that the direct expression of the people more accurately reflects the general sense of the community and is less corruptible than judgments made by small assemblies invested with only temporary authority. But the methods adopted and the results achieved, as I shall attempt to demonstrate through the historical example of the Seventeenth Amendment, appear to be far more arbitrary and less accountable than our traditional means of representation. To begin with, direct appeals to state-wide constituencies or to the entire nation are invariably mass appeals, requiring that even the most sensitive and complex proposals be addressed to the lowest common denominator. Indeed, the Madison Avenue style campaigns of today's activists and politicians have not proven to be any less cynical than the backstage dealings that took place in the smoke-filled rooms of earlier times. Furthermore, mass appeal involves an inherent expense, not only in terms of sacrificing the kind of substantive debate that it is impossible to engage in en masse, but an expense in the literal sense of the word: Money. Although every citizen is allowed, even encouraged, to take part in the political process, the issues that come up for mass ratification, the contexts in which they are set forth, and the terms in which they are phrased are more than likely to be the issues, contexts, and terms chosen by those who fund the process.

Lastly, for all its innumerable ad hoc forums which can be tuned in or out with the ease of a remote control button, mass democracy inspires a demonstrable lack of interest and participation among the eligible electorate. In large part such apathy stems from the fact that the private citizen has been asked to consider more issues and more details than he can possibly devote his time to; and I suspect also in part because he senses the insignificance of his individual ballot. And then there are probably many Americans who refuse to dignify the sham choices that mass democracy seems to be offering: They vote not to vote. Certainly, if democratization is ever carried to the point where we conduct national referenda on legislation "which the people want and the special interests want defeated," I predict that the official electoral returns will mark an all-time high in popular indifference.

In other words, mass democracy cannot even claim to promote the will of the majority so much as the agenda of those who can organize and raise money for various private and local interests. In fact, its decisions can claim no greater sanction than that of pluralities—majorities only with respect to those who respond to questionnaires and opinion polls. However "scientific" a sampling that might be, it can never be *representative* in the traditional sense of the term. It can only substitute random, usually anonymous responses to "yes/no" questions in place of the documented debates of representative assemblies, mere numbers in place of those constitutionally designated forums where the great resolves of the past were hammered out by the delegates of our ancestors. And where there is less deliberation in government, there is concomitantly less restraint.

Although I admit to a prior, somewhat vague uneasiness about the trend toward what I now call mass democracy, I had developed no formal criticism of it before my investigation into the Seventeenth Amendment. Again, the focus was historical inquiry rather than political persuasion. Nevertheless, during the research and writing of this work there were a number of political events, of which I will mention only two, which confirmed that the propensities I perceived in the Seventeenth Amendment had by no means lost their strength. The first occurred in the autumn of 1987, when I was considering whether or not the amendment would provide enough material for a master's thesis. That was also the autumn that ended the distinguished judicial career of Robert H. Bork, and I must own that what I observed in his ill-fated nomination to the Supreme Court provided no small inspiration in my decision to diagnose and describe the vices of mass democracy.

As a twenty-seven year-old graduate student, plodding my way through books and ideas that should have been taught in high school, I had only a vague understanding of the *Originalist* versus *Activist* doctrines that were being disputed, but having watched the committee hearings live on daytime public television, the one aspect of the affair that I *did* understand was the thoroughgoing character assassination that took place on the nightly news and in the daily press accounts. It was disturbingly clear that certain senators, however charming and accommodating in the committee room, were shamelessly calumniating the nominee outside the Senate chamber. Equally disturbing were those deliberating statesmen who, under the guise of refraining from judgment until all the "facts" had been ascertained, were waiting to praise or bury the man as soon as the opinion polls arrived.

I consulted the Constitution to read for myself the definition of *Advice and Consent* in matters of presidential appointments. Alas, contrary to the claims of many who supported the president's nominee, there are no restrictions or qualifying criteria on the Senate's right of rejection. Hair, height, fashion sense, or favorite color—even judicial philosophy—senators may refuse a nominee for whatever combination of reasons persuade a majority of them to do so.

But if this is so, I wondered, then why the Roman circus? Why the need to incite the fears and passions of an otherwise content and uninterested public by the vilification of a respected jurist? To say that the court—having taken upon itself the responsibility to make, as well as adjudicate, the law—must necessarily suffer the pressures of organized interests, as any other legislative body, and that the appointment of its members is therefore bound to take on the characteristics of a political campaign, is to describe a symptom, not a cause, for it is inconceivable that an institution as weakly constituted as our third branch of government could usurp such power without a corresponding abdication from those originally entrusted with the legislative function.

The fact that the federal bench has become an extension of the political process, and even possesses the final word on political issues, is largely due to the appointment and confirmation of judges who view jurisprudence as politics by other means. Apparently, Congress has found it advantageous either to have its own laws, and those of the states, nullified in court, or to pass laws so vaguely worded as to require the opinions of judges to be understood. Apparently, a nominee who believes that personal opinions are, to the extent that it is humanly possible, irrelevant to the adjudicatory application of the law, is not what Congress wants. I say apparently, because if the situation were intolerable, we would have stopped appointing politically correct judges, and those already on the bench would by now have been impeached. That would arguably be an assault on the independence of the court, but certainly less so than the national referenda to which we now subject any nominee who has ever demonstrated an independence of mind.

The salient point of the Bork hearings, as it relates to my thesis, is not that the Senate simply capitulated to the polls. Favorable or unfavorable, no public opinion really existed before the circus began. The lesson, which I would subsequently learn many more times in researching a seemingly unrelated topic, was that a few interested politicians, backed by a sufficient alliance of lobbyists, could organize a mass propaganda campaign effective enough to convince the waiverers among their colleagues as to where lay the true direction of political expediency.

I could not claim from this one instance, of course, that senators and congressmen are always manipulating the popular mood to their own ends. Sometimes they genuinely seek to surrender to that mood when it can be determined, or to one of the other branches or agencies of government when it cannot. While in the beginning of my work the Bork Affair presented the contrived semblance of surrender, the Gulf War resolution three years later, when I was writing the conclusion to my manuscript, represented the real thing.

Whatever the merits of the cause or valor of those who undertook it, the general impression that the congressional debates preceding the conflict exhibited one of the finer hours of representative deliberations is grossly in error. Compared to the unambiguous declaration of hostilities against Imperial Germany in World War I, the equivocal statement sanctioning our offensive in the Persian Gulf could well be mistaken for the handiwork of an academic committee. In both conflicts public opinion was closely divided, and for those who had to make the awful decision the political stakes were as high as the strategic ones. In the former case, the Congress "authorized and directed" the president "to employ the entire naval and military forces of the United States . . . to carry on war," pledging "all the resources of the country" to defeat the foe. In the latter, it voted not to undermine the president's hand in a game of brinkmanship. The president, of course, has the constitutional responsibility to determine how the American military should be deployed, and generally the less interference from Congress the better, but the responsibility for determining whether or not the military should be used to begin with resides exclusively with the national legislature. In the design of our checks and balances, one wields the sword, but only after the other has drawn it. The wording of the "Resolution Authorizing the Use of Military Force Against Iraq," however, belied the abdication of that congressional responsibility on two counts.

In the first place, without specifying any of the sovereign interests America might actually have had in the region, the act to authorize force was issued "in order to achieve implementation of [United Nations] Security Council Resolutions 660, 661, 662, 664, 665, 666, 667, 669, 670, 674, and 677"—pursuant to Resolution 678. From the debates came the repeated implication that the United States was bound by treaty to uphold these decrees of the U.N., as if they came from higher headquarters and Congress could not be held accountable for the decision to wage war. In the second place, the act was not even a decision to wage war, but a decision to let the president decide. A far cry from that forceful proclamation which in 1917 *ordered* the Commander-in-Chief to take the field against the enemy, the resolution of 1991 actually put Congress on both sides of the issue, for it contained the type of provisos and reserve clauses which, with no inconsistency on the part of those who supported the military offensive, would have justified their creating a Special Committee to Second-Guess the President, had the results been unsuccessful, or worse, unpopular.

The president, whose knowledge of foreign affairs was obviously greater than his knowledge of the Constitution, maintained to the end that congressional approval was a superfluity, and during the months of military build-up declared that he would initiate the use of force at his own discretion, even if Congress expressly forbade it. Not every member acquiesced, but the peculiar means they chose to defend their prerogative set a new standard for sheer congressional timidity: Threatening to stop the chief executive with a law suit. This, too, provided yet another illustration of an elected assembly shunning its responsibility, for had the president unilaterally and unlawfully committed a half million Americans to combat in the Middle East, the Constitution makes no stipulation for deciding the political consequences in district court, but rather—and I hesitate to point this out—on the floor of the Senate with the Chief Justice presiding.

I am not claiming that Congress' cowardly behavior in either the Bork hearings or the Gulf resolution was the direct result of the Seventeenth Amendment, the purported topic of this book. But the ideological premises that brought us the direct election of senators continue to manifest themselves in the undermining of candor in debate and courage in resolve among those we choose to represent us. Democracy, as it was exalted by eighteenth century theory from a mere form of government to the highest end of mankind, has created a vicious cycle in our history, in which the supposition that there must be universal and direct participation in the highest affairs of state engenders a distrust of representative institutions, which breeds untrustworthy representatives, which leads to the reduction of their authority, and as a consequence, to smaller men seeking office, men whose sights are set on what can be gotten from power, not on what should be done with it, and whose collective performance in office almost inevitably brings calls for placing further limitations on representative assemblies. In this book I have illustrated this cycle in the history of state governments up to the point where the legislatures abdicated from their role as electors of the United States Senate. In this introduction I am suggesting that the same phenomenon seems to be taking place at the federal level.

Indeed, at the time of this writing, a strong recurrence of voter discontent promises to bring to Congress many new representatives and senators who, with the humility of Uriah Heep, have run for office on what amounts to an admission of their unfitness for it. The first thing on their agenda, should they attain the majority, is to change the Constitution to save us from the abuses of power they would otherwise commit. Amid their current proposals for remodeling the craftsmanship of the founding fathers, there is a pervasive assumption, the same assumption behind changes to state constitutions in the nineteenth century, that by striking a blow against the power of representative assemblies we are striking a blow for the common man against the special interests, that we are somehow restoring the popular control of government. But the validity of this assumption is never tested against our historical experience.

However sincere in their desire to reform, the proponents of constitutional change do not trouble themselves with finding the cause of the evils they seek to redress. They do not begin with the first principles set forth in *The Federalist* and trace the point where we began to go astray of them. They only know that government has grown too large and overbearing, and that Congress is concerned more with pleasing special interests and "insiders" than with promoting the general welfare. Yet they have never contemplated the remarkable coincidence between government expansion and representative corruption on the one hand, and our increasingly plebiscitary methods of politics on the other. It has never occurred to them that the strength and character of our original system of representative checks and balances might possibly have deteriorated *because* of, not in spite of, the generations of populist intrusions we have imposed upon it, and that their complaints might better be answered by increasing, not reducing, the scope of deliberation and the authority to act in representative assemblies.

Admittedly, this prescription will strike not a few readers as utterly deranged, given the low regard in which the Congress is generally held. But I am not advocating that we endow it with anything approximating absolute powers. We should, for example, hold fast to the right of the presidential veto, and—if we could promote impartial judges—to the custom of judicial review. We should not abandon the two-thirds majority required in the Senate to ratify treaties and remove federal office-holders, nor the two-thirds majorities required of both houses to override vetoes or submit constitutional amendments to the states. All those restraints inherent in the representative processes themselves, which force compromise among the factions and which serve to delay the schemes and frustrate the ambitions of demagogues, should be maintained and insisted upon by a vigilant citizenry. Even so, within those constraints, in all those affairs (and only in those affairs) that the Constitution delegates to the federal government, Congress' supreme power to legislate must be protected from the rival forces of mass democracy, and we should view with skepticism those who seek the office for the professed purpose of degrading it.

As I have already suggested, the alternative to strong representative institutions in a political sphere as sizable as the United States, or any individual state, for that matter, is by no means a more deliberative, more accountable government. To begin with, to whatever degree representatives are shorn of their power to legislate we must excuse their failures. We cannot blame those we have entrusted with very little for achieving very little. Least of all can they be blamed for failing to reduce the burdens and impositions of government. It was not statesmanship that created the colossus, and it is not by restricting the opportunities for statesmanship that the beast will ever be brought to heel. Socialism, like bankruptcy, requires nothing more artful than the steady habit of yielding to the desires of the moment. It is the natural drift of nations, and all the labored tactics manuals of the Marxist-Leninist vanguard proved quite unnecessary to attain it. By contrast, the adjustment of interests and constituencies to the required sacrifices of retrenchment would try the wisdom and courage of the best men and women we could find to represent us. It will not likely result from simply reshuffling the deck with term limits or constitutionally mandating that Congress collect in taxes what it distributes in entitlements.

Not least among the harms resulting from such constitutional tinkering is its tantamount admission that members of representative assemblies cannot, and should not, rise above the views of the localities and interests that placed them in power. Because we have recognized the chaos and ruin that ensues with "every member out for his own," we seek to restrict what the assembly may do collectively, yet at one and the same time we consider it an undemocratic pretension for members individually not to obey their constituents, not to promote their interests at all costs, even at the expense of the general welfare.

The logical corollary is that only someone elected by all the people could possibly represent the interests of the nation, an idea which first manifest itself in the Jacksonian presidency, but a constitutional fallacy which is not any more true for having been believed and practiced for the better part of two centuries. Technically, of course, the president has never been elected by the people, and, had it been more feasible to uphold the intentions of the framers, a presidential candidate would still rest his reputation before the 538 elders entrusted with the temporary office of Elector (or 535, assuming the Federal City was to remain politically neutral). He would not be sloganeering before the masses or selling images of himself to the scores of millions who will know him only through television and the newspapers. Furthermore, not only is it wrong to think of the president as the one representative who is "elected by all the people," but with the exception of his duties in foreign negotiations, it is erroneous to think of him as a representative at all. He is, or at least was designed to be, the executor of the laws and policies laid down by Congress.

In stark contrast to today's beliefs and practices, the Congress, and particularly the House of Representatives, originally the only branch to be elected by the people, was the initiator of policy and the director of government in the early years of the republic. Besides the fact that the framers did not confuse the legislative functions (deliberation and decision) with those of the executive (enforcement and administration), they did not suffer the modern delusion that a single man, however wise and impartial, could possibly know, let alone *represent*, the vast variety of interests in the nation more comprehensively than the collective minds of locally elected legislators. The difference between then and now was that the assembled members were expected to find and promote the common interest, not simply divide the nation's resources among their constituencies. Policy worked from the ground up, achieving national consensus by first refining and filtering the local views and interests though the representative process.

Current politics tends to work the other way around. As Alexis de Tocqueville so brilliantly perceived and as Thomas Jefferson so tragically did not, democracy is ultimately incompatible with decentralized government. In emphasizing equality above all other values, it tends to the consolidation of power that both men rightly feared. Under the inviolable conviction that the people should directly influence the highest matters of government, popular attention focuses naturally on the one man "elected by the nation at large." Candidates for every other office are judged less on their individual merits than on whether they support or oppose this imperial magistrate, and locally elected bodies dwindle in power and significance as a result. But again, in the demise of local barriers and hierarchical processes of representation, the people en masse can only ratify or reject the proposals of others, while the commitment to deliberation, compromise, and the protection of interests not strong enough or loud enough to make themselves heard above the din gets sacrificed to the plebiscite.

Today's government of mass opinion, which I assert has its origin in eighteenth century ideas not shared by the wise reactionaries who framed the Constitution, was rejected by the founders long before it was conceivable to establish it on the scale now possible. Although they created a central authority strong enough for the purposes proclaimed in the Preamble, they sought to ensure that its powers could not be arbitrarily wielded by any one man, or group of men, and most certainly not by the mass of men collectively. Indeed, the great art in the edifice they constructed lies in the manner by which they succeeded in breaking up the mass, creating a system of checks and balances and various hierarchical methods of election and appointment that ultimately expressed the popular will, but not the mere reflexes of a consolidated majority.

Nevertheless, the Enlightenment ideology of the direct and universal application of popular rule was only temporarily held at bay. I have attempted in this book to chronicle the resurgence of that ideology and the triumphs it achieved up to the year 1913, by which time the mass majority had long usurped the powers of the Electoral College, and state legislators, after considerable struggle, had finally and officially surrendered to it as well, abdicating their constitutional responsibility to mediate the election of senators. Yet, while such conquests have succeeded only in diminishing the accountability of government and the impact of the individual vote, the egalitarian momentum has not been abated. I cite one more story from the recent past as a concluding example:

In one of the debates of the 1988 presidential race, a major network news organization sponsored an experiment in which a studio audience was gathered from the streets to participate in an electronic evaluation of the contestants. Each participant was given a device with a lever that could be switched fully or incrementally to the left or right, and was instructed to move the lever in one direction or the other during the debate, depending on whether the individual agreed with the Democratic candidate or with the Republican, moving it as far left or as far right as he was in agreement. The motions of each were instantaneously processed and averaged in with those of the others, and the mood of the group at any given moment could be read on a meter. The results of this experiment were shared with the nation as part of the post-debate commentary. Apparently, the meter never veered to the extreme left or the extreme right. As the major network commentator observed, it always stayed fairly close to the center, "like the American people, themselves." That the results of the attempt to judge presidential contenders by the emotional impulses of random spectators could ever be thought of as "moderate" illustrates only too well the extent to which our politics have succumbed to plebiscitary thinking. It remains to be seen whether this incident marks the high tide of mass democracy before a return to the principles of representative checks and balances, or whether it is merely the first wave of an even greater tide to come.

Nov. 1, 1994
Columbia, SC

1

The Progressive Myth

A dangerous ambition more often lurks behind the specious mask of
zeal for the rights of the people than under the forbidding appearance
of zeal for the firmness and efficiency of government.
—*Alexander Hamilton*

Under the original terms for a more perfect Union, the United States Senate was elected by the legislatures of the several states. This provision admirably suited the political conditions of the time, when considerable popular sentiment still favored a loose alliance of the former colonies, and members of Congress were looked upon less as legislators for the Union than as ambassadors for the "sovereign" states which sent them. A familiar vestige of the old Confederation, the legislative appointment of one branch of the federal legislature maintained the states as "constituent parts of the national sovereignty,"[1] and thus gave the Constitution's supporters a vital defense against the charge that they were erecting an overbearing central authority.

Yet this method was also conceived with a far more fundamental end in view. The statesmen at Independence Hall in Philadelphia, convened ostensibly for the purpose of merely amending the Articles of Confederation, shared a common foreboding that the government outlined in that document was critically ill-equipped to prevent the popular excesses which all too frequently disturbed the public tranquility. Freed from the fetters of an unresponsive and irresponsible monarchy, the new nation seemed to be heading toward an opposite extreme. Insurrection, economic chaos, and a dangerous "mutability of legislation," offered ample proof that "liberty may be endangered by the abuses of liberty as well as by the abuses of power; . . . and that the former, rather than the latter, are apparently most to be apprehended by the United States." The critical task before the men assembled in Philadelphia was to strike a balance between freedom and authority, to retain a government which was accountable to those whom it governed, yet was still capable of putting forth a restraining hand upon any and all who threatened the general welfare. At the heart of this attempt to find the middle ground was a faith that popular government was a workable possibility if the majority of citizens were given the necessary time to reflect and reconsider before committing themselves to action. Patriotism, intelligence, and fairness may not have been instinctive, but given an opportunity for second thought, such qualities would surface in most people most of the time. The Constitution's renowned system of "checks and balances" was instituted precisely for the purpose of suspending "the blow meditated by the people against themselves, until reason, justice, and truth can regain their authority over the public mind."[2]

In the scheme of 1787, therefore, the Senate played a crucial role in maintaining this governmental stability. Its check upon all legislative proposals of the lower house, its prerogative to reject any treaty or refuse any appointment desired by the president, in essence, its negative on nearly every function of government (indirectly, senatorial concurrence in appointments and the power to try impeachments checked the judiciary as well), made the Senate the figurative center of gravity in the federal sphere. Conservatism was its indispensable characteristic, and as such, every employable means was adopted to cultivate and sustain it. A six-year term permitted greater consideration of those "well chosen and well-connected measures, which have a gradual and perhaps [popularly] unobserved operation." A division of senatorial seats into three classes, elected successively in two year intervals, would "obviate the inconvenience of periodically transferring those great affairs entirely to new men." New men brought new opinions; new opinions new measures; and as the founders knew from experience, "a continual change even of good measures" was "inconsistent with every rule of prudence and every prospect of success."[3]

As a final insurance that it remain "an anchor against popular fluctuations," the Senate was elected by the state legislatures. Because the uninhibited discussions for which it was intended required a smaller membership, which in turn entailed broader, state-wide constituencies, popular election was ruled out, even in those days of sparse population, as a mockery of the true principles of representation. Candidates would have too little acquaintance with any but the largest or most vocal interests. Conversely, the individual citizen's vote, as well as the knowledge upon which it would be cast, counted for so little among the mass electorate as to favor the intrigues of a well-organized few, adept at "taking advantage of the supineness, the ignorance, and the hopes and fears of the unwary and interested."[4]

Hence, state legislators, selected with greater competence on the part of the people, served as intermediaries to raise to America's highest lawmaking body "those men only who have become the most distinguished by their abilities and virtue." Then, too, such discernment as the senators possessed was of little avail without the ability to speak candidly, a further advantage of a body one degree removed from the popular tumult. Lastly,—and for the purposes of this thesis, certainly not least—in the event that the wisdom and probity of the Senate, like all things mortal, should temporarily subside, it would be checked by a coequal branch of the legislature, drawn in its immediate respects from an essentially different constituency. In factious times, "the dissimilarity in the genius of the two bodies," each with a reciprocal hold on the other, reduced the likelihood that the same interests could gain the upper hand in both houses, and thus monopolize the legislative power for their own ambitions.[5]

Thus was the two-fold purpose of the original method of Senate elections: On the one hand, it allayed the suspicions of the Anti-Federalists; on the other, it was considered instrumental in keeping popular government on an even keel. But in 1913, the Seventeenth Amendment transferred the election of U.S. Senators directly to the people. For a number of reasons, it was thought that the nation's highest legislative body was no longer serving the country in the capacity for which it was intended. Steadily since the Civil War, it seemed whatever esteem a senator might claim lay more in "money-making talent" than in any civic or intellectual virtues, as E. L. Godkin's reform magazine, *The Nation*, complained.[6] Senatorial elections had ceased to be determined by the deliberated concurrence of the state legislators, hinging instead on the dictates of the party bosses who ruled the legislative "machines." The senators, themselves, no longer valued as the sagacious and disinterested legislators of the national welfare, more closely approximated, in the opinion of historian Henry Jones Ford, a "Diet of party lords, wielding their powers without scruple or restraint in behalf of those particular interests" responsible for placing them in office.[7]

The direct election of senators was also seen as a necessary revision to maintain the original constitutional principles against the social and economic transformations of the post-Civil War Era. Huge concentrations of business, capital and labor had diminished the significance of the individual and rendered him voiceless in many of the decisions which affected his daily existence. To restore control to the ordinary citizen, he needed to be invested with more direct methods of governing. Here, the Seventeenth Amendment was part of a sweeping reform movement that brought direct popular legislation in the form of the initiative and the referendum in many states, and in still others, an opportunity to remove unpopular officials by means of the direct recall election. Considering the wide range of a senator's responsibilities, and the tremendous effects which his decisions had upon the entire nation, the restoration of popular government would hardly have been complete as long he was allowed to retain his distance from the will of his constituents.

In the dawn of mass communications, moreover, it was now possible to disseminate the news of national events across the countryside, and reciprocally, to register the will of the people on the highest affairs without the aid of representative intermediaries. It was no longer necessary, then, to delegate the responsibility of electing senators to the legislators, when the people could now elect senators for themselves. In short, great changes had occurred since the augmentation of the original system of representative checks and balances, and the Seventeenth Amendment was deemed an important step in keeping popular government up to pace with those changes. "Our forefathers believed in a certain method of selecting senators over a hundred years ago," as one reformer stated, but "today, under present conditions, those statesmen and patriots would undoubtedly be of another opinion."[8]

Not surprisingly, the direct election of U. S. Senators has engendered very little commentary in the historiography of either the Constitution or of the Progressive Era. It has been somewhat summarily adjudged a closed case. Legislative machines elected senators whom, it was claimed, the people would not have elected themselves; senators, for their part, if not representing interests adverse to those of the people, were too out of touch with popular needs and had to be rendered more responsive; and advanced technology provided the means by which this could be done, dispensing in many areas with the need to delegate authority to middlemen like the state legislators.

But how do these reasons in any way accord with the founders' purposes? Popular appeal, for example, was never the expected criterion by which the legislators were to choose members of the Senate. Nor was it the case that interests opposed to the will of the majority were necessarily illegitimate. And of course, one of the critical points in favor of the indirect method of electing senators had been that it rendered them less vulnerable to the impulses of their constituents. In every instance, then, the traditional explanations for changing the Constitution have essentially begged the question that the Senate was supposed to answer directly to the popular majority. Between the rationale on which the Senate's original mode of election was based and that on which the present method has been adopted, lies a contradiction which precludes the generally accepted idea that the Seventeenth Amendment was somehow an improvement basically in accord with the founding premises. In other words, there is every reason to question the progressive assertion that the framers "would undoubtedly be of another opinion" concerning the need for popularly elected senators, had they but lived in a later age.

On the other hand, there is little question that most reformers of the era believed that they were upholding the Constitution's original principles. The growing influence of money and the dominance of party bosses over the electoral system were clearly not what the founders envisioned when they established the legislative election of senators. But how did these evils arise? That was a question the progressive reformer never seriously asked. He deemed it sufficient that the evils existed and had to be corrected, and when he looked for solutions, he naturally turned to the people. It was obvious *they* did not countenance the undemocratic and occasionally corrupt practices of the state machines, and so it seemed just as obvious that to give them more direct control over governmental affairs would bring about the necessary regeneration of the political system.

This, it so happens, was the very siren call from which the founders tried to protect the republic, yet to which it has steadily drifted at the hands of successive generations of constitutional reformers. Indeed, there were far fewer novelties in the "progressive" solutions than commonly assumed. The underlying assumptions on which they were based have had their adherents in every era of American history, and had been urged long before industrialism, business corporations, and all the other conditions unique to modern life had furnished the pretexts for implementing more direct methods of popular rule. In fact, the political decay manifested in the late nineteenth and early twentieth centuries—although it is not conceded that conditions were as bad as they have been portrayed—owed much less to the country's economic and social changes than to the constitutional tampering of previous ages. Yet these problems were addressed with more of the same sort of tampering. Leaving aside the historical arguments regarding the era's regulatory reforms, however unprecedented in scale or revolutionary in impact, Progressivism, insofar as many of its *constitutional* reforms were concerned, had its origins in a philosophy and form of government against which the American founders had been consciously struggling when they met to amend the Articles of Confederation.

The story of the demise of the original method of electing senators reveals just how long certain disparate assumptions have been competing for supremacy in the American political arena. Indeed, not only in America, but in the Western World more generally, a philosophical dichotomy has existed since at least the middle of the eighteenth century. A number of modern thinkers have commented upon this two hundred year conflict ranging across social, economic, judicial, and particularly political thought, a conflict that has been defined as a struggle between the "constrained" and the "unconstrained" traditions. The point at which the adherents to these respective traditions diverge is as fundamental as a disagreement over the given limitations of humanity, and from that elemental dispute extends to the degree to which governments can and should attempt its improvement. The founders can arguably be placed in the constrained tradition because of the suspicion with which they regarded the wielders of power, even when it was they who did the wielding, and because of the elaborate system of checks and balances they devised to hinder its abuses. Moreover, theirs was a philosophy much more consistent with the political traditions that had been handed down and adapted since antiquity. More democratic thinkers, such as Thomas Paine and Jean-Jacques Rousseau, who promised an almost utopian result when all power was bestowed upon the popular majority, held an obviously less constrained view of human nature,[9] a view decidedly of post-Enlightenment origin, and one which was much more in line with that expressed by proponents of the Seventeenth Amendment.

The philosophic contrasts, however, amount to far more than an intellectual curiosity. After all, philosophies *do* have consequences in the political world, and the seeds of absolutism take root in immoderate ideas. Since the initial establishment of the federal system of checks and balances, American politicians have succumbed to increasingly less judicious opinions about the rights and powers of "the people," a contention amply demonstrated by the long train of historical events, the successive revolutions in political expression, and the steady deterioration of constituted authority which finally brought about the popular election of United States senators.

Necessarily, this proposition encompasses a much broader perspective than the usual accounts of senatorial corruption in the Gilded Age and Progressive Era. Those circumstances immediately preceding the amendment, while appearing the most relevant, have in actuality been the most misleading, for they fail to represent how far the constitutional balance had already been skewed by the time such maladies appeared. The logical starting point, therefore, is the founding intent, the political tradition on which it was based, and the application of that tradition to the practical questions of governing the former British colonies. Then again, to define the intentions of fifty-five men, of various professions and backgrounds, who represented conflicting interests and diverse constituencies and who spent an entire summer trying to reach an agreement, might be considered too tall an order, especially when it is done, as it is here, in a single chapter. But discussion has been confined to the most obvious thing they held in common, the fear of democratic government.

It is unfortunate that in the dwindling vocabulary of political discourse, *democracy* has become synonymous with liberty and popular sovereignty, the only alternative to modern totalitarianism. From Plato to Madison, in the constrained tradition at least, it was actually considered an undesirable state of affairs, meaning the unchecked rule of the majority. It is perhaps a sign of the times that no such word has been retained to describe the phenomenon. In any event, clarity requires that the term be applied consistently in its classical sense, the same in which it was applied by the founders themselves. The second chapter thus seeks to illustrate the popular excesses in the various states of the newly-formed Confederation, and to trace those excesses in part to the defectiveness of existing constitutions. The alarm inspired in the founders was not simply due to the inability of the Confederation to control the states. The federal system which was called into being and given paramountcy was no less a reaction to the democratic weaknesses of the nation in general. The Senate's role in the new system, in accordance with the classical formula for checks and balances, was to maintain the political equilibrium *against* the natural weight of democracy.

There was a latent danger, however, in making the state legislatures responsible for promoting the federal government's "natural aristocracy" (not only the senators, but also the College of Electors). As the third chapter reveals, the history of state constitutions subsequent to the Federal era was a continual concession to principles the founders opposed, a steady erosion of checks and balances in state governments that inevitably rendered them incapable and unwilling to support the federal hierarchy, which had been designed to restrain the extravagance of democratic government. Indeed, the culpability of the states in establishing an increasingly imperious national power was one of the unsought discoveries of the present investigation. Little by little, state constitutions nibbled away at delegated authority in the name of popular rights, and particularly the authority of the legislators. By the early twentieth century, most states had adopted means of legislating over and around the will of their constituted lawmakers in the form of the initiative and the referendum. With "the people" thus performing many of the tasks of their legislators directly for themselves, the direct election of senators was an almost inevitable development, which would in turn diminish the senatorial checks on the capricious use of national power.

But federal repercussions became manifest well before the formal movement to amend the Constitution. The Electoral College, as an independently deliberative body, collapsed in the Jacksonian Era, and the decline in the indirect method of electing senators had its beginnings in approximately the same period. Chapter 4 chronicles this increasing democratization of Senate elections, and shows that the major problems which led reformers to advocate the Seventeenth Amendment actually had their origin in these prior attempts at popularization. If this seems implausible, one might ask whether or not the amendment has truly worked the improvements its proponents promised. Has the Senate become any more deliberative, and less scandalous, since it was handed over to "the people?" Has big campaign money from big interests ceased to be a factor in Senate elections since that alleged revival of popular rule? Are these conditions not only not better, but worse?

Chapter 5 makes a necessary digression to show that, in spite of the muckraking rhetoric, the Senate was completely incapable of inflicting the sort of harm with which it has been charged. Taking up the major issues of the era in which the amendment was urged, the chapter explains the role of the Senate in resolving them, or not resolving them, as the case may be. No matter how corrupted the institution had allegedly become, it was powerless to act in any positive way without the collusion of every other arm of government. That was the nature of checks and balances. Whatever private influences were then at work within the upper chamber, the worst that can be said of them is that the Senate delayed, or diluted with amendments, legislative or executive proposals of momentary popularity. In no instance was it ever able to withstand the sustained opinion of the public. In other words, if not always motivated by the greater national interest, the Senate nevertheless fulfilled its primary task of moderating the course of national affairs. But its power to resist the popular impulses, the quality for which it was originally most valued, was weakening steadily.

Nothing refutes the accepted wisdom more than the passage of the Seventeenth Amendment itself. The claim that the Senate, elected by the legislatures, was too unresponsive and too corrupted to address the needs of the people, does not at all square with the fact that two-thirds of the former and three-fourths of the latter concurred in a constitutional revision which supposedly ran counter to their own selfish interests. Chapter 6 resumes the story of the Senate's increasing popularization, this time in the formal movement for an amendment, which by way of illustration contradicts a number of traditional assumptions about America's popular political reforms. Conventional interpretation tends to portray grass-roots uprisings overthrowing the abusers of power, when in actuality those most clamorous for constitutional change have, as often as not, been those already in possession of political influence. Time and again, the successive episodes of democratic reform have been marked by a willingness, even anxiousness, on the part of the constituted authorities to surrender their powers to "the people," or perhaps one should not say powers, but responsibilities. It is as if they sought to be absolved from the unpopular tasks for which their authority, in part, had been granted. The paradoxical, if not hypocritical, aspect of such efforts was that democratic innovators first had to come to power using the same "machine" methods, and the same well-financed campaigns, that they proposed to supplant with direct popular rule. The further the extension of direct democracy, the further such distasteful practices became necessary to attain office and achieve reform.

Once in power, reformers typically accomplished their desired changes by invoking the specter of "the interests" against "the people." The notion of such a dichotomy has been a fundamental determinant of America's political destiny, since proponents of democracy in every era, including the present, have prefaced their desire for constitutional revision on the need of dislodging power from the one and restoring it to the other. In the view of the Federalists, however, no such concept existed, or rather it was a concept they denounced as a fiction of democratic theorists and a handy weapon for demagogues. Their own understanding, as shall be shown further, was that political battles grew out of conflicting interests among the people. Certainly, reformers of the

Progressive Era, whose popular rhetoric often belied a shrewd ability to defend their personal power, proved no exception.

Another recurring irony that has received almost no attention in the history of America's democratization, but which can not be avoided when studying the causes of the Seventeenth Amendment, is the fact that democratic reformers, try as they might, never managed to improve the popularity of representative bodies by diminishing their authority. On the contrary, as clearly evident in the history of state legislatures—the representative assemblies originally entrusted with electing U.S. Senators—the respect with which they were popularly regarded, and the quality of men they attracted, subsided proportionally with the amount of control that was taken from them.

What these contradictions ultimately point to is the traditional inability of democratic reformers to understand the democratic origins of the problems they addressed. The truth of this contention is substantially attested to in Chapter 7, in which is narrated the Senate's own debates over the question of direct elections. Primarily, the chapter focuses on the months of January and February 1911, for the simple reasons that prior to then the resolution had never been reported favorably out of committee, and thus had not received any considerable discussion, and after that point there was little new ground to be covered by either side. The speeches have been rendered in the order in which they were delivered, but for the sake of avoiding redundancy some speeches have been reluctantly but necessarily skipped altogether. Others have been paraphrased, without, it is hoped, doing any damage to the speaker's intent. Moreover, the narrative includes only those points of each speaker that were essentially new as the discussion proceeded. It is doubtful that any author's rendition, however, could convey the drama that the debates actually possessed. The senators were still the best that America had to offer in the way of eloquence, and charged with their convictions on this question, their deliberation over the direct elections resolution was at times almost Sophoclean in its intensity.

Thus, the final chapter attempts to present the debates as a clash, for the first time at the federal level, between the two contending philosophies of the eighteenth century. The recourse which speakers had on both sides to the founding era and to the founding intent, as they attempted to bolster their arguments, made the task much easier than it might at first seem. Only one side could plausibly claim Elijah's mantle, however, and it was demonstrably not the side which sought to democratize the federal Constitution.

All the same, the progressives were ultimately correct in declaring the failure of the former method of Senate elections. Their success in overthrowing it was the very proof that it could not withstand the tides it was designed to deflect. In the final analysis, the Seventeenth Amendment represented a critical defeat in the historical struggle to check and to balance the popular employment of federal power, and the Senate's undoing as an institution capable of enforcing second thought in determining the national will was, as the following chapters disclose, the result of tendencies the framers had managed to obstruct but could not halt. In the age in which they found themselves, a new but potently appealing philosophy had already positioned itself to subvert the constitutional constraints under which they had briefly persuaded their countrymen to be governed.

Notes

1. Alexander Hamilton, John Jay & James Madison, *The Federalist* (New York: Modern Library, 1938), p. 52.
2. *Ibid.*, pp. 413, 410.
3. *Ibid.*, pp. 409, 418–419, 405.
4. *Ibid.*, p. 417.
5. *Ibid.*, pp. 417, 403.
6. E. L. Godkin, "Rich Men in the Senate," *The Nation* 50 (January 16, 1890): 44.
7. Henry Jones Ford, *The Rise and Growth of American Politics, A Sketch of Constitutional Development* (New York: The Macmillan Company, 1889), p. 270.
8. Charles J. Fox, "Popular Election of United States Senators," *Arena* 27 (May 1902): 456–457.
9. Thomas Sowell, *A Conflict of Visions: Ideological Origins of Political Struggle* (New York: Quill Publishers, 1987), pp. 31–33.

2

A Precarious Balance

A paper declaration is a very feeble barrier against the force of national habits, and inclinations.
—*Noah Webster*

As initially stated, the direct election of senators, an event of the early twentieth century, had its theoretic basis in political assumptions originating a hundred and fifty years previously. They were not, however, the assumptions which shaped the Constitution of 1787. In fact, they were in many ways a direct contradiction of them. The driving force behind the Seventeenth Amendment was the furtherance of democracy, which is exactly what the founders were trying to prevent when they deliberately placed the Senate beyond the immediate popular reach. Again, democracy did not carry all the connotations in the eighteenth century that it does today. It simply meant majority rule. The men who framed the Constitution saw nothing sacred or inalienable in that form of government. It was as apt to err, to be as arbitrary and abusive in the exercise of power, as any monarchy or aristocracy, for superior numbers did not necessarily confer superior wisdom or virtue. In unchecked democracies, wrote James Madison, "measures are too often decided, not according to the rules of justice and the rights of the minor party, but by the superior force of an interested and overbearing majority."[1] Maintaining liberty for all entailed somehow balancing the interests of the majority with those of the minority, while of course preserving the rights of individuals.

This entailed the protection of certain inequalities. "The diversity in the faculties of men" made them naturally unequal in their abilities, say for example, to acquire and possess property. If they were to be free in the pursuit of it, naturally they would possess it unequally. If government was to protect freedom, it would have to protect these natural inequalities, a task which Madison considered "the first object of government." Yet this was an impossibility if all power was simply exercised by universal suffrage. Distributing political rights in equal portions, one-man, one-vote, had the paradoxical effect of creating another form of inequality—between the majority and the minority. To let the majority vote away the wealth of a minority without its consent was no less an injustice than for the few to plunder the many. The classic solution, to be discussed more thoroughly in a moment, was to devise a "mixed" constitution, giving these contending elements—majority and minority—a reciprocal hold on one another, with one arm of the state based more or less on popular suffrage, the other on some form of distinction, usually property, since that seemed to be "the most common and durable source of factions."[2] But whatever the mode of distinction, it meant that liberty required some basis of political inequality in this second arm of government.

Absolutism Post Enlightenment: Vox populi, vox Dei

While proponents of this "mixed" constitution concerned themselves with the critical question of balance, however, the eighteenth century democrat was busy forging theories for the complete overthrow of inequality, natural or otherwise. In fact, argued the democrat, it was not nature at all, but society with its perverse emphasis on material pursuits which engendered inequalities. It defied "Reason" and "the Laws of Nature" that one citizen or group of citizens should have a greater voice politically than any of the others. In the strictest sense of the term, political equality as conceived by the democrat recognized and upheld the sovereignty of every individual. But how was this to be reconciled with social harmony? The central dilemma, as Jean-Jacques Rousseau formulated it, was how to defend this individual sovereignty "with the collective force of all," that is, with a force superior to that of individuals, while ensuring that each citizen "obeys no one but himself." In his most famous work, *The Social Contract* (1762), Rousseau outlined a utopia in which it was "in no one's interest to make the conditions onerous for others," because equality of condition and political rights had made the "social contract," the agreement on which individuals entered society, the same for all. When it came to affairs of state, each member would naturally assert his voice in his own self-interest, which was intrinsically the interest of the whole. In other words, Rousseau had essentially solved the conflict of majority versus minority by denying that it would exist. The people would express the "General Will," the rational course which the citizenry would unanimously and spontaneously adopt, once equality had given them the ability to perceive it.[3]

Admittedly, Rousseau's influence on political developments in the United States has been minimal in any direct sense. But no philosopher more clearly articulated the unspoken premises of later generations throughout the Western world. His notion of the General Will corresponded perfectly to the reformer's belief that if only political power were properly derived, it would automatically result in the common good. Like Rousseau, America's democratizers assumed that there was an "infallible origin" of political will, waiting to express itself through the oracle of universal suffrage.[4] The idea was to be unconsciously echoed in subsequent eras, particularly in justifying the revocation of representative authority. Such authority was inherently unequal, since the transference of power to representatives meant subtracting it from the people universally. If society were going to see that the individual "obeys no one but himself," then obviously, Rousseau pronounced, "any law which the people has not ratified in person is void." This was why he considered democracy incompatible with any polity larger than the city-state.[5] In the twentieth century, of course, that objection was supposedly rendered moot by mass communications.

At the core of the philosophy was the unproven supposition that equality would do what the democrat said it would do. As Rousseau explained, political factionalism continued, the General Will had not yet been expressed, because "the spirit of society together with the inequality that society engenders . . . changes and corrupts in this way all our natural inclinations."[6]

Madison directly attacked this philosophy in *The Federalist*. "Theoretic politicians," by which he meant theorizers with no practical experience of politics, "have erroneously supposed that by reducing mankind to a perfect equality in their political rights, they would, at the same time, be perfectly equalized and assimilated in their possessions, their opinions, and their passions." It was simply not so. Liberty begot diversity. Diversity begot conflict. In contrast to the democrat's idea that there was somehow a perfect voice to be followed when the political system had set up the means to express it, Madison believed that "as long as the reason of man continues fallible, and he is at liberty to exercise it, different opinions will be formed." The unfortunate truth was that "the latent causes of faction" did not originate in social inequalities. They were "sown in the nature of man," and could not be removed. Public order was "only to be sought in the means of controlling [faction's] effects," in keeping one party from suppressing another. If the faction were a minority, it was easily defeated "by regular vote," but when "a majority is included in a faction, the form of popular government, on the other hand, enables it to sacrifice to its ruling passion or interest both the public good and private rights." The central dilemma as conceived in *The Federalist,* therefore, was "to secure the public good and private rights against the dangers of such a faction, and at the same time to preserve the spirit and the form of popular government."[7]

What distinguishes this from the problem as Rousseau proposed it was the moderation in terms. The acceptance of "faction" as a given element in popular government was an implicit acknowledgment of the futility of trying to divine the "General Will," and nowhere in the defense of "private rights" was it suggested that the individual would obey "no one but himself." Central to the founding view was not the universal perception of the oracle, but merely the popular recognition of the need to compromise between distinct and often conflicting interests. In questioning the infallibility of the people, however, or in counseling restraints upon individual sovereignty, the Constitution's framers proved to be in full reaction to the egalitarian premise of modern political thinking.[8] To be sure, they had overthrown the hereditary order of their forbearers, once and for all, replacing it with a representative system uniquely adapted to American conditions in the post monarchical age. But notwithstanding the novelty of the design, the most basic principles on which the founders raised their structure were hardly original. If anything, they were the inheritance of more than two thousand years of Western political experience.

The One, the Few, and the Many

The evolutionary processes which the founders upheld against the revolutionary theories of their age may be said with comparative safety to have started with Aristotle (384-322 b.c.), although Aristotle himself claimed merely to have articulated "the experience of the ages." A diligent student of the constitutions of the Hellenic world, the author of the *Politics* eventually parted ways with his mentor, Plato, whose criticism of democracy is, nevertheless, in no danger of losing its relevance. To Aristotle, however, Plato's solution of the Philosopher King seemed hardly more moderate. He also rejected Plato's communalism as the answer to the divisiveness of property disputes, arguing, as Madison would argue twenty-one centuries later, that the divisiveness was inherent in man, and that political society, the *"polis"* would always be "an aggregate of many members."[9]

Hence, it was the task of the legislator to promote the interest common to all. At the same time, investing magistrates with the power to do so was in itself a source of conflict, particularly between rich and poor. When it came to the question of rule, the rich believed "that superiority on one point—in their case wealth—means superiority on all." The poor, almost always in the majority, insisted that "equality in one respect—for instance, that of free birth—means equality all around." In their notions of which rule was proper, both professed a conception of justice, but only "up to a point . . . thinking that they profess one which is absolute and complete."[10]

Aristotle contended that politics should focus on the just exercise of power, not the abstract justice of its origins, on whether sovereignty was used in the interest of all, not where it rightfully resided. Even rule by a single man, *kingship,* was not by definition unjust. The same was true of rule by a few, *aristocracy,* or rule by the majority, which he termed *Polity.* Any one of the three forms were to be regarded as "right constitutions" when the sovereign powers were used "with a view to the common interest." On the other hand, any one of the forms could be oppressive. "Constitutions directed to the personal interest of the One, the Few, or the Masses must necessarily be perversions," which the philosopher termed respectively *Tyranny, Oligarchy,* and *Democracy.*[11]

"The final sovereign," claimed Aristotle, must be a law which transcends the partial conceptions of justice held by those in power. Any real constitution was "based on general rules," on established processes, rather than on the whim of the sovereign. "There is no constitution," said Aristotle, if "everything is managed merely by decrees." Democracy was no exception. When the demagogue stepped forth and announced, "the people ought to decide," it was the beginning of the polity's demise. The authority of the constituted magistrates was undermined and the laws were no longer sovereign. The rule of the plebiscite, therefore, was simply another form of tyranny, "a single composite autocrat made up of many members, with the many playing the sovereign, not as individuals, but collectively."[12] Of more than passing coincidence, this was exactly the situation surrounding the American Senate's consideration of the Seventeenth Amendment. When all other arguments failed, senators who opposed direct elections, despite the fact that theirs was the judgment of constituted authority, were told, verbatim, "the people ought to decide."

Following Aristotle's lead, later thinkers in antiquity began working out the concept of a *mixed* constitution, achieving the best and avoiding

the worst in each of the three forms of rule. Probably the most endur-
ing addition to the classical political thought was that put forth by
Polybius (ca. 200-118 b.c.), the Greek historian of the Roman republic
who traced the chain of calamities that beset improperly balanced poli-
ties. An absolute monarchy, he asserted, eventually degenerated into
tyranny until it was at last supplanted by the uprising of an aristocracy,
which in its turn decayed into an oppressive oligarchy. At that point,
the people revolted and established their polity. Yet when the masses
became as debauched as the aristocracy they had overthrown, taking
their liberty and power for granted, the state sank into mob rule until
some champion reestablished law and monarchy. Without balancing
these rival elements, the state was doomed to perpetual revolutions
in this "cycle of constitutions," and was ever the prey to stronger and
better organized nations.[13]

Actually, philosophers since Plato had noticed the phenomenon, this
cycle by which states seemed to fluctuate between extreme forms of
government. The question was how to break it. The Romans, according
to Polybius, escaped such a fate and mastered the world with a proper
synthesis of the One, the Few, and the Many. Their "mixed Constitution,"
of Counsels, Senate, and Tribunes secured the advantages of monarchical despatch, aristocratic wisdom, and popular contentedness, while
avoiding the extremes of tyranny, oligarchy, and ochlocracy. When they
cooperated, Rome possessed "an irresistible power to achieve any goal
it set for itself," yet "whenever one of the three elements . . . becomes
over ambitious and tends to encroach upon the others," its designs
were "blocked or impeded by the rest."[14]

The Western political evolution would owe a tremendous debt to
this ancient idea. Underscoring the need for moderation in the use of
power, Aristotle's "right constitution" was sought in a tripartite balance of power among the separate social interests. The concept had
been strongly preserved in modern thought from Machiavelli through
Montesquieu, and its influence was not lost on eighteenth century
Americans. During the Philadelphia Convention, in fact, a number of
delegates continued to refer to the Constitution's "monarchical element"
and its "aristocracy," and even after the federal system had been fully
inaugurated, Vice President John Adams continued to insist that "every
project has been found to be no better than committing the lamb to
the custody of the wolf, except that one which is called a balance of
power. A simple sovereignty in one, a few, or many has no balance, and
therefore no laws."[15] James Madison, as a young pupil, was evidently

impressed enough by one of Hobbes' unflattering commentaries on unchecked democracy as to place it among the first of his voluminous journal entries: "All Kings are Ravenous Beasts, said Cato. He did not see that the Roman People were as Rapacious & oppressive as any Tyrant. How could he think, that that was glorious in many Men, which was detestable in one?"[16]

The so-called "Father of the Constitution" would devote his entire life to rummaging through the examples of history for the perfectly balanced republic without recanting his earlier Polybian conclusion: "The natural rotation in Government is from the abuses of Monarchy to Aristocracy, from the oppression of Aristocracy to democracy, and from the licentiousness of Democracy back to Monarchy."[17]

Western political thought had obviously not petrified in the lessons of the ancients, however. The idea of separating legislative, executive, and judicial powers, now the primary feature of Western governments, was the contribution of early modern Europe. In antiquity, "each branch of the government, representing a distinct social class, was to participate in all government functions."[18] By the seventeenth century, the Europeans had begun working out the separation by function, most notably in the writings of Locke. By the mid-eighteenth century, a French Anglophile, the "celebrated Montesquieu," one of the few philosophers to be mentioned by name in the 1787 assembly, had given it the clearest and most applicable expression. According to Madison, Charles de Secondat, le Baron de Montesquieu (1689–1755), was the "oracle" most consulted on the separation of powers in the modern sense of the term.[19] Although the doctrine, having its own distinct origins, was no mere derivative of the mixed constitution heritage,[20] the two ideas were not mutually exclusive, and were actually quite compatible as a means of checking the abuse of power. Quite possibly, Montesquieu's strong appeal to the Constitution's framers stemmed from the fact that he did not reject the older idea of balancing interests, but incorporated it as much as practicable to maintain the division of legislative, executive and judicial powers. Although in his great political work, *The Spirit of the Laws,* he gave little thought to the judiciary (considering it, as did the founders, "in some measure next to nothing"), he still ascribed a separate political function to each of the social elements by means of a bicameral legislature and a single-headed, independent executive. In Montesquieu's properly balanced republic, the monarch executed the laws initiated by the representatives of the people in the first house, and approved by the peerage in the second.[21]

The monarch, solitary and independent in his power, and thus with no necessity to favor any faction in the realm, was the best guarantor of the impartial administration of the laws. But he was checked in his proclivity to ambitious schemes of personal glory, because his powers were simply executive. His legislative abilities extended no further than the veto. The laws themselves were inspired by those who had to live under them, that is, by the people, who did not legislate directly, however, but through their representatives, for "the great advantage of representatives is their capacity of discussing public affairs." For this, Montesquieu believed the people collectively were "extremely unfit." Nevertheless, they were still perfectly capable of "knowing in general whether the person they choose is better qualified than most of his neighbors."[22]

When the representatives of the people had initiated the law, it then passed for approval to the upper house, representing the nobility, which Montesquieu believed to have legitimate interests distinct from those of the ordinary citizens. "There are always persons distinguished by their birth, riches or honours." Were such a class to be "confounded with the common people, and to have only a single vote like the rest, the common liberty would be their slavery, and they would have no interest in supporting it, as most of the common resolutions would be against them." The people's representatives could not be counted on to protect the liberty of the propertied classes, which compose the minority in virtually every society. "The legislative power is therefore committed to the body of the nobles, and to that which represents the people, each having their own assemblies and deliberations apart, each their separate views and interests."[23] "Here then," wrote Montesquieu:

> is the fundamental constitution of the government we are treating of. The legislative body being composed of two parts, they check one another by the mutual privilege of rejecting. They are both restrained by the executive power, as the executive is by the legislative.
>
> These three powers should naturally form a state of repose or inaction. But as there is a necessity for movement in the course of human affairs, they are forced to move, but still in concert.[24]

In outlining his model republic, Montesquieu unabashedly admitted his admiration for the Constitution of Great Britain, attributing her unrivaled degree of personal liberty to the orderly separation of powers which accompanied the balancing of estates. In actual practice, however, the separation was not so distinct as he believed. Judicial power, for the most part, resided in the king's courts; control of the military had for all practical purposes fallen to the Commons; and by the late eighteenth century, the crown had generally refrained from using the veto, preferring instead to influence the legislature through its power of patronage.[25] But in many ways, the misconception of the British Constitution fitted the Americans more suitably than the reality. Harboring long years of animosity toward the monopoly on offices held by the king's "placemen," the trial of civil cases in the admiralty courts, and the appointment of the upper houses in the colonial legislatures by the governors, revolutionaries often adopted the Montesquieuan version as the orthodox, and the actual British practice as the corruption.[26]

In any case, whether or not the Americans received their understanding of the balanced constitution from Montesquieu, or from a first-hand knowledge of the British constitution, the resemblances were close enough. Both supported Madison's opinion that "the accumulation of all powers, legislative, executive, and judiciary, in the same hands, whether of one, a few, or many, and whether hereditary, self-appointed, or elective, may justly be pronounced the very definition of tyranny." Worthy of note, Madison considered the separation of powers as not only supplementary to the classical balance, but subordinate to it. Privately, he observed that "the best provision for a stable and free Government is not a balance in the powers of the Government," that is, in Montesquieuan separation of functions, "tho' that is not to be neglected," but rather in the much more ancient concept of "an equilibrium in the interests & passions of the country itself."[27]

Paine and Democracy in the Several States

All the same, it would take a decade of experience for the nation's political leaders to appreciate the ageless lessons of unchecked majority rule. From 1776 to 1777 the new state governments were being erected in the same year that Thomas Paine's *Common Sense* sold 500,000 copies in the United States in fifty-six editions. Benjamin Franklin, himself an accomplished author who knew the publishing business, marvelled at how quickly the pamphlet had made a "great Impression" in Philadelphia, then the hub of political influence in America.[28] And Paine had turned the classical balance on its head:

> To say that the commons is a check upon the king, presupposes . . . the king is not to be trusted . . . or the commons are either wiser

> and more worthy of confidence than the crown. But . . . as the same
> Constitution . . . gives . . . the king a power to check the commons . . .
> it again supposes that the king is wiser than those whom it has already
> supposed to be wiser than him [sic].[29]

The whole idea of balancing estates, Paine argued, was "absurd," based upon the "two ancient tyrannies" of monarchy and aristocracy, which being "independent of the people . . . contribute nothing towards the freedom of the state." Paine's advice to the Americans, therefore, was to disburden the people of checks and balances and establish the simplest and least inhibitive means of enacting their will. They knew best how to protect their own liberties.[30]

Paine had correctly gauged that the American governments would never feature "mixed constitutions" in the traditional sense. On the other hand, he and many others of the day had failed to see any possible conflict between personal and public liberty, assuming instead a homogeneity of interests in the simplest expressions of "the people." By putting government firmly and more directly in the hands of the people, the people were believed safe. They may at times have become licentious, even anarchic, but it was unthinkable that they could oppress themselves. So prevalent had the underlying assumptions in Paine's argument become during this first flush of republican liberty, that even the aristocratic John Adams, who despised Paine, declared that "A democratical despotism is a contradiction in terms."[31]

The initial idea of limited government, therefore, was seen primarily in terms of keeping a jealous popular eye upon the possible abuses of the magistrates, and giving them as little independence and authority as possible. It is not surprising, given the old colonial resentment against royally appointed executives, that what power there was resided in the legislatures. Even though six state constitutions specifically proclaimed a separation of legislative, executive, and judicial powers (Georgia, Maryland, Massachusetts, New Hampshire, North Carolina, and Virginia),[32] their independence of one another was usually nominal.

The executives, for example, were generally given a short leash. They were either dependent on the legislatures, or on the same constituency as the legislatures, which is to say the direct popular majority. Delaware, Georgia, Maryland, New Jersey, North Carolina, South Carolina, and Virginia elected their governors through the legislatures, and usually did the same for all executive subordinates and the judiciary. Of these, only Delaware and South Carolina provided an executive term longer than one year. Among governors who were popularly elected, only New York provided a term as long as three years. The rest were elected annually, often under some form of rotation. The citizens of Pennsylvania, who directly elected an "Executive Council" every three years, attempted to do without a governor altogether. Only Massachusetts gave its governor any effective degree of legislative veto power,[33] but his short tenure and direct election were hardly designed to promote an independent executor of the laws, standing aloof of the popular factions. He was still a far cry from the Montesquieuan ideal.

Meanwhile, the creation of upper legislative houses, such as they were, posed one the more perplexing quandaries for the new republics. If they represented an elevated wisdom and virtue, and yet could be popularly elected, why have an upper chamber in the first place? Such was the logic of the Georgians and the Pennsylvanians, whose constitutions rejected bicameralism altogether. If, on the other hand, they were intended to counterbalance the majoritarian tendencies of the lower branch, where were the requisite social distinctions to be found?

South Carolina elected its senate through its Assembly, which gave it a degree of independence from the popular will, but essentially no interest contrary to that of the lower house. Most of the popularly elected senates required higher property qualifications for the candidate, the electors, or both. Delaware and Virginia had no additional qualifications for senatorial electors, although the latter specified that senators themselves be freeholders of at least twenty-five years of age. Massachusetts required senate electors to have a £3 annual income or an estate of £60. New York required the possession of a £100 freehold estate over and above all debts in order to vote for senators, and a £20 freehold or comparable payment in taxes to vote for members of the lower house. New Hampshire's eligibility requirement for electing members to either house was the mere payment of a poll tax, with the stipulation that candidates for the senate possess a £200 freehold. New Jersey senators were elected by citizens with a £50 estate. In North Carolina, all taxpayers could vote in lower house elections, and a 50 acre freehold was needed to vote in the upper. It should be borne in mind that many of these distinctions were not particularly exclusive in an era of general land availability.[34]

In an interesting attempt to distinguish the interests of a majority of mere numbers from the interests of property, Massachusetts and New Hampshire rewrote their constitutions in 1780 and 1784 respectively, apportioning the senate according to the tax assessment of each district and leaving the lower house proportional to district population.[35] The rearrangement naturally left the governments open to charges of favoring the wealthier and more settled counties of the East in both houses. Since the qualification for electors remained unchanged, the revision did little to establish that "proper complication of principles" which Thomas Jefferson, writing of Virginia's political woes, felt sorely lacking in the legislature of his own state.[36] In practically all the revolutionary legislatures, the upper house was either the sibling or the offspring of the popular branch.

Only Maryland managed to devise a senate truly distinct from its lower house. Her constitution expressly stated that senators should not be "compelled" by the House of Delegates to assent to any proposal "in their judgment injurious to the public welfare." Besides serving five-year terms (Delaware, New York, South Carolina, and Virginia were the only other states to provide longer than annual terms in their upper chambers), the Maryland senate achieved a marked degree of independence from the immediate popular will, as well as from the delegates, by means of an electoral college consisting of two electors from each county (one each for the corporations of Baltimore and Annapolis) to be elected by the freeholders. These electors in turn chose fifteen men "of the most wisdom, experience and virtue, above twenty-five years of age, residents of the State above three whole years next preceding the election, and having real and personal property above the value of £1000 current money," to serve in the Senate.[37]

Of all the senates created in the post-Revolutionary governments, Maryland's had most distinguished itself for its ability to restrain the popular tides. The greatest example was in its successful resistance to the paper money agitations of the debtor interests. In a legislative confrontation lasting throughout the 1780s, the lower house Delegates charged that "The two houses are composed of 89 members, 8 of whom [the majority of the 15 member Senate] have it in their power to counteract 81. Will they submit?" They concluded with a call for "the people" to submit instructions to their representatives as a means of settling the dispute. According to constitutional historian Gordon S. Wood, "this remarkable action was to raise the most significant constitutional debate of the entire Confederation period." The delegates were more numerous and more pervasive throughout the state, "and would obviously have a greater opportunity of influencing the people in drawing up instructions."[38]

The Senate held firm, insisting that "Once . . . appeal is made from the dictates of judgment to the voice of numbers, freedom of discussion and decision," for which the Senate had been created, was essentially extinguished.[39] The popular zeal for inflated paper currency eventually waned. The senate had successfully ridden out the storm, and provided in this as in other cases a needed ballast amid the democratic fluctuations of the revolutionary period. All told, the Maryland Senate was more protective of Tory property, more responsive to the needs of Congress, stricter on government expenditure, and more conscientious in the defense of religious liberty than was true of upper houses in any other state. It was hailed as the best in the Confederation by those who began to appreciate the need for majority restraints. It would also be held out as a model for the federal Senate.[40]

Most states, by contrast, failed to establish Senates (or executives) which could check the temporary interests of the democratic lower houses. Again, in the prevailing spirit of 1776, Americans tended to see limited government solely in terms of checking the tyrannical tendencies of their officials through a frequent recurrence to the popular will. As it was, power was centered in the legislatures in unhealthy proportions, but the legislators themselves, elected annually and often bound to the "instructions" of their constituents, were little more than ambassadors, powerless to deviate from the farming, merchant or craftsmen interests that sent them. The result was a legislative chamber permeated by what Madison called "a spirit of locality." As he complained to Jefferson, "we find the representatives of Counties and Corporations in the Legislatures of the States, much more disposed to sacrifice the aggregate interest, and even authority, to the local views of their Constituents, than the latter to the former."[41] Christopher Gadsden of South Carolina deplored this "fettering" of representatives with "absolute instructions," claiming it made a mockery of legislative deliberation and undermined the atmosphere of compromise necessary to secure "the general combined interests of all the State put together."[42] And without deliberation and compromise, what could the laws possibly reflect besides the cumulative desire of superior numbers?

The people checked their government, in other words, but what checked the people? Despite the constitutional genuflections to the separation of powers, the state governments had been rendered almost entirely subservient to the first expression of the majority, and it was not long before the classic symptoms of democracy began to appear. It was exceedingly difficult, for example, to maintain any stability in the laws with an eighty-three member turnover in the Massachusetts House of Representatives in 1778, or an annual turnover rate of nearly half the Virginia Burgesses throughout the first decade of independence.[43] This constant recurrence to the people, Madison lamented in the months leading up to the convention, defeated the entire purpose of representative government. "We daily see laws repealed or superseded, before any trial can have been made of their merits, and even before a knowledge of them can have reached the remoter districts within which they were to operate." Reviewing the legislative trends of the several states, the Virginia statesman complained, "The short period of independency has filled as many pages as the century which preceded it. Every year, almost every session, adds a new volume" of what seemed to be hopelessly mutable statutes.[44]

And yet the political situation could not precisely be described as anarchic. If anything, there was too much government, too many laws. To those who suffered the butt of them, popular government had proven itself as arbitrary and capable of oppression as any unchecked monarchy. The redistribution of property, either through direct confiscation, cancellation of the public debt, or deliberately inflationary money schemes, enjoyed the general public approval. In all, according to the figures of Forrest McDonald, over $28 million of loyalist and absentee-owned property, more than a "tenth of the value of all improved real estate in the country" at the time, was seized through bills of attainder and legislative "divestment acts" that deprived the victim of his holdings without due process, right of appeal, or compensation.[45]

The confiscation craze was too strong even for the Maryland Senate to restrain. The state's political insiders, while uttering "republican pieties," managed to raise popular support for the arbitrary confiscation of $1.3 million in Tory estates, which they in turn acquired at a fraction of its pre-war value.[46] It was a classic example of the passions of the many being played upon for the profits of the few, and *The Federalist* authors may well have had it in mind when they warned that governmental acquiescence in shifting popular enthusiasms did not always benefit the common citizens themselves. On the contrary, it often gave "undue advantage" to the speculators who hovered over the seats of government. "Every new regulation concerning commerce or revenue, or in any manner affecting the value of the different species of property, presents a new harvest to those who watch the change, and can trace its consequences; a harvest not reared by themselves . . ."[47]

Ill-considered legislation in Connecticut was so confusing that public creditors occasionally found their lands on the auction block for not paying taxes which had been levied to pay the interest on the public securities they held. In Rhode Island the legislature passed a law actually disfranchising anyone who refused to accept payment in paper money which had depreciated to seven or eight percent of its original worth. Not even an executive elected independently of the legislature could guarantee any restraints on the democratic impulses, so long as he, too, answered immediately to the people, as evidenced in the example of the Massachusetts governor, John Hancock. During the war, Hancock pushed through an enormous funding bill, and then, having obtained the credit, declined to collect taxes—with no complaints from the popular majority. It was the attempt of Hancock's successor, James Bowdoin, to honor the debt, which ignited the Massachusetts tax revolt under Daniel Shays in 1787.[48]

The Restoration

In the Bay State, as elsewhere, "Public faith and private confidence were being destroyed."[49] Paper money, ex post facto legislation, laws that impaired the obligations of contract, and the mutability of the laws in general, were undermining the respect necessary for the promotion of commerce and the pursuit of property. What creditor would invest, what entrepreneur would venture any risk, under such unstable conditions? Individuals capable in the main of self-government required laws which were not "so voluminous that they cannot be read, or so incoherent that they cannot be understood," explained *The Federalist.* "Law is defined to be a rule of action; but how can that be a rule, which is little known, and less fixed?"[50] To reiterate, the problem in legislation arose not from rogue representatives acting in defiance of the will of the people, but from the fact that the people's "transient and indigested sentiments have been too implicitly adopted."[51]

Essentially, the lessons of 1776 had been overlearned in the attempt not to repeat the usurpations of the crown, and the evidence was mounting against the eighteenth century theory that popular governments were intrinsically incapable of ruling against the general interest. The public assaults on private property and individual rights had not been the decrees of arbitrary magistrates, but came from "laws enacted by legislatures which were probably as equally and fairly representative of the people as any legislature in history."[52]

It became all too apparent to those who eventually called a convention for reform that state governments had no sufficient check on the abuse of power, because "the real power lies in the majority of the

Community." In a letter to Jefferson, Madison noted that "the invasion of private rights is *chiefly* to be apprehended, not from acts of Government contrary to the sense of its constituents, but from acts in which the Government is the mere instrument of the major number of the constituents."[53]

The experience of the Confederation era reestablished the need to balance the claims of the one and the few against the preponderance of the many. In closed assembly at the federal convention, the reformers did not mince words. "The evils we experience flow from the excess of democracy," said Elbridge Gerry. "The people," Roger Sherman urged, "immediately [that is, directly] should have as little to do as may be about the [federal] Government. They want information and are constantly liable to be misled." Edmund Randolph, having submitted the "Virginia Plan," reminded his colleagues that, however much they might disagree on the particular points, their primary object was to check "the turbulence and follies of democracy." Not a single voice dissented. Even George Mason, from the beginning highly suspicious of creating a stronger central authority, agreed that in the government of the states, "We had been too democratic."[54] Indeed, regardless of where they stood on the nationalist-states' rights spectrum, most of the delegates shared this mistrust of unchecked popular majorities.

It would be a grave injustice, however, to think that these men were "against the people." To the contrary, it was their concern for popular liberties that prompted the convention, for in their classical understanding of politics, the "democratic licentiousness" that they believed they were witnessing was the ominous prelude to a reactionary swing of the pendulum back toward monarchy. "It is much to be feared," George Washington observed in a letter to John Jay, "that the better kind of people being disgusted with the circumstances, will have their minds prepared for any revolution whatever. We are apt to turn from one extreme to another. I am told that even respectable characters speak of a monarchical form of government without horror."[55]

John Dickinson was one of those "respectable characters" Washington probably had in mind. The delegate from Delaware considered a limited monarchy "one of the best Governments in the world." It was not certain, he told the Convention, "that the same blessings were derivable from any other form." But he was sure of one thing: history had not shown any long-lasting blessings in a democracy. Nevertheless, Dickinson conceded that even a limited monarchy was out of the question. "The spirit of the times—the state of our affairs, forbade the experiment." Nor could a "stroke of the pen" create a House of Nobles, which was "the growth of ages, and could only arise under a complication of circumstances none of which existed in this Country."[56]

Obviously, not all of the delegates shared Dickinson's nostalgia for limited monarchy. Still, the British Constitution, with its tripartite alignment of estates (and the Montesquieuan separation of powers which had been grafted on to the American image), provided a pattern which most of the framers almost instinctively imitated, with one fundamental difference. The entire edifice was to be erected on republican principles. Hence, the idea of devising artificial forms capable of serving in the place of the missing monarchy and aristocracy dominated the convention from the outset. A few delegates, in their desire to curb democracy, opposed even the popular election of the lower house, although both Madison and his fellow Virginian, George Mason, quickly defended the necessity of the "Commons," as Mason revealingly referred to it, as a means of securing popular attachment to the government.[57]

As for the Senate, the Virginia Plan tentatively proposed its election by the lower house, but the idea was quickly dismissed as ill-fitted to give it the necessary independence. Delaware's George Read, suspicious of the people, the state legislatures, as well as the proposed lower house, suggested a Senate appointed by the executive. Alexander Hamilton wanted senators chosen for life by a college of electors.[58] Only James Wilson of Pennsylvania proposed a popular election, hoping to prevent what in fact the overwhelming majority of delegates earnestly desired—the conflict of interests that would arise from placing two branches "on different foundations." His idea was not warmly received, and he did not press the point. Significantly, when Madison wrote to Jefferson in France about the various proposals for senatorial appointments, Wilson's was the only plan he neglected to mention.[59]

But on the third day of discussing the subject, Dickinson put forth convincing arguments in favor of electing senators through the legislatures. A "House of Lords," or at any rate, an assembly which could check the passions of the lower house, could not be elected in the same manner, for if all power were "drawn from the people at large, the consequence would be that the national Government would move in the same direction as the State Governments now do, and would run into all the same mischiefs." A system based solely on direct popular principles "would only unite the 13 small streams into one great current pursuing the same course without any opposition whatever."[60] Worthy of note, Dickinson was not defending the rights of states, per se, but advancing a means of establishing what has been called a "natural" aristocracy, an agency which would fulfill a function similar to that of the Lords in checking the runaway tendencies of popular rule, but which at the same time would remain a non-hereditary body. Charles Pinckney of South Carolina concurred with Dickinson's reasoning, adding that such a manner of appointment would make the Senate more "permanent and independent" in its deliberations.[61]

Obviously, the plan could also be justified on the grounds of states' rights. George Mason made a point of declaring that the legislative election of senators would give the states some means of "defending themselves"[62] against national encroachments. That said, for many, if not most of the delegates, the threat of encroachment was at least as likely to be apprehended from the opposite direction. The lack of national authority, not the excess of it, brought them to the convention. There, they quickly scuttled the enfeebled Articles of Confederation and contrived a new species of federalism which preserved the sovereignty of the states in all areas not delegated to the federal government, but gave the latter complete supremacy in matters of national interest. Having bequeathed this new government with sufficient power to carry out its delegated authority over so extensive a republic, they sought to minimize abuses by separating its powers, establishing checks and balances among its several branches, and "refining" the appointment process. Election of senators by state legislatures seemed consonant with these requirements. To lay too fine a point on an ideological attachment to states' rights is to overlook other crucial aspects of the Senate's composition—such as the deliberate exclusion of provisions for state recall, or for that matter, the implementation of six-year terms[63]—which suggest that Senate actions were ideally to be as free from state coercion as they would from popular whims.

But in times of intense partisanship, the jealousy of the states might be institutionally harnessed for the purpose of counterbalancing the "democracy" of the House. This reasoning naturally provoked objections from those in the convention who feared that the legislatures were not exactly free from the democratic vices themselves. Madison, no less, argued that "nothing can be more contradictory than to say that the National Legislature without a proper check, will follow the example of the State Legislatures, & in the same breath, that the State Legislatures are the only proper check."[64] A few score years would prove just how contradictory the proposition really was.

Still, it must have been unimaginable, even to the most ardent of nationalists, that the people would eventually lose their sense of local community so completely that most of the eligible electorate would not know the names of their own state legislators. At the time the Constitution was drafted there was little reason to believe that the states would not continue to challenge the consolidation of federal power, whether in spite of, or because of, their democratic proclivities. The experience of the Continental Congress had been entirely to the contrary. Naturally enough, when the founders were casting about for that proper "collision between the different authorities," Dickinson's idea of having the states, in their collective capacity, elect the nation's Senate, seemed more than plausible. Given the American historical circumstances, in which real aristocracy was unthinkable, and given the necessity of justifying a stronger national authority to suspicious localists, the scheme was as "politic as it was unavoidable." Thus, despite certain apprehensions, none of which arose from the desire for greater democracy, the convention adopted Dickinson's motion by unanimous vote on June 7, 1787.[65] The subsequent argument that nearly ruined the convention's deliberations, and that more clearly and forcefully evoked concern for states' rights, was over the manner of apportioning the senators, not the manner of electing them.

Meanwhile, the remaining elements of federal authority embodied an obvious attempt to provide stability, "repose or inaction," as Montesquieu called it, through deliberate complications of the electoral system. There was no genuine monarchy or nobility, but the only branch directly accountable to the popular majority was the House of Representatives. The executive was chosen by electors, who were in turn selected at the discretion of the legislatures, and in a direct sense, at least, answered to a distinctly different constituency than did either house of Congress. The judiciary, chosen by the president with the endorsement of the Senate, achieved its independence from the other branches, as well as from the people, through life tenures. The final result was that the "separate and distinct exercise of the different powers of government," the fundamental calculation in the "preservation of liberty," was accomplished by giving each department "a will of its own," with "as little agency as possible in the appointment of the members of the others." The Constitution, claimed Madison, fragmented the absolute power of the majority, deliberately supplying "opposite and rival interests" as a more solid guarantee of individual freedom than could be expected from a mere reliance on the good will of the superior number of citizens.[66]

The Senate was to be "the great anchor of the government," a restraint upon the democracy of the lower House, and upon the ambitions of the executive. By the same token, obstacles were laid as a precaution against its own "oligarchic" usurpations. By the provisions of Article I, Section 3, no more than one-third of the Senate body could be replaced in any one election. In the case of election fraud, a simple Senate majority had the power to investigate and expel any colleague determined to have gained office through underhanded means (Section 5). A senator suspected of crimes committed while in office could be removed by a two-thirds vote. As for the Senate as a whole, it had no power to legislate without the concurrence of the House, whose members answered immediately to the people.

On the premise, therefore, that the people responsibly exercised their constitutional duties (which remained at the local level, where they were considered most competent), the Senate was probably the least corruptible legislative body in the Union:

> It is evident that the Senate must first be corrupted before it can attempt an establishment of tyranny. Without corrupting the State legislatures, it cannot prosecute the attempt, because the periodical change of members would otherwise regenerate the whole body. Without exerting the means of corruption with equal success on the House of Representatives, the opposition of that coequal branch of the government would inevitably defeat the attempt; and without corrupting the people themselves, a succession of new representatives would speedily restore all things to their pristine order. Is there any man who can seriously persuade himself that the proposed Senate can, by any possible means within the compass of human address, arrive at the object of a lawless ambition through all these obstructions?[67]

In other words, a corrupted Senate, one which was beyond repair of all these checks, was, from the Federalist point of view, an indictment on the people too outrageous to be seriously considered.

But How Long the Balance?

Ironically enough, in 1913, when the principle of supplying "opposite and rival motives" to the interests of the majority had lost its hold upon most Americans, who were already long accustomed to electing presidents themselves, and were on the verge of directly electing senators as well, the historian Charles Beard offered the reading public an interpretation of the founding principles which was as unwittingly accurate as it was misguidedly critical:

If we examine carefully the delicate instrument by which the framers sought to check certain kinds of positive action that might be advocated to the detriment of established and acquired rights, we cannot help marvelling at their skill. Their leading idea was to break up the attacking forces at the starting point: the source of political authority for the several branches of the government. This disintegration of positive action at the source was further facilitated by the respective differentiation in the terms given to the respective departments of the government. And the crowning counterweight to "an interested and over-bearing majority," as Madison phrased it, was secured in the peculiar position assigned the judiciary and the use of the sanctity and mystery of the law as a foil to democratic attacks.[68]

Notwithstanding the widespread criticism which befell Beard for oversimplifying the Constitution as a document of class preservation (a view he moderated in later years), his observation, in this passage at least, was entirely correct. But it should have been worded more favorably: Temporary majorities were prevented from abusing their powers; the minority had the right to appeal; and these fundamental procedures were not easily altered.

While Beard's entire tone suggested the Constitution was a conspiracy to maintain the power of the privileged few at the expense of "the people," few charters of government have ever reflected such great faith in its citizens—as individuals in their private capacity—to govern themselves without the arbitrary intrusions of the state. Its framework was intended to restrain the pace of government, to force the lawmakers to consider interests beyond those of the transient majority before prescribing action. As for the minority, its powers were purely negative. "It may clog the administration, it may convulse the society; but it will be unable to execute and mask its violence under the forms of the Constitution." Hamilton, for one, was well aware that this "power of preventing bad laws includes that of preventing good ones." But anyone acquainted with the American problem, he insisted, would consider every constitutional check on the "excess of lawmaking," every instrument designed "to keep things in the same state in which they happen to be at any given period, as much more likely to do good than harm; because it is favorable to greater stability in the system of legislation."[69] The prevention of a few good laws, in short, was a cheap price for restraining a profusion of bad ones.

What must also be kept in mind is that the checks and balances were the product of prudence, not cynicism. First and foremost, the founders expected the representative system to "refine and enlarge the public views," passing it "through the medium of a chosen body of citizens, whose wisdom may best discern the true interest of their country, and whose patriotism and love of justice will be least likely to sacrifice it to temporary and partial considerations." But human nature being what it was, it was reasonable to assume that "Enlightened statesmen will not always be at the helm." The possibility could never be ruled out that "men of factious tempers, of local prejudices, or of sinister designs, may, by intrigue, by corruption, or by other means, first obtain the suffrages, and then betray the interests of the people."[70] The division of the national electorate into the People, the Legislatures, and the College of Electors tripled the difficulty of their acquiring the full power to carry out such ambitions.

In the long run, however, the constitutional machinery was not automatic. If it was true that the founders had "retained the forms of the aristotelian schemes of government,"[71] they had done so without the traditional elements. The American people promoted the One and the Few from among themselves, which could truly be described as the best and the worst feature of their novel republic. On the one hand, the accidents of birth conferred no superior political rights. On the other, the "natural aristocracy" would find its way into the nation's higher offices only as long as the majority showed an interest in promoting it, and checks on the majority will would last only until a sufficient majority had tired of them. Benjamin Franklin, whose faith in the popular instincts was greater than most, concluded that the whole intricate contraption was "likely to be well administered for a course of years, and can only end in Despotism, as other forms have done before it, when the people shall become so corrupted as to need Despotic government, being incapable of any other."[72]

Even Madison, for all his enthusiasm about America's "mixed Constitution," which for him came to mean "partly Federal, partly National," could not argue around the fact that ultimately the balance of power hinged on nothing more than popular self-restraint. Explaining the role he expected the Senate to perform, he reflected that "a people deliberating in a temperate moment" would understand "that they themselves were liable to temporary errors . . . [and] that . . . as different interests necessarily result from the liberty meant to be secured, the major interest might under sudden impulses be tempted to committing injustice on the minority."[73] Presumably, Madison expected that when the people arrived at this realization, they would cordially submit to negatives imposed on their will by a body of statesmen, chosen by others on their behalf, on the grounds that the wisdom, virtue, and patriotism of such an assemblage was superior to their own.

So what happened when the people were not "deliberating in a temperate moment?" What if, instead, they demanded more than this government of stasis could readily provide? What assurance was there that the *demos,* attracted to this new and greater authority, would not find means of overcoming its restraints and capturing its powers in the absolute? As it was, the Few and the One were separated from the Many in this classical illusion by the state legislatures, and by the Electors chosen by the legislatures. Yet in the infancy of the republic, the legislatures had hardly shown themselves independent of the Many. The constitutional solution thus proposed that democracy be checked by institutions already proven to be incapable of doing so. Throughout the nineteenth century, popular reformers would reassert the ideas against which the founders had contended, insisting that the direct vote was the inalienable right of every citizen, and one which applied to the highest spheres of government. The legislators were hardly in a position to refuse.

Notes

1. Alexander Hamilton, John Jay & James Madison, *The Federalist* (New York: The Modern Library, 1937), p. 54.
2. *Ibid.,* pp. 55–56.
3. Jean-Jacques Rousseau, *The Social Contract,* Maurice Cranston, trans. (New York: Penguin Books, 1968), pp. 60, 73.
4. Walter Lippmann, *Public Opinion* (New York: The Free Press, 1965), pp. 196, 162.
5. Rousseau, p. 141.
6. Rousseau, *Discourse on the Origins and Foundations of Inequality Among Men,* Maurice Cranston, trans. (New York: Penguin Books, 1984), pp. 136–137.
7. *The Federalist,* pp. 55–59.
8. Lippmann, p. 176.
9. Aristotle, *Politics,* Ernest Barker, ed. and trans. (New York: Oxford University Press, 1958), pp. 51, 54.
10. *Ibid.,* pp. 117–118.
11. *Ibid.,* pp. 113–114.
12. *Ibid.,* pp. 168–169.
13. Polybius, *The Rise of the Roman Republic,* from *The Histories,* Ian Scott-Kilvert, trans. (New York: Penguin Books, 1986), pp. 307–310.
14. *Ibid.,* pp. 311–318.
15. John Adams to Roger Sherman, July 17, 1789, *The Works of John Adams,* Charles Francis Adams, ed. (Boston: Little Brown & Company, 1856), vol. 6, p. 431.
16. James Madison, *The Papers of James Madison,* William T. Hutchinson and William M. E. Rachal, ed. (Chicago: University of Chicago Press, 1962), vol. 1, p. 16.

17. *Ibid.*, Robert Rutland, et. al., ed. (Charlottesville: University Press of Virginia, 1983), vol. 14, p. 162.

18. George W. Carey, "The Separation of Powers," *Founding Principles of American Government: Two Hundred Years of Democracy On Trial*, George J. Graham, Jr. & Scarlett G. Graham, ed. (Bloomington: Indiana University Press, 1977), p. 103.

19. *The Federalist*, p. 313; Gilbert Chinard, "Polybius and the American Constitution," *Journal of the History of Ideas* 1 (1940): 42, 44.

20. W.B. Gwyn, *The Meaning of the Separation of Powers: An Analysis of the Doctrine from Its Origins to the Adoption of the United States Constitution* (New Orleans: Tulane University Press, 1965), pp. 24–27; *See also*, M. J. C. Vile, *Constitutionalism and the Separation of Powers* (Oxford: Clarendon Press, 1967).

21. Charles de Secondat, Baron de Montesquieu, *The Spirit Of The Laws, Great Books of the Western World*, Thomas Nugent, trans. (Chicago: Encyclopedia Britannica, 1952) vol. 38, pp. 70–72.

22. *Ibid.*, pp. 72–73, 71.

23. *Ibid.*, p. 71.

24. *Ibid.*, p. 74.

25. Forrest McDonald, *Novus Ordo Seclorum, The Intellectual Origins of the Constitution* (Lawrence, Kansas: University of Kansas Press, 1985), p. 82–83.

26. Gordon S. Wood, *The Creation of the American Republic 1776–1787* (New York: W. W. Norton & Company, 1969), pp. 42, 44.

27. The Federalist, p. 313; Madison, *Papers*, vol. 14, p. 158.

28. Benjamin Franklin, *The Papers of Benjamin Franklin*, William B. Wilcox, ed. (New Haven: Yale University Press, 1982), vol. 22, p. 357.

29. Thomas Paine, *Common Sense* (New York: Penguin Books, 1968), p. 67.

30. *Ibid.*, pp. 67–69.

31. Adams, "Novanglus," *Works*, vol. 4, p. 79.

32. Francis Newton Thorpe, ed. *The Federal and State Constitutions, Colonial Charters, and Other Organic Laws of the States, Territories, and Colonies, Now or Heretofore Forming the United States of America* (Washington, D.C.: Government Printing Office, 1909), vol. 2:778; 3:1713; 5:2787; 7:3815.

33. *Ibid.*, vol. 1:563; 2:778; 3:1696; 5:2596, 2791; 6:3243; 7:3816; 5:2632, 3084; 3:1900–1901.

34. *Ibid.*, vol. 2:778; 5:3084; 1:562–563; 7:3816; 3:1896; 5:2631, 2459, 2595, 2790.

35. *Ibid.*, vol. 3:1895, 1898; 4:2459, 2461.

36. Thomas Jefferson, *Notes on the State of Virginia*, William Peden, ed. (Chapel Hill: University of North Carolina Press, 1955), p. 120.

37. Thorpe, vol. 1:562–563; 5:2631; 6:3244–3245; 7:3816.

38. Wood, p. 252.

39. Ibid., p. 255.

40. Jackson Turner Main, *The Upper House in Revolutionary America* (Madison: University of Wisconsin Press, 1967), pp. 111–114.

41. "Madison to Jefferson, October 24, 1787," *The Writings of James Madison*, Gaillard Hunt, ed. (New York: G. P. Putnam's Sons, 1904), vol. 5, pp. 25–26.

42. Wood, pp. 193–194.

43. *Ibid.*, p. 405n.

44. Madison, "Vices of the Political System of the United States (1787)," *The Writings of James Madison*, vol. 2, pp. 365–366.
45. McDonald, pp. 91–92.
46. *Ibid.*, p. 91.
47. *The Federalist*, p. 406.
48. McDonald, pp. 173–177.
49. Wood, p. 406.
50. *The Federalist*, pp. 405–406.
51. Quoted in Wood, p. 410.
52. Wood, p. 404.
53. Madison to Jefferson, October 17, 1788, *The Papers of Thomas Jefferson*, Julian P. Boyd, ed. (Princeton: Princeton University Press, 1958), vol. 14, p. 19.
54. Madison, *The Debates in The Federal Convention of 1787*, Gaillard Hunt & James Brown Scott, ed. (Buffalo: Prometheus Books, 1987), vol. 1, pp. 31–32, 34.
55. General Washington to John Jay, August 1, 1786, *The Writings of George Washington*, Worthington Chauncey Ford, ed. (New York: G. P. Putnam's sons, 1891), vol. 11, p. 55.
56. Madison, *Debates*, vol. 1, p. 47.
57. *Ibid.*, pp. 32–33.
58. *Ibid.*, pp. 24, 70, vol. 2, p. 609.
59. *Ibid.*, vol. 1, p. 70; Madison to Jefferson, October 24, 1787, *Jefferson Papers*, vol. 12, p. 273.
60. Madison, *Debates*, vol. 1, pp. 70, 72;
61. Max Farrand, *The Records of the Federal Convention of 1787*, (New Haven: Yale University Press, 1966), vol. 1, p. 155.
62. Madison, *Debates*, vol. 1, p. 74.
63. *Ibid.*, p. 66.
64. *Ibid.*, p. 73.
65. *Ibid.*, pp. 72, 65, 74.
66. *The Federalist*, pp. 336–337.
67. *Ibid.*, pp. 413–414.
68. Charles Beard, *An Economic Interpretation of the Constitution of the United States*, 2nd ed. (New York: The Macmillan Company, 1935), p. 161.
69. *The Federalist*, pp. 57, 478.
70. *Ibid.*, pp. 59, 57, 59.
71. Wood, p. 604.
72. Madison, *Debates*, vol. 2, p. 578.
73. *Ibid.*, vol. 1, p. 167.

3

The Tilt in the States

Without the intervention of the state legislatures, the president of the United States cannot be elected at all; and the senate is exclusively and absolutely under the choice of the state legislatures. The representatives are chosen by the people of the states. . . . How is it possible, under such circumstances, that the national government can be dangerous to the liberties of the people, unless the states, and the people of the states, conspire together for their overthrow?
—Justice Joseph Story

In the ebb tides of public spiritedness, interests temporarily in the majority, or claiming to speak for the majority, were supposed to face an imposing obstacle in having to gain the support of the greater number of states, as well as of the people directly, before they could attain the full legislative power of the Union. That was but one purpose, however, in recommending the indirect election of senators. The founders also believed that the legislators commanded a higher and broader view of their state, and were thus deemed more competent than the electorate at large in selecting "the most respectable men in the State," as James Iredell reasoned in the North Carolina ratifying convention, "men who had given strongest proofs of their attachments to the interests of their country."[1]

The Initial High Ground

For at least the first half century under the Constitution, the legislators had, on the whole, fulfilled the latter and higher function. In 1834, Alexis de Tocqueville marvelled at the Senate's "eloquent advocates, distinguished generals, wise magistrates, and statesmen of note, whose arguments would do honor to the most remarkable parliamentary debates of Europe."[2] A few years later, another celebrated visitor, Harriet Martineau, recorded that "the stamp of originality was impressed upon every one, and inspired a deep, involuntary respect."

The widely-travelled English noblewoman confessed to having seen no assembly of hereditary dignitaries whom she considered "half so imposing as this collection of stout-soled, full-grown, original men, brought together . . . to work out the will of their diverse constituencies."[3] Another observer, having remarked upon a certain senator's second-rate abilities, was quick to add that, in the constellation of the Senate, "to be 4th rate is no mean praise."[4]

At the same time, the illustrious chamber which then hosted the likes of Henry Clay, Daniel Webster, and John C. Calhoun, contrasted starkly, in de Tocqueville's estimation, with the "vulgar demeanor" of the lower house, filled as it was with "obscure individuals," "village lawyers" and "persons belonging to the lower classes of society." It puzzled the Frenchman that "Both of these assemblies emanate from the people; both are chosen by [*through* would have been a more accurate preposition] universal suffrage; and no voice has hitherto been heard to assert in America that the Senate is hostile to the interests of the people. From what cause, then," he queried, "does so startling a difference arise?"[5]

He ventured that the only conceivable explanation was in its indirect method of election:

> This transmission of the popular authority through an assemblage of chosen men operates an important change in it by refining its discretion and improving its choice. Men who are chosen in this manner accurately represent the majority of the nation which governs them; but they represent only the elevated thoughts that are current in the community and the generous propensities that prompt its nobler actions rather than the petty passions that disturb or the vices that disgrace it.[6]

It was de Tocqueville's belief that this indirect method of election was the "only means of bringing the exercise of political power to the level of all classes of the people." With an eye toward the expansion of territory, population, and economic diversity that was obviously in the young nation's destiny, he calculated that the "American republics will be obliged more frequently to introduce the plan of election by an elected body into their system of representation, or run the risk of perishing miserably on the shoals of democracy."[7]

Notwithstanding this admonition from one of the modern world's truly brilliant and often prophetic political philosophers, the American republics embarked on a course that was completely inimical to the continuance, let alone the expansion, of the system of indirect elections.

In fact, M. de Tocqueville himself had already observed disturbing tendencies. "The man of a democratic age," he noticed, "is extremely reluctant to obey his neighbor, who is his equal; he refuses to acknowledge superior ability in such a person; he mistrusts his justice and is jealous of his power."[8] In other words, the individual citizen, in obeying "no one but himself," as eighteenth century theorists conjectured, tended to withhold the requisite portion of power which had to be delegated in order to make representative deliberations truly effective. Instead, he favored successive constitutional innovations that purported to give him an equal voice in the broader realm of public affairs. This millennial quest continually eluded him, and often bore consequences directly contrary to his expectations. But it seemed to daunt him not the least, so steadfast was his faith in the absolute power of "the people."

The federal Constitution had been designed in forthright repudiation of such leveling impulses. It will be recalled, on the other hand, that the hierarchical elements it contained, the checks on popular whims that it created, were in some manner or other dependent on the popular assemblies in the states. The Senate, for one, was chosen by the state legislatures. The president, for another, was promoted by electors who were chosen by the legislators, or by agents designated by the legislatures; while the federal judiciary was appointed by the president in concurrence with the Senate. Even the House of Representatives, elected by direct popular vote, originally relied on the suffrage laws of the respective states. And here was the chink in the armor, for as already demonstrated, the states suffered from those very propensities which, in the workings of the federal government, they were supposed to counteract. Closer within the popular grasp, state governments in the nineteenth and early twentieth centuries would yield ever further to the claims of democracy, impairing in the process the representative checks and balances of the federal system.

Thus, even as de Tocqueville wrote the praises of indirect elections, forces were gaining strength in the states which spelled their eventual doom. If democracy, as he observed, seemed so well restrained in his day at the national level, perhaps it was merely smoldering in the states before the general conflagration spread to the structure of federalism as well. It would be instructive, therefore, to trace the history of state democracy in fuller detail, for as the states have gone, so eventually has gone the Union. Problems in federal governance have often had their parallel in the governance of the states, and the unravelling of checks and balances in the latter has been the legacy of a similar phenomenon in the former. If the U.S. Senate was intended to represent the states in their "deliberative capacity," it is appropriate to ask what had happened to that capacity, that it could allow the forces of democracy to pull the Senate directly within their sway.

The Resurgence of Sovereign Individualism

The undeliberative, often capricious, use of popular power manifested under the Confederation had been curtailed to some extent by the federal Constitution's prohibition of ex post facto legislation, bills of attainder, and laws impairing the obligation of contracts, as well as by strongly implied proscriptions against paper money (which was seen as being more easily inflated for political purposes). Judicial review ensured compliance on the part of both Congress and the state legislatures. No doubt, the widespread respect and personal abilities of the founders themselves had also contributed an initial resistance to the republic's democratic propensities. In due time, however, those propensities inevitably reasserted themselves, and the impetus came, quite naturally, from the states.

Universal suffrage was the first step. Beginning with Vermont in 1791, it was adopted by all the new states, except Tennessee, which entered the Union in 1796 with an unspecified "freehold" requirement. By the mid 1830s, all of the original states had adopted the all-male standard, or a close approximate, except New Jersey (1844), Virginia (1850), and South Carolina (1865). Property qualifications for voting were replaced across the country with the prerequisite of paying taxes, or serving in the militia, and these, in turn, were supplanted by mere residence requirements of increasingly shorter duration. By the mid-nineteenth century, in the overwhelming majority of states, the vote was the inherent prerogative of any twenty-one-year-old white male, except an "idiot or insane person, or person convicted of any infamous crime."[9]

There can be little doubt about the efficacy of a suffrage broad enough to secure the responsibility of the rulers to the ruled. Yet there is also a rational but not absolute line to be drawn, beyond which a voice in determining the general laws is mistaken for an inviolable right, rather than a privilege earned with respect to established community standards. The former property qualifications, for the lower houses at least, were not particularly stringent, while they offered proof of an individual's permanent attachments, his investment, as it were, in the common enterprise. And as long as the honest attainment of property remained open to all, it could not be claimed that the political franchise was a caste monopoly.

On the other hand, the pursuit of happiness in the nineteenth century was obviously not confined to the romantic rusticity of the Jeffersonian ideal. The vote could not indefinitely be reserved to the possessors of land, as if the "numerous and respectable body of citizens" in the burgeoning centers of commerce and manufacturing were utterly "destitute of interest." This was the complaint of the non-freeholders of Richmond, Virginia. The petition which John Marshall submitted on their behalf to the state constitutional convention of 1830 was certainly reasonable, for it conceded that "the right of suffrage [was] a social right," not a natural one. It was not inherently universal, but was "of necessity . . . regulated by society." Quite sensibly, the Richmond petitioners did not premise their request for extending the suffrage on any absolute principles of right, but on the simple question, "Is the existing limitation proper?"[10]

But amending the rights of suffrage, as James Madison had once cautioned, was "a task of peculiar delicacy."[11] Voting qualifications were not to be modified upon transient provocation; yet, at the same time, the question of who should vote was, and is, relative to changing circumstances. Exactly where to draw the line was supposed to remain an open question. Universal suffrage, as it soon came to be applied, essentially ended the discussion, once and for all, for although the vote would never be "universal" in the literal sense of the word, particularly not when qualifications of race and sex were applied, the community was left with no admissible criteria for distinguishing the responsible, committed and contributing citizen from the prodigal, the transient and the indigent.

In popularly elected offices throughout the country a noticeable decline in statesmanship ensued. A variety of reasons for the phenomenon have been ascribed. One group of historians, echoing de Tocqueville, claimed that, "To elect one's betters to office was to admit one had betters. To throw one's betters out of office was to rebuke for their pretensions those who thought themselves superior, and to prove that the people really ruled."[12] De Tocqueville himself had added that the feeling was mutual, that the able men of America were beginning to retire from an arena in which it was "so difficult to retain their independence, or to advance without becoming servile."[13] Yet another explanation has been that the great increase in the number of voters caused by universal suffrage made it impossible to manage politics informally, and that the drill and muster of mass party politics "called for talents that were by no means restricted to the gentry."[14]

In any event, the fact of the decline has been roundly conceded. "A race of pygmies came to infest the public councils," according to one recent account.[15] To another still more recent, politics fell under "the sway of the Lilliputians."[16] One of the modern textbooks on American history, which usually applaud the nation's egalitarian progress, noted in the wake of universal suffrage the "lowered . . . moral and intellectual tone of American political life," but managed to conclude, rather sanguinely, that at least "it was possible for the ordinary man to feel a sense of participation."[17] That comment belies the highest good in democratic thinking: Universal participation, regardless of the consequences. Indeed, it is significant that the process of universalizing the suffrage was in many states followed by constitutional amendments that detailed the penalties for voting fraud, bribery of officials, and a host of other unethical practices beyond the need of mention in earlier times, when the the right to cast a ballot was bestowed as a mark of merit.

Of course, if the aim of constitutionalism is stability, then the importance of popular attachment to the government cannot be overestimated, and it might be plausibly argued that a certain leveling in the caliber of statesmanship was a necessary compromise toward that end. There were still branches of government, such as the Senate, capable of exercising some restraint. But democratic theory assumed the suffrage as a right. And if the right was assumed to be absolute and universal, what was the justification for any representative hierarchy at all? This was the question faced by the defenders of "mixed constitutions" in the state conventions of the 1820s and '30s. For the average citizen, to be represented in the lower house had once been considered sufficient, so long as it retained a complete check on the actions of government. But what eventually triumphed, in Chancellor Kent's words, was "the notion that every man that works a day in the road or serves an idle hour in the militia, is entitled as of right to an equal participation in the whole power of government." Conceding the legitimate extension of the all-male vote in the lower assembly, Kent saw no reason, as he told the New York constitutional convention of 1821, why, on purely theoretic grounds, the state Senate should also be sacrificed to "the idol of universal suffrage."[18]

The same egalitarian principle was raised eight years later in Virginia, that one-time bastion of free-hold conservatism. In this first skirmish, however, it was temporarily defeated, largely through the genuine persuasiveness of delegates such as Abel P. Upshur, who argued that to base legislative representation solely on universal suffrage was not to establish true equality (the equal protection of "diverse and unequal faculties"), but to give undue power to the majority. "I have been forcibly struck with the fact, that in all the arguments upon this subject here and elsewhere," said Upshur, "this right in a majority is assumed as a postulate. It has not yet been proved, nor have I heard an attempt to prove it."[19]

His intractable colleague, John Randolph of Roanoke, opposed even the slightest modification of the suffrage. Undeniably eccentric and irascible, but just as undeniably brilliant—a rebuke, rather than an example, to the statesmen of his age—this relic of the planter aristocracy had an uncanny sense of the far-reaching consequences that would result from the commonwealth's concessions to democracy. Randolph held that the overextension of voting rights would weaken Virginia's system of checks and balances, and thus remove those constitutional constraints which forced the people of the state to deliberate. By default, the absence of strong, deliberative authority in the states would invite a larger, more intrusive, and more irresponsible federal government. To the would-be levelers of the Virginia constitution, therefore, he professed, "It is because I am unwilling to give up this check [of the states upon the general government], or to diminish its force, that I am unwilling to pull down the edifice of our State government from the garret to the cellar; aye to the very foundation stone."[20]

To extend the suffrage, declaimed the old planter, was simply "the entering wedge." The rule of "King Numbers," as he called it, would inevitably triumph on a national scale, for it was Randolph's strong conviction that no rational restriction on the privilege of voting would hold, once it ceased to be based on the land. Property had always been and would always remain the basis of power (he believed them inseparable: one would always go in search of the other as soon as they were estranged). Hence, in answer to the Richmond nonfreeholders, Randolph protested that their willingness to make political distinctions was not a sufficient safeguard. To extend the suffrage beyond the holders of real property, but only so far, was tantamount to asking "an industrious and sagacious Hollander if you may cut his dykes, provided you make your cut only of a certain width. A rat hole will let the ocean in."[21]

Randolph's invective did not prevent Virginia's expansion of the suffrage, although its extension to all white males would have to wait until twenty years later. All the same, he correctly predicted that, once the vote was assumed as an *a priori* right, there could be no limits at which its direct and universal application could be halted. As with

New York in 1821, when the Old Dominion finally adopted universal suffrage in 1850, it was applied to both houses of the legislature. And Virginia was rather a latecomer. All of the new states had entered the Union with no difference in the electoral qualifications for either branch of the legislature, except Kentucky, which abolished a college system like Maryland's within seven years of its admission (and technically Vermont, which had a unicameral legislature until 1836). In most of the original thirteen states, the "mixed" character of the legislatures had been obliterated by the mid-1830s. Virginia held out until 1850; Rhode Island, 1842; New Jersey, 1844; North Carolina, 1856; South Carolina was finally forced to yield after the Civil War.[22]

At approximately the same time, the governorships became the property of the popular majority, as did all or parts of the judicial branch in most states. By the end of the century, in fact, only eleven states did not elect at least some portion of their judiciary (Connecticut, Delaware, Maine, Massachusetts, Mississippi, New Hampshire, New Jersey, Rhode Island, South Carolina, Vermont, and Virginia). Moreover, the judicial tenure of "good behavior"—which the English-speaking world had considered progress in the Revolution of 1688—was shortened in most states to eight or ten years, but often to as few as six.

In this second era of state constitution-making, accomplished for the most part between the early 1820s and the mid-1830s, the advocates of extending the direct popular influence could cite few specific abuses of power, and not one which could be traced conclusively to inequalities in the political structure. Notably, the biggest scandal in the young republics, Georgia's "Yazoo Land Fraud" of 1795, occurred after that state, which already had one of the more democratic constitutions of the former colonies, had extended the vote to all white male tax payers for both legislative houses.[23] But given the premise of democracy, under which inequality in the political structure was an abuse in itself, the logic of such a transformation in state constitutions was irresistible, and the changes irreversible.

On occasion, the degree of imperviousness to any legitimate, rational distinctions which might have existed among "the people" was plainly ludicrous. A Louisiana champion of popularly elected state Supreme Court justices, for example, declared to the state's constitutional convention in 1844 that he could care less "where a candidate may address the people, be it in the midst of a tavern, where a mob may be collected together," as long as they had "the opportunity to have the shallowness of his capacities detected. The humblest among them will say, 'Well that man has no more sense than I; how can he pretend to such an office?'"[24]

Crass and simplistic as such reasoning was, it carried the unmistakable echo of those fine-sounding theories from the eighteenth century. Reformers of the early nineteenth century essentially continued where Thomas Paine had left off in the American Revolution, insisting that the only means of preventing political abuse was to keep the full power of government in the immediate grasp of the people. Even though this idea had already been tried and found wanting during the initial years of independence, constitutional tinkerers in subsequent ages consistently reasserted that the proper direction for the political order was "invariably, an extension of the range of popular power." And typically, such leveling was mistakenly understood as a progressive contribution to the separation of powers. By placing the legislative, executive, and judicial officers under the direct control of universal suffrage, so the reasoning went, "you divide and separate these powers," and thereby "advance from monarchy to republicanism."[25] Madison, by contrast, had stated in no uncertain terms that such an arrangement was not a separation of powers at all, but rather a consolidation of power in the hands of the many. His exact words were, "the very definition of tyranny."

A contemporary of this democratic transformation, John C. Calhoun, described the phenomenon as a move from the rule of the *"concurrent* or *constitutional* majority" to that of the *"numerical,* or *absolute* majority."* In his tersely written political masterpiece, *A Disquisition on Government* (1851), the senator from South Carolina observed that "the division of government into separate, and, as it regards each other, independent departments," while essential, could not, in and of itself, counteract "the tendency to oppression and abuse of power." If all branches were based exclusively on universal suffrage, the entire government would still be under the direction of the numerical majority, without any realistic check to protect legitimate minority interests. The separation of powers was merely nominal without first making "the several departments the organs of distinct interests or portions of the community" and clothing "each with a negative on the other."[26] A constitutional majority rested not on strictly numerical decisions, but on the concurrence of the separate and distinct interests that were represented in the various divisions of government.

Although the *Disquisition* treated the concept of the concurrent majority in general terms, without reference to specifically American conditions, Calhoun undoubtedly believed that it vindicated the rights of states. His fears of an impending mass democracy at the national level led him time and again to assert that the states not only checked the federal government, but were in fact superior to it. Yet the object of such fears could not be realized unless at the instigation of the states. To repeat, the states controlled the Senate, the presidential electors, the congressional voting qualifications, and even had the final word in the process of amending the federal Constitution. In terms of preserving the Union from mass democracy, the true difficulty stemmed from the fact that by the time Calhoun took up his pen against it, the states had already exchanged the constitutional distinctions necessary for the concurrent majority in favor of the purely numerical form of government. The full legislative, executive, and judicial authority had been placed in the hands of the popular majority, or as often as not, in the hands of those adept at organizing majorities out of all the private and partial interests that called themselves "the people."

The Evils and Follies of Democracy, Again

During the second quarter of the nineteenth century, the states were arming the popular majority with far greater powers than it had possessed before 1787, and naturally enough, their governments came to be increasingly characterized by majoritarian excesses and abuses. For example, the majority of white citizens in the South, "the people," as they no doubt thought of themselves, had made the manumission process virtually impossible for the dwindling minority who felt ill at ease with "the peculiar institution." In point of fact, it became far more difficult to free slaves *after* the constitutional reforms than it was in the days when the Virginia aristocracy fretted over what to do with them.[27]

Meanwhile, democratic constitutions in the Old Northwestern states were prohibiting the immigration of free blacks. Indiana's legislative, executive, and judicial power, for instance, answered completely and directly to the popular majority when the state constitution was written with the declaration that:

> No negro or mulatto shall come into, or settle in the State, after the adoption of this constitution.

> All contracts made with any negro or mulatto coming into the State, contrary to the provisions of the foregoing section, shall be void.[28]

It is arguable that nothing in these provisions violated the federal Constitution as it then existed, and that judges must uphold the decisions of the people when acting through their legislatures or in conventions, no matter how foolish or unfair they seem, unless the higher law of the Constitution expressly forbids them. Otherwise, there is no separation of powers, properly speaking. Yet the subject at hand is not judicial, but legislative restraint, the wisdom and impartiality that goes into the making of law. Whether or not such discriminatory legislation could be judicially sustained, it demonstrated that "the people," expressing themselves through universal suffrage, were not inherently protective of minority interests and individual rights (in the second half of the nineteenth century, constitutions of the Pacific states contained similar clauses, adopted by universal suffrage, against the Chinese).[29]

Admittedly, this sort of constitutional bigotry represented the extremes. Popular government was not usually guilty of malice, merely imprudence. "There is more feeling and less design in the movements of masses," reflected James Fenimore Cooper, after his seven years among the aristocracies of Europe.[30] He returned in 1835 in time to witness what has been called a "wild frenzy for internal improvements to be constructed at state expense."[31] The voters clamored for turnpikes, canals and railroads, and the legislators in most states spared no means to satisfy the demand—except taxation. As Governor William Seward reminded the lawmakers of New York, the levying of taxes for such projects "finds no advocates among the people."[32] He was preaching to the choir, of course, for politics dictated, as representation without taxation is wont to do, a spree of deficit spending.

The states raised bonds, invested existing revenues in the stocks of private companies, chartered banks, and otherwise pledged the public credit for literally scores of enterprises that they were incapable of executing or supervising. Total state indebtedness jumped from under $13 million in 1825 to more than $170 million in 1838, to nearly $204 million in 1842.[33] Anticipating a net profit from toll fees, many states ended up owing payments on bonds for railroads never completed, or holding stock in canals too infrequently traveled to return a profit. A number of projects undertaken directly by the states, such as the Pennsylvania Railroad, had to be sold at considerable loss to private enterprises.[34]

The fact that private interests could capitalize on public misfortune was hardly the fault of governmental elitists defying the will of the people. On the contrary, the recklessness that engendered the failure of so many projects stemmed from that resurgent "spirit of locality" to which democracies are particularly vulnerable. A case in point was the New York legislature, which, intoxicated with the success of the Erie Canal, completed in 1825, proposed the construction of seventeen others that same year, most of them of dubious value to the common welfare, but of decided interest to the majorities in their respective constituencies. Meanwhile, localities which did not benefit immediately from the canals petitioned incessantly for railroads. In response, the legislators extended loans to no less than ten separate companies, four of which went bankrupt without ever building their roads. And while New York legislators, in their haste to satisfy constituents, were proceeding to quadruple the state deficit in five years (1837–1842), Pennsylvania's legislature found itself powerless to construct its vital main line route across the Appalachians without considerable appeasement of the local "branch line" advocates.[35]

West of the Appalachians, the "feeder line" mania was undertaken as if every farmer had to have his property directly linked to the eastern harbors. The gross commitments of public expenditure and enormous grants to private construction corporations cannot be viewed, therefore, in simplistic terms of a speculative minority seeking gain at the public expense, for such occurrences, whenever they happened, were results, not causes. After all, state legislatures had committed these extravagant outlays so that farmers, manufacturers and mine owners would earn higher prices, consumers would get more for the money, real estate values would climb, and favorably located brokers and middle men would enhance their profits.[36] In other words, regardless of the outcome, which turned out to be catastrophic in many cases, the popular majority had been behind such spurious projects from the very beginning.

The excessive undertakings in public works were but the larger part of the financial recklessness of an unchecked majority in the states. With the death of the Bank of the United States under President Jackson, the burdens of fiscal regulation had fallen to the state legislatures, most of which were incapable of restraining the demand for easy credit. Of the $170 million state deficits in 1838, close to $53 million had been incurred in the chartering of state banks (specifically called for in a number of popularly ratified constitutions), whose lending policies were often risky enough. Then, too, the states did little to regulate the practices of those private lending institutions tellingly referred to in the parlance of those days as "wildcat" banks. The indiscriminate extension of credit touched off a wave of speculation in the 1830s. Most of the loans went to the internal improvement corporations, and to real estate companies (there were, traditionally, few restraints on the use and sale of public lands).[37] In the race for credit, however, even the venerated common man behind the plow had to bear a portion of the blame for the disaster that followed. Farmers often mortgaged their lands for loans from local banks to buy more land, and then turned around to borrow an even greater amount on the strength of their larger deeds. The Arkansas Constitution of 1836, for example, provided for a state bank specifically "calculated to aid and promote the great agricultural interests of the country,"[38]—which happened to be the interests of the Arkansas majority.

As with internal improvements, excesses in state banking systems resulted in a number of failures. The speculation they inspired, particularly in land, contributed to the soaring inflation of the '30s, until the boom collapsed in the Panic of 1837. When depression followed, Indiana, Louisiana, Maryland, Michigan, Mississippi, and Pennsylvania had made outright repudiations on their debts. Other states arbitrarily suspended interest payments on their "improvement bonds." Creditors, foreign and domestic, had good reason to doubt the "full faith and credit" guarantees of popular government.[39]

More Power to the People: The Solution

To be sure, the people of the states sought earnestly to put the anarchic conditions of their finances in order. Their reaction was not as harsh as that of the Athenians in time of war, who put their unsuccessful generals to death, but the principle was the same. As one historian of state government described, "The people insisted upon legislative policies that resulted in disaster, and then, after the injury had been done, they imposed strict limitations upon their legislatures." From the late 1840s into the 1870s, more or less, another generation of constitutional reforms was undertaken, greatly prohibiting the power of the legislatures to embark upon internal improvements or to incorporate banks. In states where the results of indiscretion had been most severe, absolute strictures were placed against either or both. New states that entered the Union during the period, capitalizing on the experience of the older ones, placed similar constitutional restrictions on their own legislators.[40]

In the short term, these amendments instituted a needed restraint on state expenditures, but failing to strike at the root of the problem, they also introduced precedents detrimental to the long term effectiveness of checks and balances. The true source of the trouble was a fictional perception of the popular will, that imaginary oracle which would guide the body politic if only its medium, the people, was left unhindered to express itself. As the previous examples show, there were, in reality, only individual wills within districts, wills of districts within regions, and so forth. E Pluribus Unum was not the result of mere expression, but of setting priorities, subordinating, and at times even suppressing various private and local demands for the good of the common welfare. Such power frankly contradicted the egalitarian creed, and was therefore rarely delegated (the practice of "instructing" representatives lasted well into the Jacksonian Era, at which time local party platforms fulfilled a similar function). Thus, as Herbert Croly wrote in *The Promise of American Life* (1909), "local representative government was poisoned at its source." The people expressed their will in every town and county, but the state legislator, "even if he were an honest man, represented little more than the local powers constituting his district."[41]

The problem with the constitutional restrictions on the legislators, then, was that they did nothing to restrain the popular majority which had prompted the folly to begin with. Without interests constitutionally distinct from that majority, with power to check its impulses, as had been attempted in the earlier versions of "mixed" systems, political restraint was no longer inherent to the form of government. Instead, it had to be reinforced by expressly worded constitutional limitations on the power of the delegated authorities. But as there was a limitless field for placating special and local interests, (that is, the people), where would such restrictions finally end? And more importantly, exactly *who* was imposing the limitations?

In answer to the first question, state constitutions in the second half of the nineteenth century necessarily dropped all pretense of establishing a minimal, flexible framework in which representatives forged the common will out of the vast and diverse interests of the state. Instead, they were transformed into monstrous catalogues of do's and don'ts, encumbering every conceivable aspect of the legislative process. As the details expanded, and representative authority correspondingly diminished, state constitutions necessarily ventured from the realm of fundamental law into that of ordinary statutes: spending limits, tax collection, property laws, divorce laws, establishment of regulatory commissions, the salaries, wages and working hours of state employees, veteran's pensions, and the location of state universities. Virtually any power that the legislator might be tempted to use in advancing the local and private interests of his constituents, even the most petty authority that he could possibly abuse, was liable to be taken from his discretion and rendered a part of the "fundamental law." Many state constitutions, for instance, outlined the contract bidding process for state repairs and purchases, even to the point of specifying how the state would buy its furniture and stationary. Some constitutions went so far as to prescribe the daily allowances for legislative expenses, the number of staff the legislatures could employ, and the rules of legislative proceedings.[42]

In answer to the second question, the constitutional conventions which made these reforms were called for by the legislators themselves, and like the regular legislatures, they, too, were essentially representative bodies, with delegates elected by the people. Almost inevitably, conventions were subject to the same special interest pressures as the legislatures had been. In 1870, a substantial debtor interest in Virginia, hard-pressed from the ravages of the Civil War, secured a "usury clause," which set constitutional limits on interests rates. Colorado's convention of 1876 gave a constitutional tax exemption to the mining interests. In many of the southern and western states, the constitutions prohibited "rebates" and "drawbacks" on railroad rates.[43] A rebate was a partial refund by the railroads to large shippers who threatened to take their business elsewhere. The biggest shippers could extort drawbacks, that is, a rebate on their competitors' shipping. Thus, constitutional prohibitions against such practices, while they served to protect smaller shippers, were hardly against the interests of the railroads.

As events would prove, "the people," as represented in the conventions, were hard to distinguish from "the interests" represented in the legislatures. One such event was the Louisiana convention of 1879, which, after proposing a fair and uniform system of taxation, exempted:

> All public property, places of religious worship or burial, all charitable institutions, all buildings and property used exclusively for colleges or other school purposes, the real and personal estate of any public library and that of any other literary association, used or connected with such library; all books and philosophical apparatus, and all paintings and statuary of any company or association kept in a public hall; provided, the property so exempted not be used or leased for purposes of private or corporate profit or income. There shall also be exempted from taxation household property to the value of five hundred dollars; there shall also be exempt from taxation and license for a period of twenty years from the adoption of the constitution of 1879, the capital, machinery and other property employed in

the manufacture of textile fabrics, leather, shoes, harness, saddlery, hats, flour, machinery, agricultural implements, manufacturer of ice, fertilizers and chemicals, and furniture and other articles of wood, marble or stone, soap, stationary, ink and paper, boat-building and chocolate; provided, that not less than five hands are employed in any one factory.

It was "submitted to the people and adopted," a fundamental charter with hardly any interests overlooked, and a life span of twenty-two years.[44]

After "the people" had been exempted, it was imperative that "the interests" should not escape taxation. The Illinois constitution of 1870 therefore announced a governmental policy of vigilance in procuring the due portion of revenue from the state's "peddlers," "auctioneers," "brokers," "hawkers," "showmen," and "jugglers," the sort of interests who—until recently, at any rate—were not likely to be well represented in a popular political convention.[45]

These examples hardly begin to scratch the layer of minutia which the people began to include in their state constitutions. It almost goes without saying that they became the prey of perpetual innovation, amendments, and repeals, partly because so little of their bulk had to do with fundamental law, and necessarily shifted with the exigencies of politics, and partly because, like the governments they were supposed to outline, they were hardly respected bulwarks against the transient mood of the popular sovereign. Between 1789 and 1848, the people in their respective states adopted thirty-six new constitutions. Excluding the seventeen constitutions creating the new states of that period, and two which revised colonial charters in use since the mid-seventeenth century (Connecticut's and Rhode Island's), the remainder leaves seventeen rewritten constitutions out of thirty states, a little over one out of two in sixty years. In the sixty years that followed, that figure was greater still, with more than fifty constitutional overhauls among forty-six states.[46]

But on the whole, constitutional conventions were too unwieldy as a means of change. Adding amendments to existing constitutions was far easier. Nearly all of the states which had provisions for amendments had originally required two successive legislatures to make a change, many requiring two-thirds majorities in each house or a popular referendum upon legislative approval, or both. Even under these restrictions there had been enough amendments to refute later claims that the legislators were not "responsive" to the needs of the people. Nevertheless, in the late nineteenth century most states had reduced the amendment process to passage by a single legislature and a popular referendum; and by the fateful year of 1913, eleven states (Oregon, Oklahoma, Missouri, Michigan, Arkansas, Colorado, Arizona, California, Nevada, Nebraska, and Ohio) were amending their constitutions through what amounted to little more than a straw poll, the popular "initiative," by which a petition, endorsed by the signatures of anywhere from eight to fifteen percent of the electorate, could be placed on the ballot in the state's next general election.[47]

The results were prolific. Louisiana's 7th constitution, a closely printed, seventy-five page charter of fundamental law that had been instituted in 1898, was not so comprehensive, apparently, as to preclude the need for twenty-six more amendments by 1907. That was about par with Oregon, whose constitution changed twenty-three times between 1904 and 1910. California had averaged one amendment per year since becoming a state in 1850 (embracing such cardinal principles as the eight hour work day for public employees and tax exemptions for fruit trees under four years old), but in the early twentieth century, California's average multiplied seven-fold, with twenty-three amendments passed in 1911 alone. A year later, Ohio surpassed that single-year figure with thirty-four constitutional revisions.[48]

To be fair, some states, particularly in New England, made comparatively few changes in their constitutions, but the trend was clearly marked toward easier and more frequent amendments. In the twenty years between 1889 and 1908 only two states, Wyoming and Tennessee, left their constitutions in tact (and Wyoming had not entered the Union until 1889). Even Lord Bryce, who knew state constitutions better than the overwhelming majority of the citizens who lived under them, admitted that he had "not found it possible to keep abreast of the changes" made between the time of professor Thorpe's 1909 publication and the 1914 edition of his own exhaustive study, *The American Commonwealth*.[49]

Contemporaries saluted the fact that the people were no longer "gripped by the dead hands of antiquated, fundamental law,"[50] impervious to the contradiction in terms. The law was either antiquated or fundamental, not both. Moreover, it was quite ironic that a generation which would not be gripped by the "dead hands" of the past would have burdened posterity with constitutions tenfold the length of those drafted in 1776. Victims of a "specious present," as Walter Lippmann called them, democratic reformers showed an incredible zeal for amending their constitutions with "all kinds of rules and restrictions that, given any decent humility about the future, ought to be no more permanent than an ordinary statute."[51]

It was becoming increasingly difficult to maintain the distinction, because both the constitutions as well as ordinary statutes were subject to change at the same hands and in the same manner. The initiative and referendum could be used for either (for ordinary legislation, a petition signed by as few as five percent of the electorate was usually sufficient to place it on the general election ballot). By the end of the first decade of the twentieth century, the people in twenty-five states were in one form or another making laws directly for themselves at the state level. Executives had no veto power in such cases, and even if they did, it would have been suicidal for them to have exercised it. If popularly passed laws were not constitutional, the constitution could be easily changed, or the judge who challenged the direct legislation of the people could simply be voted out in the next election, or dropped from the party ticket in the nominating process. To add further restrictions, a number of states implemented the recall election of unpopular officials, including judges. Admittedly, this last innovation was not widely used, but then the mere threat of its use was enough to discourage independent deliberation on the part of elected authorities.[52] Many states, in short, made rapid strides toward that state of affairs in which, as Aristotle once said, "everything is managed merely by decrees."

William Allen White, in his widely read *The Old Order Changeth* (1910), gloried in this progress of direct democracy as the beginning of the overthrow of checks and balances. "The friends of the movement for direct legislation," wrote White, "should frankly admit that the purpose of their cause is two-fold: first, to *compel* the legislatures to act quickly and without evasion; and second, to *circumscribe* the veto of such courts as are elective, and hence dependent upon popular majorities." White, like his contemporary, Charles Beard, conceived that the principles espoused by the founders flatly contradicted the progressive notions of constitutional government. "But nevertheless," he declared ecstatically, the tendency of the states represented "a strong movement away from the Constitution." The political order was triumphantly "drifting toward democracy." Unlike the elitism of the federal charter, the new forms of governing instituted by the states more fully secured "the rights of the individual" by offering him a direct and wider range of participation. By some process White did not explain, the American people had progressed in wisdom and patriotism, and were fully prepared to exercise the greater role which democracy now held out to them. He assured the Doubting Thomases in politics that the direct methods of governing would be "the instrument of a self-restrained people."[53]

Less Power to the People: The Result

White's contentions were palpably false on almost every count. State governments under these newer methods were, if anything, even less restrained than previously. Nor did they defeat "the interests," at least not in the manner in which reformers were accustomed to thinking of them. The settlement of the fishing controversy in Oregon's general election of 1908 presented a classic refutation of such expectations. Interregional competition for the Columbia River's diminishing supply of salmon had grown increasingly fierce during the early years of the twentieth century. Catching the fish in the upper narrows involved use of an instrument called the "fish-wheel." The lower river was fished by a method known as the "gill-net." Taking advantage of the state's recently established direct legislation amendments, the "fish-wheel" operators managed to obtain enough signatures to place an initiative on the ballot that would ban all salmon fishing at the river's mouth. The stated object of the proposal was to protect the fish from "commercial greed." In retaliation, the "gill-net" fishers, having affiliated themselves as the "Columbia River Salmon Protective League," proposed their own initiative to prohibit their rivals from fishing upstream. "Because special privilege and unjust monopoly had so often threatened the will of the people in the Legislature," the gill-net interests reminded the electorate, "the initiative and the referendum was [sic] adopted—the people's direct rule was established." As if the league were not attempting to do precisely what it accused its enemies of doing, the petition urged the voters to "apply the people's rule" in favor of its bill. "A vote against this bill," the league warned, "means that a few rich wheel owners of the upper Columbia River will be able to pile up great wealth for a few more years" before ruining the industry altogether.[54]

As it turned out, the voters of Oregon defeated both "interests," with the simple result that no commercial fishing for salmon was permitted on the Columbia River. Proponents of direct legislation claimed victory, the people having seen fit to preserve the salmon for the long-term good of the industry, but it is highly doubtful that this was a widely shared motive among the voters. For one thing, both bills were passed by a minority of the total electorate. A significant portion of voters chose not to cast their ballots for either side in the dispute. For another, the initiatives had originated out of wholly selfish interests intent on using the plebiscite as a means of eliminating the competition. Although it may have been poetic justice that the leaders of both parties should suffer for their demagoguery, the negative effects extended to the entire community. Perhaps as many as five thousand fisherman faced unemployment, and Oregon was suddenly confronted with the possibility of losing at least $3 million dollars in annual revenues.[55] Fortunately for everyone involved, the legislature intervened in a timely effort to undo the damage and balance the claims of the competing interests.[56] The episode was a rather shaky vindication of the General Will.

Not only did direct legislation fail to guarantee legislative restraint, as White asserted, it demonstrably failed to enhance the voter's control over political decisions. After all, the extension of the voting power into higher echelons of governmental affairs reduced the significance of the individual vote: The higher the echelon, the more massive the constituency, and the less the importance of any one vote. The right of the people to choose the laws under which they lived, and in the unfortunate wording of many constitutional preambles, "to alter, reform or abolish their form of government, in such manner as they think expedient," relied on an increasingly narrower definition of "the people." On the face of it, the direct and universal vote on initiatives and referenda hinged on the will of a mass majority, which was not the whole people. Yet in reality, the victorious factions often composed no more than a plurality, a majority only with respect to those who bothered voting on a given issue. To take yet another example from Oregon: in 1910, 123,000 voters showed up at the polls on general election day. A mere 44,000 votes on one particular initiative was sufficient to pass a sweeping constitutional amendment:

> providing for verdict by three-fourths of the jury in civil cases; authorizing grand juries to be summoned separate from the trial juries, permitting change of judicial system of statute, prohibiting retrial where there is any evidence to support verdict; providing for affirmance of judgment on appeal notwithstanding committed in lower court, directing the Supreme Court to enter such judgment as should have been entered in lower court; fixing the terms of [the] Supreme Court; providing for judges of all courts to be elected for six years, and increasing the jurisdiction of [the] Supreme Court.[57]

How much thought "the people" had given to such sweeping proposals, and what their qualifications were to make such judgments, were not matters of public record, as would have been the deliberations of the legislature. According to one observer, even lawyers were confused by the measure and what its long-term effects were likely to be. The voters probably understood the three-fourths jury verdict, but certainly little else.[58] Even on this point, the longstanding individual right to a unanimous jury verdict had been thrown to the wayside by an anonymous minority.

In the following year California held a referendum which added twenty-three amendments to her constitution. Every registered voter in the state was sent an information pamphlet, a large sheet closely printed on both sides, which some critics claimed was not intended to be read by anybody. Despite the importance of the issues—among which were the initiative for statutory as well as constitutional law, and the popular recall of judges—the turnout in this nonpresidential election year was minimal. The amendments passed on average with 60,000 votes. This was hardly a landslide, considering that in the previous presidential election, William Jennings Bryan failed to carry the Golden State by 90,000 votes[59]

The fact that plebiscitary government often resulted in minority rule evidently held little weight, however, with Mr. Bryan himself, one of the movement's foremost crusaders. Addressing the Ohio constitutional convention of 1912, he scoffed at the idea that popular consent should consist of a majority of the total electorate, rather than a majority of votes cast on a specific proposition. As Bryan saw it, the only people who counted were those who voted:

> A reform that secures a majority of the votes cast on the subject certainly has the presumption of right on its side. The most that can be said of those who do not vote is that they are indifferent, and, if so, they ought not to be counted either way. If they fail to vote because they are too ignorant to understand the subject there is less reason why their voice should be made effective in defeating a proposition which has secured the support of a majority of those who have studied the subject and expressed themselves upon it.[60]

The "presumption of right," as it were, was purely Bryan's. He presumed that such dubious majorities had no interests adverse to the interests of the rest of the community; that only those who "studied the subject" would vote on it; and that those who did not were simply ignorant. Quite possibly, the latter were more sophisticated, aware of their own limitations, or more industrious, too occupied with making a living, raising a family, and otherwise providing for their own necessities, to keep abreast of every "issue" on which they were supposed to render their sovereign opinion.

In order to fulfill his entire obligation at the polls, the average voter in the early twentieth century would have to have been no less than the "omnicompetent citizen."[61] As part of the legacy of the Jacksonian Era, in which much of the appointive powers were revoked from representative authority, dozens and even scores of state and local officers had to be elected from among an army of candidates. In addition to the legislators, the governors and the judges, there were also the lieutenant governors, the attorneys general, the secretaries of state, treasury and education, comptrollers, state printers, internal improvement commissioners, school board officers, county coroners, court clerks, sheriffs, ad infinitum. By the early twentieth century, as government grew simultaneously with the popular mistrust of it, an average ballot in rural and suburban Illinois presented over fifty offices to be filled from nearly two hundred candidates, while in Chicago the total number of offices to be filled through popular election was about five hundred in a four year period. The same was true of New York and Philadelphia. To be fair, Progressivism accomplished an excellent reform in many states and urban areas by reducing the list of elective offices in the so-called "short ballot movement," although the higher, state-wide offices—in which the individual vote counted for far less than the ability to organize—would generally remain in the hands of direct universal suffrage. In any event, to the duty of keeping up with all the candidates was eventually added the task of making decisions on a host of legislative and constitutional questions which the people would no longer trust to their representatives.[62]

Faithful democrats answered with the miracles of modern technology. In the approaching millennium of improved communications and universal education, perhaps representative checks and balances could be done way with altogether, an idea which Bryan virtually espoused on a number of occasions. "What with our daily newspapers and our telegraph facilities we need not delegate our powers."[63] Assuming it was ever feasible to hold a town meeting for an entire state, however, it did not change the fact that such an arrangement rested on the absolute rule of numbers, as unchecked majorities or pluralities. The democracy of Athens, where the entire polity could assemble and vote, had been derided in *The Federalist* as the government that decreed "to the same citizens the hemlock on one day and statues on the next."[64] Then again, the entire polity could *not* assemble and vote in the extensive, populous territories that comprised the states. The range and depth of issues far exceeded the capacity of ordinary citizens to judge intelligently. True, many states published voters' pamphlets to "educate" the public. Oregon, for instance, distributed 126 pages of information to voters in the election of 1908, 208 pages in 1910, and 256 pages in 1912, mostly in highly technical and legal language, with the pros and cons offered by their respective partisans and antagonists. But even if the voter read from cover to cover, his direct participation came down to a yes or no vote—no discussion, no amendments—on proposals conceived and promoted by people whose motives were not the least bit known to him.

Very telling, in fact, was an Ohio law enacted in 1902, the Longworth Act, under which initiatives and referenda, or opposition to them, could be made part of the party ticket. When faced with a proposal to change a statute, or even the fundamental laws of the constitution, the bewildered voter could simply "go with his party," as he often did when casting his ballot for the annual hoard of petty officials whose names presented an overwhelming mystery at the voting booth. By means of this enactment and the subtle omission of the "no" from the ballot, Ohio politicians finally managed to get the voters to endorse their repeated call for a constitutional convention, which met in 1912 and (with Bryan's encouragement) reduced the requirement for passing direct legislation from a majority of electors "voting at said election" to a mere majority of those voting on the specific proposal.[65] The Longworth Act effectively pointed up the contradiction of direct democracy: There would always be hierarchy, regardless of the forms. Not one idea found its way among the masses, not one initiative, referendum, nomination, or recall, without first being formulated and articulated within a much smaller circle of citizens. The mass could not initiate, nor could it deliberate. Barring the mythical dispensation of the General Will, it could only approve or reject the proposals of some concerned interest or party leader.

Even in popular governments, therefore, and particularly in large republics, political power would always be exercised in the hands of the few, regardless of democratic appearances. The essential point was not whether the people governed universally, but whether they concentrated their focus upon the few who were constitutionally accountable for the general welfare. In the governance of the states, the legislature was the most logical source of popular attention. No other institution combined in the same degree such prominent visibility, yet local accessibility, which made it the ideal body to consider those affairs which affected the whole community, yet were beyond the daily scope of the individual citizen.

But turn-of-the-century legislatures were no longer the repositories of popular confidence. The movement for direct democracy claimed to be a reaction against their subservience to special interests. Yet the actual workings of the legislative process, as observed in the earlier accounts of internal improvements and banking policies, expose at once the striking resemblance between those interests and "the people." After generations of trying to overthrow the interests with more democracy, the net result was that legislatures were more than ever the creatures of the partial and local interests that elected them. Lord Bryce, in a scrutinous survey of American political institutions made more than half a century after de Tocqueville's, concluded that the average legislator was not:

> a member for his State, chosen by his district, but bound to think first of the general welfare of the commonwealth. . . . His first and main duty is to get the most he can for his constituency out of the State treasury, or by means of State legislation. . . . What is more, he is deemed by his colleagues . . . to be the sole exponent of the wishes of the spot, and solely entitled to its affairs. . . . Each member being the judge of the measure which touches his own constituency, every other member supports that member in passing the measure, expecting in return the like support in a like cause. . . . He who in the public interest opposes the bad bill of another, is certain to find that other, and probably with success, opposing his own bill however good. . . .
>
> Nothing is more remarkable about these State legislators than their timidity. No one seems to think of having an opinion of his own. In matters which touch the interests of his constituency, a member is, of course, their humble servant. In burning party questions—they are few, and mostly personal—he goes with his party. In questions of general public policy he looks to see how the cat jumps; and is ready to vote for anything which the people, or any active section of the people, cry out for . . .[66]

If, as the saying went, the legislatures represented every interest but the public's, then making them *more* responsive to the people was not the solution. If anything, the direct methods of legislation merely relieved them further of having to settle the difficult questions of public policy while they continued to cater to the narrow interests of those who placed them in office. Indeed, Bryce's study of state laws in the first decade of the twentieth century reveals that in the very years when the initiative and referendum were instituted to halt the rule of special interests, approximately eighty percent of the 15,000 statutes passed annually were of a purely local or special nature.[67]

The decline in the character and caliber of the legislatures really should not have come as much of a surprise. As Herbert Croly remarked, they became "corrupt and incapable, chiefly because they have not been permitted any sufficient responsibility." Croly, who believed in nationalism over federalism, and managerial bureaucracy over the mayhem of elective politics—which earned him high marks with progressive reformers—was nevertheless acutely perceptive of the deleterious effects that democratic ideology had wrought upon the representative systems of the states. The long train of popular encroachments, he concluded, could not have been more "admirably calculated to debase the quality of the representatives and to nullify the value of their work." State constitutions "gradually hemmed them in with so many restrictions . . . [that] they offered no opportunity for a man of ability and public spirit." Indeed, constitutions which delineated, as many did, the various forms of bribery and graft forbidden to the legislators, and the various penalties such crimes incurred, could hardly inspire the more self-respecting citizens to enlist for the office. It was a simple case of cause and effect, argued Croly, that legislatures had become "more corrupt and incompetent in proportion as they have been increasingly deprived of power."[68]

Given the egalitarian desideratum, however, reformers entertained no idea of restoring the legislative authority. The interests would supposedly be defeated when the proper means of popular expression had been established. But in actuality, direct democracy gave an even broader scope to the rule of special interests than had been the case under more hierarchical forms of representation. Constituted authority, in the shape of the legislature, was increasingly losing control. It might even be said to have abdicated its control, for until the advent of the initiative, at least, it was the legislators who called for conventions and submitted referenda, "putting into the constitutions by way of amendment restrictions upon their own powers."[69] In any event, if authority would no longer be exercised by the few who were constituted to wield it, then the door was open to organized cabals outside the representative process. Any interest which could not get its way through ordinary representation was free to try its luck with the plebiscite, under which, as a few examples have already shown, the popular assent was much more ambiguously expressed.

Moreover, if those in the constitutional hierarchies designated to hold the reins would no longer do so, the task would necessarily revert to those in hierarchies *outside* the constitution. While reformers insisted on simpler, less complicated means of expressing the popular will, there were no inherently shared ideas waiting to be expressed. Some organized few, more adept at the real workings of politics, would have to generate the issues and nominate the candidates, and by satisfying as many partial and local interests as necessary, forge majorities out of the great mass of voters. More will be said of the infamous political "machines" in the chapters ahead. For now, it suffices merely to remark that they were the product of over-popularized state governments, and that in some fashion or other they would inevitably survive the reformer's attacks against them, because they provided the necessary hierarchy behind the facade of mass democracy.

The most incontrovertible fact in the history of state governments is that their disorders in the early twentieth century, disorders that reformers proposed to remedy with more democracy, had already been preceded by successive generations of democratic reforms. Having started with the premise that all men were by the laws of nature equal in their political rights, it was a short step to supposing that the ordinary voter was the equal of his representative in determining the general laws, and from thence to the notion that the representative had no power to deviate from the will of his constituents. In the absence of the General Will, the reforms that lashed the legislatures more tightly to the demands of "the people" threatened to produce representative bodies that amounted to no more than the sum of the states' partial interests.

The danger was that the dissolution of constituted authority, the inability to restrain the mass of private and local interests, might not stop with the states. The fate of the Union, after all, was inextricably bound to that of its co-sovereign commonwealths.

Notes

1. Jonathan Elliot, *Debates in the Several State Conventions on the Adoption of the Federal Constitution as Recommended by the General Convention at Philadelphia in 1787 Together wyth the Journal of the Federal Convention...* (Philadelphia: J.B. Lippincott, 1836), vol. 4, p. 40.
2. Alexis De Tocqueville, *Democracy in America*, Henry Reeve, trans. & ed. (New York: Vintage Books, 1945), vol. 1, pp. 211–212.
3. *Harriet Martineau, Retrospect of Western Travels* (New York: Greenwood Press Publishers, 1969), vol. 1, pp. 301–302.

4. Lucian Minor, "A Virginian in New England Thirty-Five Years Ago." excerpted in *The Leaven of Democracy*, Clement Eaton, ed. (New York: George Brazillier, 1963), p. 73.

5. De Tocqueville, vol. 1, p. 211.

6. *Ibid.*, p. 212.

7. *Ibid.*

8. *Ibid.*, vol. 2, p. 312.

9. Francis Newton Thorpe ed., *The Federal and State Constitutions Colonial Charters, and Other Organic Laws of the States, Territories and Colonies, Now or Heretofore Forming The United States of America* (Washington D.C.: Government Printing Office), vol. 6:3418; 5:2601; 7:3832–3833; 6:3276; 1:393.

10. *Proceedings and Debates of the Virginia State Convention of 1829–1830* (Richmond: Samuel Shepherd & Co., for Ritchie & Cook, 1830), pp. 25, 26, 30.

11. James Madison, Note to the speech on the 7th Day of August, *The Debates in the Federal Convention of 1787*, Gaillard Hunt & James Brown Scott, ed., vol. 2, p. 619.

12. John D. Hicks, George E. Mowry & Robert E. Burke, *The Federal Union: A History of the United States to 1877*, 5th ed. (Boston: Houghton Mifflin Co., 1970), p. 384.

13. De Tocqueville, vol. 1, p. 209.

14. Richard P. McCormick, *The Second American Party System: Party Formation in the Jacksonian Era* (Chapel Hill: University of North Carolina Press, 1966), p. 30.

15. Forrest McDonald, *Novus Ordo Seclorum: Intellectual Origins of the Constitution* (Lawrence: University of Kansas Press, 1985), p. 292.

16. Merrill D. Peterson, *The Great Triumvirate: Webster, Clay, and Calhoun* (New York: Oxford University Press, 1987), p. 6.

17. Irwin Unger, *These United States: The Questions of Our Past*, 2nd ed. (Boston: Little, Brown & Co., 1982), vol. 1, p. 249.

18. *Reports of the Proceedings and Debates of the New York Convention of 1821*, N. H. Carter, ed. (Albany: W. L. Stone & M. T. C. Gould, 1821), p. 220.

19. Ritchie, p. 66.

20. *Ibid.*, p. 315.

21. *Ibid.*, p. 319.

22. Thorpe, vol. 3:1265–1266, 1279; 5:2601; 6:3230, 3271.

23. *Ibid.*, vol. 2:779, 789.

24. *Proceedings and Debates of the Convention of Louisiana which Assembled at the City of New Orleans January 14, 1844* (New Orleans: Besancon, Ferguson & Co., 1845), p. 268.

25. *Ibid.*, p. 744.

26. John C. Calhoun, *A Disquisition on Government*, Richard K. Cralle, ed., (New York: Peter Smith, 1943), pp. 28–34.

27. Henry W. Farnum, *Chapters in the History of Social Legislation in the United States to 1860* (Washington, D. C.: Carnegie Institute of Washington, 1938), pp. 200, 209–210.

28. Thorpe, vol. 2, p. 1089.

29. *Ibid.*, vol. 1:446–447; 5:3015.

30. James Fenimore Cooper, *The American Democrat* (New York: Alfred A. Knopf, 1931), p. 62.

31. Walter F. Dodd, *State Governments* (New York: The Century Company, 1922), p. 98.
32. Carter Goodrich, *Government Promotion of Railroads Canals, 1800–1892* (West-port, Ct.: Greenwood Press, 1960), p. 57.
33. James Bryce, *The American Commonwealth*, 3rd ed. (New York: The Macmillan Company, 1914), vol. 1, pp. 528–529, 529n.
34. Goodrich, p. 69.
35. *Ibid.*, pp. 57, 72–73.
36. George Rogers Taylor, *The Transportation Revolution, 1815–1860* (New York: Holt, Rinehart, and Winston, 1951), p. 88.
37. Bryce, vol. 1, p. 529n.
38. Thorpe, vol. 1, p. 285.
39. Hicks, et. al., p. 470.
40. Dodd, p. 100.
41. Herbert Croly, *The Promise of American Life* (New York: Bobbs-Merrill Company, Inc., 1965), pp. 121–122.
42. Thorpe, vol. 1:161, 366; 3:1353.
43. *Ibid.*, vol. 7:3896; 1:496.
44. *Ibid.*, vol. 3, p. 1505, 1471n.
45. *Ibid.*, vol. 2, pp. 1035–1036.
46. See Thorpe, Table of Contents.
47. James Quayle Dealy, *The Growth of American State Constitutions from 1776 to the End of the Year 1914* (New York: Ginn & Co., 1915), p. 147; Bryce, vol. 1, 473.
48. Dealy, pp. 90, 99, 105–107.
49. Bryce, vol. 1, pp. 434, 435n.
50. Dealy, p. 90.
51. Walter Lippmann, *Public Opinion* (New York: The Free Press, 1922), p. 89.
52. William Allen White, *The Old Order Changeth* (New York: The Macmillan Company, 1910), pp. 59–62.
53. *Ibid.*, pp. 56–57, 34, 2.
54. *Oregon General Election Measures Voter's Pamphlet*, (Salem, Oregon: Willis S. Duniway State Printer, 1908), pp. 48, 109.
55. "Initiative and Referendum Measures, 1902–1953," *Oregon Blue Book* (Salem: Secretary of State's Office, 1954), p. 346.
56. Allen H. Eaton, *The Oregon System: The Story of Direct Legislation in Oregon, A Presentation of the Methods of the Initiative and Referendum, and Recall, in Oregon, with Studies of the Measures Accepted or Rejected, and Special Chapters on the Direct Primary, Popular Election of Senators, Advantages, Defects and Dangers of the System* (Chicago: A.C. McCurg & Co., 1912), p. 68.
57. *Ibid.*, pp. 76–77.
58. *Ibid.*, p. 77.
59. Nicholas Murray Butler, "Why Should We Change Our Form of government?" *Senate Document 238* (62nd Congress, 2nd Session), 1912, pp. 14–15.
60. William Jennings Bryan, "The People's Law: Address Delivered at Columbus, Ohio, March 12, 1912, upon Invitation of the Constitutional Convention," *Senate Document 523* (63rd Congress, 2nd Session), 1914, p. 6.
61. Lippmann, p. 173.

62. Albert M. Kales, *Unpopular Government* (Chicago: University of Chicago Press, 1914), p. 29; Richard S. Childs, "The Short Ballot," *American State Government*, Paul S. Reinsch, ed. (New York: Ginn & Co., 1911), p. 374.

63. *Congressional Record* (53rd Congress, 2nd Session): 7775.

64. Alexander Hamilton, John Jay & James Madison, *The Federalist* (New York: The Modern Library, 1937), p. 410.

65. Dealy, p. 99.

66. Bryce, vol. 1, pp. 549–550, 552–553.

67. *Ibid.*, pp. 551–552.

68. Croly, p. 321.

69. Ronald M. Peters, "The Written Constitution," *Founding Principles of American Government: Two Hundred Years of Democracy on Trial*, George G. Graham, Jr. and Scarlett G. Graham, ed. (Bloomington: Indiana University Press, 1977), p. 192.

4

Federal Repercussions

*Tickets for the impeachment trial of Pres. Andrew Johnson
were very much in demand, and it was one of the best-attended
events of the capital's season.
—Ripley's Believe It Or Not*

Given the American constitutional structure, the egalitarian momentum in the states was bound to affect the balance of the Union. As state governments became more directly controlled by popular influences, the legislators were correspondingly weakened in their ability to promote the countervailing elements of the federal system. When they formally abdicated as electors of the United States Senate, it marked the most notable milestone, perhaps, in the states' historical retreat from representative checks and balances, but in that the amendment proposed to make the Senate of the United States similarly more "responsive" to popular impulses, it stands as a major bridgehead for the democratic advance on federal authority as well.

Traditionally, the Seventeenth Amendment has been justified by the intrigue and corruption which attended the former method of electing senators, and by the fact that the Senate used its formidable powers to protect the interests which elected them. The image of shady politicos, in league with greedy capitalists to feast on the public spoils, conforms to the conventional portrait of the Gilded Age in general, the age of the "Great Barbecue," as Vernon Parrington reproachfully termed it. Over the past generation, however, a number of historians have attempted to moderate the muckraking excesses which taint the historical legacy. Arguing that the accounts of pious reformers and yellow journalists have typically been handed down without critical examination, their revisions call to mind the maxim of George H. Hoar, one of the age's more sagacious statesmen. A lifelong political career had taught the senator from Massachusetts that "The history of no people is heroical to its Mugwumps."[1]

As valuable as such reappraisals may prove in reaching a more balanced understanding of the age, there is no intention here to dispute the degree of the Senate's moral decline, nor the extent to which the "bosses" allegedly manipulated its elections, nor still the amount of corporate influence upon its politics, such as can actually be proven. For present purposes, this is to strain at gnats when camels must be disgorged in the accepted wisdom that the evils sprang from some deficiency of democracy in the constitutional structure. The truth is, that in electing senators, the legislators were as tethered to the wishes of their constituents as they were in making the laws, and well before any widespread call for changing the Constitution. As had been the case with the history of state institutions in general, it was the steady democratization of the Senate which actually created the problems that more direct popular control proposed to solve. Despite all the evidence to the contrary, the American people had come to believe that the Constitution was a democratic instrument,[2] and when it failed to work as such, it was the Constitution, not the assumptions, that had to be changed.

The Popular Reach

In fact, the people were reaching for the Senate as early as the Jacksonian Era, the same era which inaugurated the popular presidency. It is worth recalling that when the College of Electors operated with some degree of its intended autonomy, it selected presidents who by most accounts have eclipsed all but a few of their successors. According to the Jacksonian Democrat, Senator Thomas Hart Benton, the electors were supposed to be citizens of "superior discernment, virtue and information," who elected the president "according to their own will." Yet owing partly to the absence of any constitutional guidelines for presidential nominations, and partly to the efforts of each state to consolidate its electoral votes upon a single candidate, there was from the outset a degree of external influence on the electors which the framers had clearly sought to avoid. Even so, the very idea of such independence was, in Benton's words, "wholly incompatible with the safety of the people," an affront, as it were, to the democratic sensibilities of the age.[3]

Originally, the manner of choosing electors was almost completely within the purview of the states. At first, electors were chosen in a variety of ways: By popular vote with property qualifications, by popular voting through electoral districts rather than at large, or by some combination thereof. In 1800, the electors in five-eighths of the states were appointed directly by the legislatures. After 1824, merely one-fourth of the states retained the legislative appointment. Only the South Carolina legislature held out after 1832 (until after the Civil War).[4] The change was yet another manifestation of the eroding hierarchy among representative institutions throughout the states. At the very time when most governors, state senators, and judges were becoming the direct property of the popular majority, the electors were being unceremoniously stripped of their created role as wise, patriotic elders who elevated the chief executive from among the nation's worthiest citizens, and were given in exchange the bit performance of loyal party men who could be counted on to vote for one of the candidates already nominated in popular party conventions. By the end of the seventh administration, the college had in effect become what it is today: The numerical shorthand for popular election returns (many states having dropped the names of Electors from presidential ballots altogether).

In the founding attempt to raise the executive on an electoral basis which was distinct from those of the other branches, the college was a hapless solution to a problem which dogged the three-month convention into its final week. By contrast, the original system of Senate elections, resting on the less tenuous ground of preexistent legislatures, managed to survive the indirectly elected presidency by some eighty years. Yet the fall of the Senate, while less precipitous, began at approximately the same time. In fact, the direct election of senators was initially proposed in the House in 1826—two years before the accession of Andrew Jackson, and two years after the first presidential election in which popular voting was ever recorded.[5]

The 1826 proposal was tabled without discussion, as was a similar proposal in 1835, followed unsuccessfully by five more in the early 1850s. Two of these last five were submitted by the Tennessee congressman, and subsequently senator, Andrew Johnson, who made further attempts throughout his legislative career, and by no means relinquished the cause upon inheriting the White House.[6] In his 1868 message to Congress, he urged the adoption of a direct election amendment, basing his argument exclusively on those *a priori* convictions which had been chaffing at the limits on popular sovereignty since the founding of the republic. Without citing any of the abuses which became part of the battle cry against the Senate a generation later, the president simply insisted that the intrusion of intermediaries on the popular choice of senators was not "consistent with the genius of our form of Government." (A stickler for such consistency, his message also included proposals for abolishing the Electoral College and limiting the tenure of the federal judiciary.)[7] For its part, the Congress was preoccupied with the perhaps more pressing amendments of Reconstruction. Furthermore, as Johnson's impeachment (by the popular House) and near expulsion (saved by the single vote of a legislatively appointed senator) dramatically demonstrated, it was little disposed to follow the president's lead in any event. Once again it took no action. But if senatorial elections remained unchanged in form, a significant metamorphosis was nevertheless taking place in substance. In a collapse of the representative hierarchy very similar to that which befell the electors, state legislators were beginning to be chosen less on their own merits than on whom they professed to support in the federal elections.

It is widely acknowledged that one of the most significant results of America's democratization was the creation of permanent party machinery. "With frequent elections decided by large numbers, democracy forced politicians to build large organizations to influence voters."[8] And what soon proved to be the machinery's greatest asset was the United States senator. In the first place, he was the state's chief arbiter of the federal patronage and spending projects, the "loaves and fishes" which maintained the corps of party faithful. In the second, he was perfectly positioned to thwart any federal initiative which ran counter to the interests of the organization's supporters. More importantly, and even more ironically, his power and prominence were in themselves the most compelling sources of popular support for the legislative machine. The parties discovered a peculiar vote-getting method in nominating senatorial candidates prior to the state elections, then publicizing the nominations. With the senatorial nominee thus dangled before the public, the organizations hoped to entice the people to elect legislators in the same party as the most popular candidate.

Hence, as early as 1834, George Poindexter, the Whig incumbent to the Mississippi Senate seat, stumped the crowds at a series of outdoor banquets arranged for the purpose of denouncing the Jacksonians. On the first such occasion, Robert J. Walker, a Democrat, gave such a rousing rebuttal that the banqueters resolved upon his nomination to defeat Poindexter in the upcoming election. Walker successfully ousted the senator from his incumbency, but only after both candidates had engaged in unprecedented personal campaigning before the Mississippi public. Their tactics were repeated and refined in subsequent elections throughout the states, and became known in campaign vernacular as "canvassing the public." West of the Appalachians in particular, the public "canvass" by Senate contestants had become a standard feature of state politics. It was already well established by 1841, when Governor Polk declined to convene a special session of the Tennessee legislature to fill a Senate vacancy on the grounds that in the last election of the legislators, members "had not been chosen [by the people] with the selection of Senators in view."[9]

Nor is history likely to forget the race for the Illinois seat in 1858. An obscure lawyer named Lincoln was catapulted to national fame and the presidency for taking on the most prominent politician of the day, Stephen A. Douglas. Understandably, the principal issue of the election has distracted historical attention from the means by which it was conducted. The candidates toured the countryside, publicly debating the solemn question of slavery's expansion while garnering "pledges" from prospective legislators whose preference for senator would be the biggest popular issue in the upcoming state elections.[10] The Lincoln-Douglas debates brought the canvass to a new level, reducing the Illinois legislature to a mere registering body with little more power than the presidential electors.

Few Americans at that time shared the sense of alarm with the editorialist who found it "difficult to conceive of anything more illegitimate" than the campaigns of Lincoln and Douglas. "The Senator . . . is the representative of the state, as an independent polity, and not . . . of its individual citizens."[11] But by then, perhaps, the states were already leaning too far in the direction of ad populum politics to make a reversal. What is more, the partisan machines had everything to gain from tilting the process even further. The more the senator was looked upon as the direct property of the masses, the more bound were the legislators to those who did the nominating.

The legislators found themselves even more restricted in their deliberations with the advent of the party primary. The primary is essentially an intra-party election held before the general election, intended to make nominations more democratic. Implemented at the local level in many states as early as the 1860s, and extended in time to state-wide offices, the primary "merely duplicate[d] elections and intensifie[d] party demands for subsistence," as Henry Jones Ford complained, calling the reform "a case of change without improvement."[12] It was not just change, but an actual decline, for with the advent of the primary, the same laws against bribery, fraud, and intimidation of voters which were supposed to maintain the sanctity of the general elections had to be rewritten and expanded to incorporate the nominating process as well.[13] When the primary was extended to senatorial elections, the parties polled their rank and file to ascertain the majority preference for U.S. Senator. As with direct legislation, direct senatorial primaries rarely drew a majority of the eligible voters, but the legislators, as a rule, were guided by the results. Otherwise, they incurred the risk of losing the party's backing for reelection.

Because party caucuses and party conventions had previously nominated the senators, it has been a post hoc ergo propter hoc assumption that the primary was an invention of popular reaction against the intrigues of nominating bodies that excluded the general voter. In 1875, Nebraska was the first to adopt the senatorial primary, having attained statehood only eight years previously.[14] Colorado, becoming a state in 1876, adopted primary elections eleven years later. Montana instituted "local primaries" within five years of its statehood, Oklahoma within one. Wyoming entered the union with them.[15] (Local primaries often included some form of voter "preference statement" for senators, and legislators rarely hesitated to adopt the choice of their constituents as part of their own nomination campaigns). Within a few years, these newer states almost invariably extended their primary systems to include direct, state-wide nomination of senators as well. In other words, the primary system made its first appearance in states which hardly had time to have developed a sophisticated apparatus for corruption, let alone to have waged a popular "reaction" against it. Moreover, even in the older states which eventually adopted the senatorial primary, it was the legislators, as ever, trimming their sails to the popular winds, who initiated and passed the laws needed to put the system in effect.[16] In reality, the primary was yet another surrender of representative will to the dominion of numbers.

Whether it was the old party caucus, the convention, or the primary, the party objective from the Jacksonian Era until 1913 was to nominate a senatorial candidate whose popular appeal was strong enough to drag a majority of the legislators on his coattails in state elections. But it was like trying to put a square peg in a round hole. The Senate was never intended to represent the people in their individual capacity, and practically every problem pursuant to its election in the late nineteenth and early twentieth centuries stemmed from a mistaken popular belief to the contrary.

Deadlocks

Perhaps the most distressing problem in senatorial elections was the "legislative deadlock" that ensued when the two political parties were closely balanced. If the party in power was sundered by internal factions, it was impossible to obtain a majority vote for senator. In 1882, for example, Oregon's legislators argued over their Senate seat for almost the entire session without resolve. Washington, Montana, and Wyoming went without electing a senator for almost two years starting in 1893. In all, during the fifteen years from 1891 through 1905, there were forty-five such deadlocks, fourteen of which resulted in no election for an entire legislative session or more.[17] Although press accounts often gave the impression that these deadlocks brought all legislative business to a standstill, the truth was that most legislatures took one vote at the beginning of each day and continued with their normal affairs. Noted in the previous chapter, after all, was the swell of legislation that the states managed to pass, amend, and repeal during the same period in which the deadlocks had grown worse. Still, the frequent vacancies in Senate seats, depriving the national deliberations of the full sense of the states, were a nuisance which argued for reform.

Reformers, however, seemed to see no correlation between the frequency and duration of the deadlocks, and the amount of popular restrictions placed on the legislators' prerogatives. Notably, the most extreme deadlock occurred in Delaware, when the state had one representative in the Senate from 1899 to 1901, and none from 1901 to 1903. These were the first two elections under which Delaware had implemented the legislative primary (there was as yet no direct, state-wide senatorial primary in Delaware, but senatorial preference polls were usually included in the primary campaigns of the legislators). The Missouri legislators were under similar constraints in 1905, when the struggle over a Senate seat erupted into a fist fight on the floor of the assembly.[18] To end such disgraces, as one editorialist unwittingly put it, legislators would have to take the unprecedented step of *"disregarding the verdict of the primary* [emphasis mine]."[19]

Reformers complained to no end about these contests between the interests which deprived the people of their due representation in the Senate. And of course, what was meant by "interests" were the political dealers and their corporate backers. Yet behind every member of every cabal in every legislature was a popular constituency, and often the bitter stalemates within the assembly merely reflected the party violence

75

threatening without. In Kentucky's election of 1896, for instance, the governor had to impose martial law in the capital city to keep a public riot from breaking out over the Senate contest. In 1905, Denver police who supported the Democratic candidate came close to bloodshed with the troops called out by the Republican governor.[20]

Admittedly, the Seventeenth Amendment brought an end to the deadlocks between a few score legislators when it allowed the parties to submit the decision to hundreds of thousands, or millions, on a statewide ballot. Less drastic solutions were available. In 1866, Congress had passed a law requiring a concurrent vote of both houses of the state legislatures on the first ballot, and joint balloting thereafter, if no clear majority had prevailed concurrently. However, a viva voce requirement exposed at the outset the preference of every member, as well as the differences between the two houses, enabling minorities to devise strategies at least to prevent an election they could not control. An amendment of this statute, in the opinion of Senator Weldon Heyburn of Idaho, would have been sufficient to end the deadlocks. Congress already possessed the regulatory power over federal elections. Observing that some states had adopted rules which dropped the low man from the contest after a certain number of ballots, Heyburn suggested that national legislation make the practice uniform in all the states. New York's Senator Elihu Root proposed allowing victory by plurality vote if there were no majority to elect a senator within thirty days of the convening of Congress. Root contended that majorities would therefore be obtained "in order to avoid those elections by pluralities."[21] Direct elections would later confirm his hypothesis, since the states subsequently had to make provisions in their primary laws either to declare plurality winners the party candidate, or to hold runoff elections between the two highest contestants. Then after all the favorite sons had fallen by the way in the nominating process, most voters, in avoiding plurality elections, were usually left with a choice of senatorial evils on general election day.

Corrupt Elections

Deadlocks were not the only charge against the former method of electing senators; bribery was another. But here again, the occasions rose with the democratization of the elective process. Up to 1872, there had been only one proven instance of bribing the legislators. The perpetrator, Senator Alexander Caldwell of Arkansas, resigned his seat in the face of certain expulsion by his colleagues (Article I, Section 5 of the Constitution states that "Each House shall be the Judge of the Elections, Returns and Qualifications of its own members . . ."). Over the next three decades, the number of bribery attempts in Senate elections increased to fifteen.[22] Among the most infamous were those of Montana's Senator William A. Clark in 1899, and Illinois' notorious "Lorimer Case" of ten years later.

Clark confessed to a "personal disbursement" of over $140,000 to the legislators of Montana. The Senate Committee on Privileges and Elections reported that he had obtained more than half of his apparent majority through bribery.[23] Lorimer's election ended a deadlock after ninety-nine votes. The Republicans, though comprising the majority in joint assembly, were divided four ways as the result of a direct senatorial primary which produced no popular majority. With no headway after four and a half months, a bipartisan coalition of Democrats and Republicans ended the stalemate by electing William Lorimer, a dark horse candidate acceptable to both parties, by a vote of 108 to 94 (split among all of the other candidates). A year later, with Lorimer comfortably in his Senate seat, *The Chicago Tribune* broke the shocking story of four legislators who had been bribed to change their vote on his behalf.[24]

The vindicators of direct elections tended to overlook the fact that in both of these scandals the senators, in all their supposed aloofness from the popular will, expelled the offending colleagues. Actually, Clark resigned during floor deliberations of a unanimous committee report recommending his expulsion. The people of Montana, stated the report, had a "right to expect a prompt and decisive remedy from the action of the Senate." Before resigning, Clark vowed angrily on the Senate floor to take his case to the people of Montana himself. His boast was not in vain. Receiving the unanimous endorsement of his party's popular convention, Clark was returned to the Senate in the election of 1901.[25]

A decade after the Clark affair, William Lorimer endured the most sensationalized, politicized, and humiliating investigation in the history of the Senate up to that time, before being expelled in 1912, halfway through the completion of his term. The incident is worth relating in some detail, because it has generally been considered the final outrage perpetrated under the former method of electing senators, when in truth the free agency of the Illinois legislators had been subverted by popular intrusions on the senatorial election process. Not only that, but if the benefit of the doubt belongs to the accused, Lorimer's election was probably legitimate, according to the standards and precedents of the times. Ironically, and cruelly, "a crusade supposedly devoted to more honest and responsible government claimed a victim in a case where there was no evidence that he had broken the law."[26] Nevertheless, no Senate election generated more popular fury, and certainly no Senate controversy could have come at a less propitious time. The validity of Lorimer's election was debated during the same sessions in which a Senate minority was fending off the "insurgents" in their attempt to push through a resolution for the Seventeenth Amendment. Rarely was one subject discussed without the other. In the closing days of the Sixty-first Congress, resolutions for the amendment and for Lorimer's expulsion were both defeated. Outside the Senate chamber, it was easy to jump to conclusions: A corrupted Senate was simply looking out for one of its own.[27]

The actual votes on the two resolutions were hardly convincing proof. Senators Elihu Root and Henry Cabot Lodge, for instance, were two of the most outspoken opponents of direct elections. Both voted for Lorimer's expulsion. Nearly half of the votes retaining the senator were cast by amendment supporters. Besides confusing the two issues, the press accounts also overlooked an honest disagreement over how to interpret the bribery evidence, which blurred all the usual distinctions between Republicans and Democrats, and to a certain extent, between progressives and conservatives. And regardless of where they stood, the senators were only too aware of the verdict which popular opinion was returning on the basis of hearsay. Indeed, casting his vote against Lorimer, Senator Wesley Jones of Washington felt compelled to offer a disclaimer to his colleagues. "Newspaper reports and outside statements I have thrown in the wastepaper basket without reading or consideration. Letters from my constituents I have, of course, read, but they have not influenced me in making my judgment." He meanwhile expressed his profoundest respect for those who disagreed with him, such as Thomas Paynter, the senior senator from Kentucky, who supported Lorimer with the declaration that "if I knew my vote would retire me from public life, it would not alter my course in this matter."[28]

As far as the investigating subcommittee was concerned, all that the evidence really proved was that a corrupt legislature elected the senator from Illinois. This was not the same thing as proving that he was corruptly elected. It was never shown, nor even charged, that Lorimer participated in, or had knowledge of, the alleged bribery. But the subcommittee was not even satisfied that the bribery which took place was even committed on the candidate's behalf. Three of the confessed bribe-takers were, by their own admission, "grafters" and "boodlers" who at the end of a legislative session usually divided a "jackpot" of funds delivered by various interests for successfully defeating legislation. Yet initially all three had sworn that they had not received money to vote for Lorimer. Two of them reversed their statements after perjury charges were dropped in an unrelated case. The third was intimidated by the state's attorney into changing his story also.[29]

The fourth bribe taker, Charles A. White, was the former legislator responsible for bringing the scandal to public attention. A high-living, freeloading, chronically indebted reprobate who sold his story for $3,500 to *The Chicago Daily Tribune,* White had previously tried to obtain a much higher figure from other possibly interested parties, including Lorimer. In a letter to the newly elected senator, he pointedly mentioned that he had written an account of his life in the Illinois legislature, that he had been offered $75,000 for it, and that Lorimer might be interested in making a better offer, implying that Lorimer would want to keep it from being published. Lorimer, who claimed never to have divined what White was hinting at, replied at the time that he was not interested in purchasing his story, but congratulated him on his good fortune at finding someone who would pay so handsomely for it. Eventually, White found a publisher in the *Tribune.* It was surely a remarkable coincidence that the only paper in Illinois that was willing to break the story was the lifelong political nemesis of Senator Lorimer, who had often referred to its editors as the tax-dodging "Newspaper Trust." In the sensational headlines which hit the newsstands on April 30, 1910, White stated that he and the three other legislators were paid $900 from the jackpot, along with $1000 more to change their votes for Lorimer. His own role in the affair, he claimed audaciously, was to infiltrate the bribery ring and expose it, a civic undertaking he did not seem to want do for free.[30]

Besides the four legislators alleged to have taken bribes, including himself, White implicated three other legislators as having offered the money to fix the election. In the ensuing state investigation, the latter consistently denied the allegations under oath. Not only were they not convicted, but all three were subsequently reelected. Furthermore, before any of the alleged bribes had been paid, Lorimer had already been elected. That election had then been certified by the Governor, and Lorimer's credentials had been initially accepted by the Senate. He had been in his seat nearly a year before the scandal became public. Assuming the burden of proof rested with the accuser, senators charged with examining the affair were not sufficiently convinced that the state of Illinois had sent the wrong man to represent it in Washington.[31]

The investigating subcommittee was criticized, nevertheless, for hastily making its conclusion without pursuing all the testimony pertaining to the "jackpot." But the 748 pages of testimony taken over three months of investigation can hardly be considered the result of haste. True, the subcommittee considered opening the jackpot question, without direct reference to the Lorimer election—for the sole purpose of discrediting the legislature which elected him—an unwarranted use of Senate authority. "The Senate may inquire into the personal fitness of a man elected by a State to sit as a Senator and may determine such questions within the exercise of its exclusive powers," concluded the report, "but in doing so it may not inquire into the personal character of the officers through whom the State acts. That question belongs to the people of the State exclusively."[32]

The recommendation that Lorimer retain his seat was agreed to with only one dissenting vote by the senators who actually heard the testimony, the Burrows Committee, comprised of direct election proponents and opponents alike. There was disagreement when the report reached the floor, but even among those who did not accept the committee report as to the validity of the evidence, there was substantial division over exactly what constituted a corrupt vote. Were there four corrupt votes, or seven, including the alleged bribe givers? The latter may have been corrupt, but were their votes corruptly "influenced"? It was presumed they intended to vote for Lorimer all along. And what were the disposition of such votes? If only four votes were judged corrupt, Lorimer still had a majority by two votes. If all seven were invalid, should their votes be discounted from Lorimer's tally only, or from the total number of votes? In one case, he would have been one vote shy of a majority of the voting quorum, although he would still have had a large plurality over his opponents. In the other, he would have had a majority of the "untainted votes."[33]

None of these distinctions mattered in the end. The Senate had already been infiltrated by a handful of politicians of the *vox populi, vox Dei* persuasion, and their numbers promised to increase in the succeeding Congress. Robert La Follette of Wisconsin gave an indication of how they would settle the Lorimer case as soon as they they had the power to do so. "The American people are waiting," he declared, himself out of patience with any more discussion on behalf of Lorimer. "The principal facts are as clear in the public mind as they are clear in the minds of senators here, and no discussion of technicalities as to how many tainted votes are needful to corrupt an election will affect their judgment." Likewise, Senator Robert Owen of Oklahoma believed Lorimer's fate had already been decided in the recent elections. His expulsion, like the direct elections resolution of the previous day, had been defeated, as Owen uncourteously remarked, by the lame ducks, "Senators whose seats on this floor are no longer acceptable to the people of their States."[34]

Indeed, the campaign to expel Lorimer had been headline material nationwide, a popular issue in the senatorial canvasses and primaries the previous autumn. The new members of the Senate, contributing twenty-one votes against their beleaguered colleague and only two in support, gave the expulsion forces the necessary votes to declare the Illinois seat "vacant" on July 13, 1912. It was the only time in history where a member's claim to a Senate seat had been upheld by one Congress, then denied in the next. As one Senate historian asserted critically of the newer members, "each had a career before him in a new forum, and . . . knew the strength of the 'anti-Lorimer' sentiment outside the Senate Chamber." Regardless of whether the Senate's decision was just, it was unquestionably a "political verdict."[35]

The final settlement of the Lorimer case illustrates just how amenable the Senate could be to popular opinion. A small assemblage with a wide range of responsibilities, its scandals were bound to attract public attention. But beyond a handful of instances like Caldwell's and Clark's, proof of corruption in senatorial elections was hard to pin down. In popular governments the cry of foul is the ready ploy of the defeated, particularly in close elections. While the concern for technicalities invoked the ire of Senate purists who argued (hypocritically, as it turns out) that even promises of patronage, committee assignments, and votes on pet legislation, all of which played a part in Lorimer's election, were forms of bribery, the quest for purity could only go so far before degenerating into a political witch-hunt.

In the House of Representatives, for example, the mere hint of misdoing served as a partisan pretext to unseat a minority member. From 1789 to 1907 there had been three hundred and eighty-two contests submitted to the House, and only three were not decided in favor of the majority party. Most of those investigations occurred after the Civil War, averaging twelve to fifteen contests per election year.[36] Senator Hoar, reminiscing on his service with the House elections committee, remarked that "wherever there was a plausible reason for making a contest the dominant party in the House almost always awarded the seat to the man of its own side."[37] Even Thomas B. Reed, the House Speaker in the 1890s, could not recall "an instance on record where the minority ever benefitted" in the settlement of a House election dispute.[38]

By contrast, the Senate, which traditionally favored the existing occupant of a contested seat, may have seemed less zealous in defending its honor, but it cannot be said that its decisions were any less just. Reformers tended to disregard the fact that the upper house represented the states, not the people. On the premise that it was more important to have the states fully represented than to chase down every charge of graft, the Senate's longstanding precedent, as opponents of Lorimer's expulsion tried to maintain, was to restrict investigations to two questions: Did the candidate participate in, or have knowledge of, the alleged corruption? If not, of those votes "free of taint and corruption," did the candidate still have a majority of the quorum?

The Muckrakers

This predisposition to accept a senator's credentials was not at all shared, on the other hand, by that generation of journalists who founded the business of reporting political scandal for handsome profits. Naturally, the "muckrakers" found a good deal more "taint" than the Senate ever bothered to investigate. In 1907, *Arena* accused Simon Guggenheim of blackmailing the Colorado legislature, charging him with threatening to publish a list of every person to whom he had "paid a dollar, and what it was paid for," if he was not chosen for the senatorship.[39] In *Cosmopolitan*, George Creel's "Carnival of Corruption in Mississippi" told a lurid tale of money, whiskey and women, proffered by the "lumber trust, oil-mill trust, and the rest," in order to install Le Roy Percy to the Senate in 1910.[40] Previously, in 1906, *Cosmopolitan* had run the most famous "exposure" of senatorial perfidy in a series of articles entitled, "The Treason of the Senate," written by a popular social novelist named David Graham Phillips.[41]

One can only speculate as to the impact of the muckrakers on the movement for direct democracy, a movement predicated in large part on the enlightening possibilities of the modern press. Certainly, their stories sold. Phillips' articles, for instance, were reprinted and reviewed in small town newspapers across the country. City newsstands were sold out two months in a row. By the third issue in the series, *Cosmo-politan's* subscriptions were up by fifty percent, no doubt satisfying the magazine's owner and publisher, William Randolph Hearst, one of the founding fathers of yellow journalism.[42]

Although these reports were generally founded on sly distortions and mendacious innuendo, their truth is not of primary concern here. Assuming the public took any stock in what it read, why should it have sought the remedy in direct elections? The candidacy of Le Roy Percy, like Lorimer's, was the result of compromise, necessitated by a senatorial primary in a one-party state which split the popular votes among six candidates with no majority. Guggenheim (the same corrupted Guggenheim who established, in memory of his son, the John Simon Guggenheim Memorial Foundation for advanced study abroad) had also made his public "canvass," and what is more, he voted for the Seventeenth Amendment when the question was finally put to the Senate in 1911. Phillips' "Treason" indictments were leveled against twenty-one senatorial corruptionists who supposedly could not have been chosen in a fair election by the people, but among them were six former members of state legislatures, eleven former members of the House (serving repeated terms), one lieutenant governor, four governors, and one vice president of the United states, all of whom held their former offices by popular vote.[43]

Another fact often disregarded about Senate elections is that corruption was simply more sensational, but certainly not more frequent than in other elections at the time. The people of Adams County, Ohio, effectively demolished the premise that direct elections were inherently purer elections. During the months of December 1910 and January 1911, more than fifteen hundred people were indicted for taking bribes at the polls. It was revealed during the trials that an average of two thousand voters, approximately a third of the eligible electorate, had been selling their votes to the highest bidder for more than thirty-five years. It was not the usual case of untutored freedman or illiterate immigrants falling prey to the party ward-heelers; a generation of native-born farmers, lawyers, merchants, doctors, even ministers, had, "made a business of selling votes."[44] Yet while this pitiful spectacle of corruption in the American heartland was being brought to light, the Lorimer case was reaping even larger headlines, and would go down in far greater infamy as one of the catalytic events which prompted the people to take the election of senators into their own hands. It was an article of faith that popular control would cleanse the Senate, yet no one ever explained how the river was supposed to rise above its source.

Money and Machinery

Somewhat aloof from the loose accusations of the muckrakers, a more genteel reform element conceded that the open buying of legislators was not the norm. Nevertheless, it was obvious that money was becoming an increasingly important factor in the election of senators, and fashionable journals like *The Nation, Outlook, Independent, Forum* and *The North American Review* arrived at editorial conclusions which were similar in theme, if not in their degree of provocativeness, to those of the muckrakers, insinuating that senators reached their position primarily by virtue of their connections to corporate wealth. To those who thought it sufficient cause for alarm, the "Rich Man's Club," or "House of Dollars," as the Senate came to be known, had become disproportionately representative of the moneyed few.

For instance, Philetus Sawyer, the Senator from Wisconsin (1881–1893), had made millions in the lumber industry. Leland Stanford, whose Central Pacific Railroad took up a sizable portion of the California map during the Gilded Age, managed to get elected for two senatorial terms beginning in 1885. Rhode Island's Nelson Aldrich, whose wealth stemmed from a host of banking and corporate connections, not the least of which was his daughter's marriage to the son of John D. Rockefeller, retained his Senate seat for thirty years (1881–1911). Arthur Gorman of Maryland had presided over the Chesapeake and Ohio Canal Company before the state elected him to the Senate in 1881, 1886, 1892 and 1902. James G. Fair struck it rich in the famous "Comstock" silver lode before taking the senatorship of Nevada. The list goes on: Chauncey Depew, president of the New York Central; gold mine owner George Hearst; Henry Payne of the Standard Oil family, and Stephen Elkins, a coal and railroad baron. According to *The Nation*, the men who occupied the Senate at the turn of the century represented a plutocracy of a scale not seen since "the Roman procurates came home laden with the plunder of the provinces."[45] As one populist proverb had it, it was "as difficult for a poor man to enter the Senate of the United States as for a rich man to enter the kingdom of heaven."[46]

Where there was smoke, fire was inevitably assumed, but prudent editors asserted that outright bribery was less to be found, since it was a tactic too likely to challenge public notice. "The rich man who has more delicacy of feeling and a clearer perception of popular sentiment," so the logic went, managed to keep "the process of bargain and sale from the public eye." Rather, he began by "buying his senatorship years before the seat [was] to fall vacant," contributing funds in every party contest, paying the campaign expenses of legislators who would respond to the call in senatorial elections. It was not bribery "in the usual sense of the word." He did not "send out agents openly to hand over hundreds of thousands of dollars to an individual member for his vote," but the seat was bought and paid for all the same.[47]

The nomination of William Sheehan was often cited as a case in point. In the November elections of 1910, Sheehan, the former lieutenant governor of New York and a state-wide celebrity, gave Democratic legislative candidates his valued public endorsement. He also contributed a considerable amount of campaign money to the party war chest. In an agreement allegedly made with Tammany boss Charles Murphy, if Sheehan's organizational efforts and financial support, particularly in traditionally Republican districts, could wrest a controlling majority in the legislature for the Democrats, the U.S. Senate seat was his. Sheehan's efforts apparently paid off, and he was subsequently nominated. If there actually was a "deal," however, it was not one which the party had bothered to keep confined in the smoke-filled room. Before the session which was to conduct the election had even assembled, one legislator-elect told *The New York Times,* "Mr. Sheehan may not be exactly the kind of man we believe should be sent to the United States Senate, but he has done a lot for the party by turning control of the Legislature over to us, and I believe he is entitled to his reward."[48]

Entitled or not, Sheehan's election was snatched from the jaws of victory when twenty-six "insurgent" Democrats, led by the young Franklin Delano Roosevelt, refused to attend the party's legislative caucus. As it turned out, these twenty-six were themselves divided five ways over who should replace Sheehan, and the most they could unite on was a pledge to oppose his election. The Republicans, refusing to play king-maker, stood behind the incumbent, Chauncey Depew, and a six-week deadlock ensued, during which *Outlook* magazine reproached the Tammany Democrats for obstructing the election of Edward M. Shepherd. Shepherd was considered to be above machine politics, a reputation his election committee routinely underscored with half-page campaign ads in the daily papers. It can be argued that his political rectitude, not machine politics, was the true obstruction, since Shepherd could only muster a scant fourteen votes in the legislature in opposition to Tammany's ninety-one. On the other hand, since Murphy's machine could not control a legislative majority either, the Democratic factions finally compromised with a vote for Judge James A. O'Gorman.[49]

Deplorable as it might have seemed, however, any such arrangement between Sheehan and Murphy would not have been unconstitutional. Furthermore, if it was indeed an arrangement, it had been initially backed by the overwhelming majority of the majority party in a popularly chosen assembly. If the alleged deal proved anything, therefore, it was not so much the surreptitiousness of Senate elections as the desperate obscurity which had befallen state legislators in the age of mass democracy. If Sheehan's money purchased the sort of publicity that could actually affect the outcome of local contests, it signified just how little the people, who could elect governors and presidents, were concerning themselves with elections closer to home.

Over the years, the legislators compensated for their obscurity by pooling their resources. Party treasuries were collected purely for the purpose of winning elections, and once in office, the legislators in the majority party supported one another's designs with little apparent concern for general effects. Not wanting to bite the hand that fed them, they understandably went along with the organization in matters— such as the election of senators—which were beyond the immediate interests of their constituencies. Otherwise, they were isolated, without the means of fulfilling their goals (or schemes) in office, let alone of retaining their seats. A maverick legislator, unless favored with a rare degree of personal charisma or an almost equally rare spirit of voter insurrection against the bosses, could be scratched from the ballot at the next nominating caucus. And states which had devolved the power of nominating directly upon the people only increased the difficulties of his original predicament. To finance his candidacy, he had to pay for two campaigns, one in the primary, and one in the general election.

Yet despite the increasing importance of financing elections, the contention that Senate seats were generally up for auction was grossly off the mark. To begin with, the "Rich Man's Club" of the Gilded Age was not significantly larger than in previous periods in American history. Traditionally, the Senate had always had a higher proportion of the well-to-do than other legislative bodies. After all, most of the Constitution's framers had considered independent means an essential asset for shouldering the burdens of high public office, and the only substantial change over the generations had been toward more democratic sources of wealth, as senators with hereditary fortunes gave way to the self-made men. Even so, at the turn of the century the approximate number of senators who could honestly be ranked as millionaires may have been as low as ten. The 1902 *World Almanac* set the number at eighteen. "To two-thirds of the members," on the other hand, "the annual salary of $5000.00 [was] a consideration not to be despised."[50]

Regardless of how affluent or well connected an aspirant might be, the path to the Senate was never an easy one. Rich or poor, a senatorial candidate had almost invariably served an apprenticeship in the party machinery of his state. Sheehan, for example, was not merely a wealthy campaign donor to the Tammany cause. He was himself a veteran politician who had held the second highest office in the state of New York. His campaign, far from that of the big business reactionary, was the standard Democratic fare in those days—tariff reform, anti-monopoly legislation, *the direct election of senators.* He made light of the mugwump sentiment against him by expressing his hope that the time had not yet arrived "when loyalty to and belief in efficient political organization" was considered a "disqualification for exalted trust."[51]

By the same token, Nelson Aldrich, the most influential Republican in the Senate at the turn of the century, had started in politics as a city councilman, and worked his way through the positions of assembly-man, state speaker, and U.S. Congressman. Arthur Gorman, the leading Senate Democrat, had served twelve years in the Maryland legislature before coming to the Senate.[52] Historian David Rothman's study of senators who served from 1869 to 1901 reveals that the vast majority of them had "painstakingly mounted the political ladder" of party organization. Adhering to the demands of party discipline, they followed, and if successful, inherited the leadership. In a process which left many behind on the ambitious ascent, the United States senator had reached the pinnacle of the party apparatus in his state.[53] As "survivors of the fittest," to use Senator George Hearst's description, senators were the chosen favorite, if not themselves the "Bosses" of the "State Machine."[54]

Machinery and the Interests

Too often reformers denounced the political machines in the same breath with the "moneyed interests" that supported them. If the big corporations did not inherit the Senate directly themselves, they were believed to have surrogate control of its elections through the financial contributions they made to party campaign funds. The oft-heard refrain about state machines was that they were "in the pay of the corporation." Obviously, inter-state businesses had strong motives to exert their influence on Senate elections. Encumbered by commerce laws which varied from state to state, they preferred more uniform and possibly more favorable regulation at the federal level, not to mention the protection from foreign competitors in the form of tariff duties, which only Congress could provide.

Although they could hardly deny contributing to the machines, big businesses naturally disavowed any intention of influencing elections. Contributions were made with "no placation or obligation at all," protested the sugar monopolist, Henry Havemeyer, amid grilling questioning by the Senate Special Committee to Investigate Bribery Attempts (an odd investigation for allegedly corrupt politicians to be conducting against their alleged benefactors). During the 1894 hearings, Havemeyer and his executives in the American Sugar Refining Company maintained that they had absolutely no designs on senatorial elections when they contributed to state and local campaigns. In fact, they expected nothing from the federal government "in any manner, shape or form." The company merely desired good state government for its own sake—the best safeguard of legitimate business interests.[55]

It would be naive to take the corporate claims at face value, especially when business contributions to state party organizations typically increased during years in which federal elections were being held. Nonetheless, moneyed influence before the adoption of the Seventeenth Amendment was much less than popularly supposed. This is not to say that business contributions were not steadily growing throughout the era, or that legislators never turned their heads at the offer of campaign money, but rather that the possibility of controlling the Senate through state campaign donations was somewhat remote. It would have entailed paying the election expenses of a majority of the legislators in a majority of states. Even a single legislature could not reliably be controlled through such means, because very few states consisted of a single "interest." The machines took funds wherever they were offered: from rival railroads, for instance, or from a railroad company trying to maximize profits on the one hand, and manufacturers seeking to minimize transportation costs on the other. The parties needed the funds, because welding majorities in a mass democracy was an inherently expensive proposition. Yet it stands to reason that the more varied the sources of contributions, the more independent they were of any single contributor.[56]

It might even be argued, up to a point, that the traditional impression has reversed the actual relationship between the party machines and the corporations. No business could feel secure, knowing its rivals financially backed the parties. Everybody contributed, Henry Havemeyer explained in his defense, "every individual, corporation and firm in existence does it in their respective States."[57] The Sugar Trust did not want to be excluded. At the state level, large corporations could expect not only to compete against one another, but against local businesses and local citizen's groups, in the fight to influence legislative affairs.

At times their largess thus belied an effort to appease, not control the legislatures, for as the limited successes of the Granger Laws, the Farmer's Alliance, and the Populist Party clearly confirm, the states were not the most dependable bastions of support for interstate corporations. Aware of the strong popular antipathies toward them in some states, corporations frequently gave money to the party most likely to prevail, that is, to the party least in need of their assistance. In close elections, they gave to both parties, or withheld funds until the outcome was virtually assured. The strategy, in the words of railroad president Collis Huntington, was at all costs not "to be too openly for the man that loses."[58] In short, the ability of mere wealth to influence Senate elections was, at best, limited. The outcome still hinged on the majority vote of the legislators, many of whom had won in their constituencies precisely because they supported the most popular senatorial candidate.

Herbert Croly was one of few contemporaries to appreciate the distinct and somewhat less than subservient role played by the state machines. The disposition to treat the machine politician "chiefly as the political creature of the corrupt corporation," Croly wrote, overlooked the fact that he had made "an embryonic appearance long before the large corporations had obtained anything like their existing power in American politics." The real creator of permanent political machinery was the democratic revolution of the first half of the nineteenth century. The proliferation of elective offices, the severe limitations on representative authority, and the incessant changes and cumbersome details of the fundamental laws, Croly argued, had been intended by state constitution-makers "to keep political power in the hands of the 'plain people,'" but the attempt had obviously backfired. "The ordinary American could not pretend to give as much time to politics as the smooth operation of this complicated machine demanded; and little by little there emerged a class of politicians who spent all their time in nominating and electing candidates."[59]

With the rapid growth of industry during and after the Civil War, businesses also came to depend on the advantages of specialization and organization that already characterized the state machines. There was certainly a connection between the two, as campaign contributions clearly indicated, but Croly maintained that "this alliance between the political machines and the big corporations . . . was an alliance between two independent and coordinate powers in the kingdom of American practical affairs." The captain of industry, like most other Americans, was content to leave politics to politicians, except where his own interests were directly involved. He "did not create the machine and its 'boss,'" but if anything, had "done much to confirm the latter's influence" by contributing the financial means of successful vote-getting. Not only did the political machine exist prior to and independent of the modern business corporations, but Croly predicted it would "survive in some form their reduction to political insignificance." Dedicated to capturing and maintaining power in a mass democracy, the professional electioneering machinery could be expected to make whatever protean adjustments the popular climate demanded.[60]

In sum, the senator who represented, if not controlled, the party apparatus of his state was as much the offspring of democracy as of plutocracy. True enough, financial backing played an important part in his rise to power, but the money, it will be recalled, was used for the canvass, the primaries, mass advertisements, and the campaign expenses of legislators who publicly promised to support him. The evidence that even the wealthiest senator was not in some way the result of popular choice is, on closer inspection, exceedingly thin. "There were millionaires in Washington," wrote Rothman, "but their presence reflected political efforts. No matter who entered the game, winning demanded devoted attention."[61]

The more the democratization of the electoral process, the more attention—in the form of organization and money—would have to be devoted. The range of interests in any one state were usually too broad to make direct appeals without a well financed structure of coordination. What James Madison observed a century previously with regard to the size of an assembly, therefore, proved equally true for the size of a constituency. The larger the electorate, "the fewer, and often the more secret, will be the springs by which its motions are directed." In form, "the government may become more democratic, but the soul that animates it will be more oligarchic."[62] In short, the historical trend toward greater popularization of Senate elections, by transferring direct responsibility from the legislators to the electorate en masse, had given rise to the very conditions which reformers hoped to end with even more popularization. Inevitably, big spending, the pressure of organized interests, and backstage maneuvering would continue to characterize the campaigns of senators long after the nostrum of direct elections had been administered.

More could be said about the relative limits of "moneyed interests" upon Senate elections prior to the Seventeenth Amendment, and about the fact that the much-maligned machines they supported were actually the phenomena of democratic progress. At this point, however, it would be more productive to focus instead on the Senate's fundamental inability to compel the nation down any path in opposition to the popular will. The checks and balances, after all, premised the tendency of power to be abused, senatorial power not excepted. The Constitution's framers did not aim for perfect statesmen, but for equilibrium in the making and conducting of public policy. They therefore equipped the Senate to restrain an errant majority, but they gave it no power whatsoever to coerce it. It was a constitutional fact which received scant attention among critics whose sole concern was the "interests" that the Senate represented.

Notes

1. George F. Hoar, "Has the Senate Degenerated," *Forum*, 23 (April 1898): 144.
2. Walter Lippmann, *Public Opinion* (New York: Free Press, 1922), p. 179.
3. S.Rep. 22, *Congressional Globe* (19th Congress, 1st Session), 1826, p. 4; Richard P. McCormick, *The Second American Party System: Party Formation in the Jacksonian Era* (Chapel Hill: University of North Carolina Press, 1963), p. 23.
4. McCormick, p. 28.
5. H. V. Ames, *The Proposed Amendments to the Constitution During the First Century of its History*, 2nd ed. (New York: Burt Franklin, 1970), p. 61.
6. *Ibid.*
7. *Congressional Globe*, (40th Congress, 2nd Session): 4209–4210.
8. Ari Hoogenboom, "The Spoils System," *The Gilded Age: A Reappraisal*, H. Wayne Morgan, ed. (Syracuse: Syracuse University Press, 1963), p. 82.
9. William H. Riker, *The Development of American Federalism* (Boston: Kluwer Academic Publishers, 1987), p. 148.
10. *Ibid.*
11. *Ibid.*, p. 149.
12. Ford quoted in Charles Edward Merriam, *Primary Elections: A Study of the History and Tendencies of Primary Legislation* (Chicago: University of Chicago Press, 1908), p. 129.
13. *Ibid.*, pp. 7–8.
14. Winfred A. Harbison, Alfred H. Heely, *The American Constitution, Its Origins and Development*, 4th ed. (New York: W. W. Norton & Co., 1969), p. 629.

15. Charles S, Lobingier "Popular Election of Senators," *Nation* 80 (June 1, 1905): 435; *Congressional Record* (61st Congress, 2nd Session), May 31, 1910, pp. 7113–7120.

16. Merriam, pp. 18–19.

17. John H. Mitchell, "Election of Senators by Popular Vote," *Forum*, 21 (June 1896): 390, 393–394; "A Proven Failure." *Outlook* 86 (May 4, 1907): 17.

18. George H. Haynes, *The Senate of the United States: Its History and Practice* (Boston: Houghton Mifflin Co., 1938), vol. 1, pp. 86, 90, 92.

19. "The Senatorial Primary," *Nation* 80 (March 2, 1905): 167.

20. Haynes, pp. 90–91.

21. *Congressional Record* (62nd Congress, 1st Session): 1542; (61st Congress, 3rd Session): 2242.

22. *Congressional Record* (61st Congress, 3rd Session): 2179; Haynes, vol. 1, pp. 127–129.

23. Haynes, vol. 1, p. 130.

24. *Senate Report 942* (61st Congress, 2nd Session), 1911, pp. 1–3.

25. Haynes, pp. 130–131.

26. Joel Arthur Tarr, *A Study In Boss Politics: William Lorimer Of Chicago* (Urbana: University of Illinois Press, 1971), p. 307.

27. "Popular Election of Senators," *Outlook* 97 (March 11, 1911): 521.

28. *Congressional Record*, (61st Congress, 3rd Session), February 28, March 1, 1911, pp. 3639, 3760, 2057.

29. *Ibid.*, pp. 2060–2066, 3756; *S.Rep. 942* (61st Congress, 2nd Session): 7–9, 11–13.

30. Tarr, p. 298; *S.Rep 942*, pp. 4–5, 10–12; *The Chicago Daily Tribune*, April 30, 1910, p. 1; *Congressional Record* (61st Congress, 1st Session): 2060, 3756.

31. *Congressional Record* (61st Congress, 3rd Session): 2060–2066.

32. *S.Rep. 942*, p. 16.

33. *Congressional Record* (61st Congress, 3rd Session): 2056.

34. *Ibid.*, pp. 3759, 3756.

35. Haynes, vol. 1, p. 135.

36. De Alva S. Alexander, *History and Proceedings of the House of Representatives* (Boston: Houghton Mifflin, 1916), p. 324.

37. George F. Hoar, *Autobiography Of Seventy Years* (New York: Charles Scribener's Sons, 1903), vol. 1, p. 268.

38. Alexander, p. 324.

39. Ellis Meredith, "The Senatorial Election in Colorado," *Arena*, 38 (October 1907): 358.

40. George Creel, "Carnival of Corruption in Mississippi," *Cosmopolitan*, 51 (November 1911): 725–735.

41. David Graham Phillips, *The Treason Of the Senate*, with intr. by George E. Mowry and Judson A. Grenier (Chicago: Quadrangle Books, 1964).

42. George E. Mowry and Judson A. Grenier, "Introduction" to *The Treason of Senate*, p. 28.

43. Lewis Baker, *The Percy's Of Mississippi, Politics And Literature In The New South* (Baton Rouge: Louisiana State University Press, 1983), p. 40; Phillips, 47–50.

44. *The New York Times*, December 24, 1910, 1:4; December 25, 1910, 1:1, 2; December 30, 1910, 2:4; January 15, 1911, pt. 5, p. 3.

45. "Rich Men in the Senate." *The Nation*, 50 (January 16, 1890): 44.
46. *Congressional Record* (55th Congress, 2nd Session): 4810.
47. "Money and Senatorship," *The Nation*, 70 (April 1900): 295.
48. *New York Times*, December 31, p. 3:4–5.
49. "How we elect Senators," Outlook, 97 (February 25, 1911): 389–392; *New York Times*, December 30, 1910, p. 6:4–7.
50. Henry L. West, "The Place of the Senate in Our Government," *Forum*, 31 (June 1901): 430.
51. *The New York Times*, December 30, 1910, pp. 1:1; 2:6.
52. *Biographical Directory of The United States Congress, 1774–1989* (Washington, D.C.: Government Printing Press, 1989), pp. 519, 1079.
53. David J. Rothman, *Politics and Power: The United States Senate, 1869–1901* (Cambridge: Harvard University Press, 1966), p. 128.
54. Hearst quoted in Richard Hofstadter, *The American Political Tradition and the Men Who Made It* (New York: Vintage Books, 1974), p. 217.
55. *S.Rep.* 606, 53rd Congress, 2nd Session (1893–1894): 365.
56. *Ibid.*, p. 352; Rothman, p. 186.
57. *S.Rep.* 606, p. 366.
58. *Ibid.*, p. 311–316, 357–366; Huntington quoted in Rothman, p. 185.
59. Herbert Croly, *The Promise of American Life* (New York: The Macmillan Company, 1911), pp. 118–120.
60. *Ibid.*, pp. 123, 118.
61. Rothman, p. 131.
62. Alexander Hamilton, John Jay and James Madison, *The Federalist* (New York: Modern Reader, 1938), p. 382.

5

The Anomalous Counterweight

*Caesar must come, or must fail to come, which means our
failure to reach the next stage of life. The Senate is already
an imperious obstacle to concentration.*
—Henry Adams

As a consequence of state democracy, the federal Senate was already an all-but-popular assembly by the time the public campaign was formally undertaken to wrest it from the legislative "machines." Indeed, the amendment for direct elections could not have been the victory over political manipulators that tradition supposes, in view of the fact that for decades party organizers had staked their success on the popularity of Senate candidates. Seeking office on the coattails of senators, establishing the senatorial preference vote in legislative primaries, or—taking the process even further—mandating the direct primary nomination of Senate candidates, to whom they then pledged themselves in their own campaigns, state legislators had steadily abdicated their federal responsibilities in favor of the popular expedient. Whether or not this abdication was the sole cause of problems such as deadlocks and corrupt elections, exaggerated though they were, it had certainly preceded them, just as it had preceded the senator's increasing reliance on partisan financing to gain and hold his office. In view of how much popularization had already been accomplished, as one retired senator skeptically pronounced, any senator unfit for the office was there because the people had been "grievously negligent [at the polls] or else [were] fairly represented."[1]

The possibility that democracy was in any way culpable was, of course, completely anathema to those who accredited "the people" with an infallibility long since denied to aristocrats and kings. In the words of one constitutional reformer:

> The people are honest and intelligent. The people would vote for the public interest alone and would not vote for purely selfish private

interests. . . . The people know more than their Representatives do and . . . are worthier to be confided in than any individuals entrusted with temporary power.[2]

But the Senate stood in the people's way, perverting government in its service to special interests. Putting that assembly under direct popular control was imperative if politics was ever to return to the straight and narrow course of determining the general welfare. Given this tautology, "the public service would be purified" only when the federal Constitution embraced an "absolute government by the people," toward which the Seventeenth Amendment was obviously a fundamental step.[3]

At the risk of redundancy, this was not at all the philosophical legacy of the founding fathers. It echoed Rousseau, Paine, the demagogues of the revolutionary legislatures, and generations of constitutional reformers in the states, but the founders had never postulated "purity in politics," as more than one progressive phrased it, because they had observed no such purity among men. "We must take human nature as we find it: perfection falls not to the share of mortals," wrote an apprehensive General Washington in 1786, as crisis upon crisis brought fresh arguments for a government capable of restraining the wants and passions of its citizens.[4] And if perfection was not to be found in individuals, it was no more likely to be found in majorities. "Bodies of men," insisted James Madison, "are not less swayed by interest than individuals." En masse, they were even "less controlled by the dread of reproach and the other motives felt by individuals." Who, asked Madison, "would rely on a fair decision from three individuals if two had an interest in the case opposed to the rights of the third? Make the number as great as you please," fairness would not be increased, "nor any further security against injustice be obtained, than what may result from the difficulty of uniting the wills of a greater number."[5]

Making it difficult to unite the greater number against the general interest was the essential purpose of checks and balances. Granted, the indirect schemes of election were also designed with the hope of refining the appointment to higher office, but it was never asserted that any branch, no matter how it was selected, would be permanently insulated from factionalism and self-serving ambitions. Thus, by dispersing the federal powers among separate agencies, and maintaining their separation by distinctly different modes of election, those powers were thought less likely to be combined, to recall John Dickinson's metaphor, "into one great current pursuing its course without any opposition whatever."[6]

Ambition Counteracting Ambition:
The Senate and Executive Power

The limits of senatorial power were aptly illustrated in the problem that had developed in the system of federal patronage. The process of selecting civil servants had been a staple complaint among political reformers well before a disappointed office-seeker brought the issue to public attention in 1881 by assassinating President Garfield. Constitutionally, the president had to make appointments with the Senate's "Advice and Consent," thereby hindering him from establishing a personal following in the government. But after the Civil War, the danger was apprehended from the opposite direction. In what *The Nation* called the "silent compact of patronage," the Senate was believed to overshadow the executive completely in the matter of appointments, indeed, to have him "by the throat." Under the chamber's unwritten "Rule of Courtesy," the Senate majority refused to confirm a nominee in, or from, a given state over the objection of a party colleague who represented that same state. Hence, the objection of a single senator was often sufficient to wear the president into submission.[7]

Grover Cleveland made the mistake of nominating the eminent New York attorney, W. B. Hornblower, to the United States Supreme Court, without consulting the state's Democratic senator, David B. Hill. The nomination never made it out of the judiciary committee. Again ignoring Hill, Cleveland nominated another New Yorker, and again came up empty-handed. The Senate foiled his attempt to fill a vacancy in the highest court of the land, arguably the gravest appointment that a president must make, and had done so for what seemed to be purely a matter of New York politics. Of course, senators were equally jealous of the lesser offices. The armies of postal carriers, port inspectors, patent officers, census takers and petty clerks who owed their sinecures to a U.S. Senator generally consisted of the same political soldiers who had campaigned for his election. In the tacit understanding of senatorial courtesy, one senator generally supported the territorial claims of another, in order to retain his own dominions with the patronage. Perceived to have a lock on virtually all the available officers in their respective states, the senators, according to the reform journalist Henry Loomis Nelson, enjoyed "the most perfectly developed trust in the country."[8] Placing them under popular control would help break up their monopoly.

Or at least this is what reformers argued. As usual, they ignored the popular origins of the very abuses they wanted democracy to correct. The rotation of appointed officers under each new administration had been inaugurated with President Jackson in order to prevent the entrenchment of a privileged bureaucracy. Instead, it further entrenched the party machines and the political bosses. It should be recalled that, at precisely the same time that the civil service became rotational and more democratic, the American people had also done away with the elitist pretensions of the Electoral College. Discerning politicians, on the other hand, understood the sheer impossibility of choosing a president without some form of political hierarchy. An upper few had to settle on the candidate with the greatest mass appeal. Lieutenants had to orchestrate attractive spectacles, with songs and slogans and souvenirs, while the rank and file worked the wards and rural districts drumming up the vote. Simply having the chance to cast a ballot for "Log Cabin & Hard Cider," "Manifest Destiny," or "Honesty & Grant," might have gratified the ordinary citizen, but hard-working campaigners took a less exalted view of political duties and compensation. With every presidential contest offering vast rewards in federal offices, Boss William Marcy's immortal dictum aptly expressed the attitude of the great majority of party politicians: "To the victor belongs the spoils."

While the "spoils system" originally issued from the popularization of the presidency, it fell upon the senators to administer it for a number of reasons. For starters, a senator represented the states, where excessive democratization had created the sort of extra-constitutional hierarchy that could be called upon in the quadrennial election of presidents (and the choosing of electors was also a state responsibility). Presidents were thus in some measure obligated to support the sundry state machines which had helped promote them, and could generally do so by deferring patronage matters to the regional party chieftains in, or represented in, the U.S. Senate.[9]

This political necessity aside, democracy was also expanding the number of civil offices beyond the appointive capacities of a single executive. In theory, Americans traditionally subscribed to laissez-faire economics and the yeoman ideal, but in practice they demanded their fair share of the governmental resources: protective legislation, rail subsidies, homestead grants, veteran's pensions, Indian removal, and so forth, all of which had to be regulated and overseen by a burgeoning corps of civil servants, approximately fifty thousand by the end of the Civil War, over a quarter of a million by the end of the century. The president could not possibly fill all the vacancies created by his own accession, and over the decades had all but ceded the responsibility to the senators as necessary intermediaries.[10]

Then again, dispensing the federal patronage could be a dubious privilege, as likely to engender enmity as much as loyalty. Despite the expansion of offices, there were never enough for everyone, so that "for every ally attracted through some sinecure, ten others went away angry." Even before the big push to popularize the Senate at the turn of the century, the members themselves had already grown weary of "the persistent demand of persons for place," as California's Stephen White told the newly appointed civil service commissioner, Theodore Roosevelt. "It is a question," complained the senator, "whether we were elected to legislate, or procure employment." To be sure, senators continued to prevent the patronage from falling into the hands of their political enemies, and this was almost invariably the case when they invoked the rule of courtesy against the president. But it was an advantage most senators seemed willing to trade. Indeed, the landmark civil service reform bill of 1883 had been initiated and formulated in the Senate. The legislation passed unamended in the House, and bore the name of its sponsor, George H. Pendleton, the senator from Ohio.[11]

The Pendleton Act initially "classified" ten percent of the civil offices; that is, it took ten percent of the offices out of the process of political appointment, and made hiring and promotion a matter of merit determined within a professional and supposedly nonpartisan bureaucracy. Although nine out of ten offices remained open to the abuses of the "spoils system," the Pendleton Act gave the president broad discretion to increase the percentage of professional civil servants. By the beginning of Theodore Roosevelt's term, politically appointed officials had been whittled down to a one-third minority of all federal office-holders, and the Senate had meanwhile taken the lead in passing follow-up legislation to strengthen the independence of the bureaucrats from the politicians.[12] Whatever advantage there was in removing public appointments from the direct control of the constitutionally designated representatives, the Senate's surrender of so large a prerogative did not exactly square with the image of a political "trust" perpetuating its power over the popular will.

Even without the reforms, however, presidents had never been helpless in the battle over patronage. Ultimately, there was no reason, other than usage, for their deference to senatorial courtesy. Appointments still required presidential concurrence no less than that of the Senate, and obstinacy was a tactic which could be employed on either side. The longer the contest, in fact, the more it was likely to turn in favor of the president, whose base of support was usually broader than that of any one senator. In 1881, when the spoils system was at its very worst, President Garfield's bitter struggle over a New York port collectorship with Roscoe Conkling, generally considered the most powerful man in the Senate at the time, resulted in the latter's humiliating retirement from public life. If, twelve years later, Grover Cleveland could not install appointees of his own choosing, he could at least exact the price that senators paid for installing theirs. His ruthless, albeit effective, refusal to provide patronage to any senator who did not support—to the letter—his proposal for repealing the Silver Purchase Act, was a classic application of the institutional checks that the Constitution offered him.[13] Such confrontations were never pleasant, and rarely noble, but they epitomized the intended workings of checks and balances, when necessary. Although he could no doubt appreciate the gritty realism of the political axiom, "that loaves and fishes must bribe the demagogues," it did not originate with Cleveland, nor with any other president in the Gilded Age; it had been the unblushing advice of Gouveneur Morris in the federal convention of 1787.[14]

In addition to the patronage, the Senate traditionally locked horns with the president over the ratification of treaties, although, unlike appointment disputes, such conflicts were not as often the subject of popular complaint. Usually, both sides maintained a certain secrecy over their deliberations (the Senate sometimes closing its doors in "Executive Session"), while detailed delineations of whaling rights and reciprocity agreements did not exactly inspire page-burning headlines. Still, to many political observers, diplomats, and certainly to the president, the Senate's role in foreign policy was viewed as being unnecessarily obstructionist, often protective of the special interests it represented at the expense of the national or international welfare. Foreign policy was, like the patronage, being held hostage to the "oligarchy of the Senate," and gave reformers yet one more reason to remove its electoral insulation, and thereby its ability to circumvent the national will.[15]

The roots of complaint, however, had little or nothing to do with the Senate's mode of election. Rather, they stemmed from the distribution of the treaty power itself. The likelihood was intrinsically high that long, hard negotiations by the executive branch would founder on the Senate floor, since ratification required a two-thirds majority.

The states comprised a variety of economic and political interests, and each state had an equal voice in the nation's upper house. A successful treaty, therefore, necessitated not only extraordinary cooperation with the president, but among the senators themselves. It is not at all clear, in fact, how making the senators more "responsive" to the discordant demands of their constituents was supposed to lessen the friction in the process of making treaties.

John Jay, no less, had argued the contrary. The need for "perfect secrecy and immediate despatch" in foreign policy, wrote the architect of America's first peace agreement, precluded sharing the power with any "large popular Assembly" such as the House. On the other hand, consideration of the nation's myriad interests could not be entrusted to the president alone. Treaties, after all, were binding on the entire citizenry, the "supreme laws of the land," and because they also bound a foreign sovereign, it was all the more reason that they should not be lightly entered into, nor lightly repealed. In making such "supreme laws," Jay insisted, the Senate's duty was to safeguard "each of the parts or members which compose the whole"—manufacturing and commercial no less than agricultural. Negativity was deliberately built into the process. A corrupted Senate, therefore, might possibly prevent a good treaty. It could not impose a bad one, at least not without a two-thirds majority and presidential acquiescence, an idea Jay considered "too gross and too invidious to be entertained."[16]

Over a century later, the only significant change in the treaty making process was that both the presidency and the Senate had become far more popular institutions than was constitutionally intended. Their relationship to one another, on the other hand, was fundamentally the same. At the very worst, the two institutions came to a draw, and were forced to compromise. But there were sufficient examples, such as McKinley's handling of the Spanish-American settlement (in which the president sent senators to help with the negotiations, and adroitly dangled the carrot of patronage), to show that an executive truly desirous of foreign accord was more likely to succeed by also offering the olive branch to the ambassadors from the several states.

Ambition Counteracting Ambition:
The Senate and Legislative Power

Senatorial impediments were obviously felt beyond the realm of executive affairs. Proposals for legislation, sometimes quite popular proposals, routinely passed away in Senate committees, or surviving the committees, languished under the dilatory tactics of floor debate until the Congress expired. The Senate could also ensure the death of legislation through its considerable power to amend; it could alter a bill into such a caricature of the original proposal as to make it unacceptable to the majority in the House of Representatives. "They debate . . . interminably; they amend . . . to their taste," complained *The Nation,* and for the House to make revisions would "defeat it altogether." Although the Senate's power was constitutionally more limited when it came to revenue bills, that is, taxation, toll fees, and tariffs, which had to be initiated in the House, this amounted to a mere technicality. As an editorial in *The North American Review* explained, the Senate "strikes out all except the enacting clause, writes in and returns to the House a new bill, which that body is compelled to accept." It was essentially creating the law.[17]

And compounding the grievance was the growing belief that the Senate created the law, as it were, on behalf of that perennial bugbear of democratic reformers, "the interests." As tradition has it, while Americans were crying for relief from the railroad barons, high tariffs, and the trusts, the senators were harrying reforms in a concerted effort to aid and abet the economic oppressors who paid their campaign expenses. Property was concentrating in the hands of the few, wrote David Graham Phillips apocalyptically, and "little children of the masses [were] being sent to toil in the darkness of mines." Erstwhile, the Senate would permit no legislation that was not "either helpful to, or harmless against the 'interests.'"[18]

A quick review of the Constitution suffices to show the patent absurdity of this Senate versus "the people" thesis. The upper house could pass no law without the majority consent of the lower one, and even then could be thwarted by presidential veto. As for its ability to obstruct, that, too, had its constitutional limitations. It took six years, or three elections, to bring about a complete turnover of the Senate's membership, but a maximum of four years to bring in a fresh majority. Meanwhile, the senatorial electors, namely, the state legislators, had shown time and again their easy pliability in the shifting winds of popular sentiment. Assuming, then, that the American people felt compelled to legislate at the national level, all that was constitutionally required of them was a sufficient degree of consistency at the local polls—one election to secure a favorable majority in the House of Representatives, and one election of the legislators, but carried out in two stages among the states, to bring the Senate into conformity.

The movement for tariff reform was a case in point. Under the four tariff bills submitted by the House between 1890 and 1909, import duties were consistently, often steeply, raised by the Senate. The motive, as ascribed by Senate critics, was to give the great trusts a "license to loot" the consumer by adding a prohibitive tax on competing imports, and thus permitting domestic industries to maintain prices at artificially high levels. While there is no denying that a number of interests energetically lobbied for and received such benefits, their actions were not wholly unpopular, and certainly not new. Ever since the War of 1812, it had been Congress' forthright intention to foster industrial self-sufficiency by nursing along the nation's "infant" manufactures with protective duties. Interestingly enough, free traders in the Senate, who advocated tariffs for revenue only, had been as much of an impediment to the initial implementation of the protective system as high tariff senators were to be two generations later, when the first attempts were made to dismantle it.[19] There was no real irony in this, however. Given constitutional intent, the Senate could hardly be reproved for lagging behind the popular desire for change.

Notwithstanding the vehemence with which reformers denounced the protective system as the buttress of corporate power, it had enjoyed tremendous popular support throughout most of its history. Wage earners, for instance, were as likely as their employers to espouse its blessings, believing their prosperity depended to a large degree on keeping the products of foreign labor out of the domestic market. Near the industrial sectors of the country, produce and dairy farmers with big-city markets were not inclined to take sides against their leading customers. The staple growers—wool and wheat in the Midwest and West; sugar, cotton and tobacco in the South—all insisted on high tariffs against like products from abroad.[20] (Not surprisingly, tariff duties often bore a striking resemblance to the tax exemptions in a number of state constitutions at the time). Many of the duties, such as those on most agricultural products, were altogether superfluous in light of the negligible competition from foreign producers. But whether or not it made sense economically is beside the point. "All the popular debates of the last generation," wrote the early twentieth-century tariff historian and former U. S. Tariff Commissioner, F. W. Taussig, "had inculcated the belief that the mere imposing of a duty served at once to benefit the domestic producer."[21]

By 1890, however, as evidenced by the Populist revolt, reaction to the tariff had erupted throughout much of the staple growing regions.

Distressed farmers with huge surpluses decried the injustice of having to sell competitively on the export market while bearing the tariff-enhanced cost of manufactured goods. In the conspiratorial theories that circulated in western and southern meeting halls, the honest tillers of the soil had gone bankrupt subsidizing the monopolists who owned the legislative process. The "sham battle over the tariff," declaimed the National People's Party platform of 1892, was a "vast conspiracy" of standpat politicians "to destroy the multitude in order to secure corruption funds from the millionaires." Direct election of senators was part of the 1896 platform.[22]

It was a consoling explanation which obviated their own culpability. Trying on the one hand to maintain an elusive ideal of yeoman independence, and on the other the higher living standard conferred by the very collective life they spurned, the agrarian interests had bought into the tariff system when they accepted eastern capital and credit to further their own aims, and in the rough and tumble democracy of the frontier, they had been as acquisitive and as speculative as any other sector of the economy. Notoriously overextending themselves in the boom years, it was not until they had created surpluses too large for the domestic market to absorb that they voiced any scruples about free trade.[23]

But if in humanitarian terms the suffering of the farmers argued for tariff reform (of course, in economic terms the extent of damage caused by the tariff is open to debate), the fact that it was delayed for over two decades was not necessarily the fault of the U.S. Senate. The militant farming element composed a small, if vocal, minority of the national voting population at the turn of the century. Majority opinion on the tariff question was, at the very most, a theoretic commitment to free trade which quickly broke down amid political realities. For starters, there was the inevitable log-rolling common to all representative bodies, but further exacerbated by the equal representation of states, under which lesser interests from less populous states were sure of obtaining their share of protection. During twenty years of reform discussion, senators seemed willing to adopt the principle of reduction, except where their own constituents were concerned.[24]

There was also a tendency to lose sight of tariff reform among other issues. Although Democrats had made lower duties part of their national agenda since the mid-1880s, they managed to obtain a Senate majority only once before 1913 (1893–1895). Even then, it was not large enough to prevent a few defectors from defeating the lower duties proposed by the House. Otherwise, Republicans retained their Senate hegemony, and with it, their high protective posture. In Taussig's estimation, this was not because there was any strong mandate for the Republican position on the tariff, which was comfortably *status quo*, but because other issues, such as Free-Silver, the Spanish American War, as well as the general prosperity which lasted throughout most of the Republican era, kept tariff reform in the rear of the public agenda.[25] In other words, regardless of how Americans felt about it as an isolated issue (as an attack on the "interests" in general, not their own in particular), reform did not come unalloyed with other important considerations of national policy.

When tariff reform did arrive, it is hard to say whether it was prompted by consumer revolt against the "interests," or by a change of heart among America's industrialists themselves. In a number of key industries, such as coal, lumber, steel, iron, and the articles manufactured from those materials, American production had become efficient enough and cheap enough to compete abroad. Reducing tariff barriers and promoting international "reciprocity" promised new outlets for production surpluses. Thus, free trade, or at least lower duties, made increasingly more sense for many industrial interests.[26]

On the other hand, students of American history should be wary of giving too much credit to rational economic analysis in the making of public policy. When depression struck the economy in 1907, the Democrats, seizing upon the general discontent, were quick to blame the crisis on Republican tariff policies, and were at last able to present reform as a credible priority on the national agenda. Of great assistance to their campaign was the harsh reaction of the press to the allegedly exorbitant Payne-Aldrich tariff of 1909. Although the average rates decreased from fifty-seven to thirty-eight percent, publishers were antagonized nonetheless by the doubling of duties on newsprint—a provision inserted by the otherwise progressive senator, Robert La Follette, to protect Wisconsin's lumber interests. In the Senate elections of 1910, the Democrats succeeded in cutting a sixty to thirty-two Republican advantage in the Senate down fifty-one to forty-three. In 1912, fifty-one Democrats and one Progressive put Republicans in the minority with forty-four. It had taken, in other words, merely two elections to reverse the Senate majority, despite the medium of the state legislators (correspondingly, in 1910 the Republicans lost the House in a single election).[27]

Although there were certainly additional reasons for the Democrats' ascent to power, reduction of the tariffs had long been the one issue on which the party was most united, and which had most distinguished it from the Republicans. In negotiating their first tariff in 1913, the new Senate majority not only approved, but actually reduced the duties proposed by the House.[28] Prior to that point, apparently, opposition to the protective system had never been broad enough, nor sustained enough, to carry the Senate.

What tariff reform demonstrated was that the Senate *could* be moved, and that ultimately the people, albeit indirectly, controlled the levers. In matters less divisive than the protectionist-free trade controversy, its performance on reform was hardly unreasonable. In 1890, senators not only endorsed, but sponsored, drafted, and with the exception of one vote, unanimously approved the first federal antimonopoly statute, the (Senator John) Sherman Anti-Trust Act. It had already undertaken the civil service reforms of 1883, and had consented to the Interstate Commerce Act in 1887. From 1900 to 1906, the span of one Senate term, it passed two railroad regulation bills, and concurred with the House in establishing the National Forestry Service, the Food and Drug Administration, and the Department of Commerce and Labor with an overseeing Bureau of Corporations. In sum, the Senate had sanctioned all, and initiated many, of the major reforms of the Gilded Age and Progressive Era. Even when it did resist, as the records of its proceedings testify, it was usually to dispute the details, not the principle, of federal regulation. Either way, historians are at a loss to cite a single proposition, supported by persistent public opinion, which was ultimately defeated at the hands of the U.S. Senate.

Yet despite its role in bringing the rule of law to the anarchy of industrialized America, the Senate could not assuage its declining popularity. Longstanding institutional customs, such as senatorial courtesy and the (then) absence of any rules for cloture during debate, continually frustrated those who sought a quicker pace of reform. Constitutional devices like the equal representation of states and the two-thirds requirement for approving treaties, overriding presidential vetoes, and removing federal office-holders only further ensured delay of Senate action. And long terms in office, rotating elections, and indirect appointment necessarily dulled the Senate's sensitivity to popular feelings. But then, that was the whole point of its creation. Whereas the courts were intended, in part, to uphold the individual's *civil* rights (an admittedly debatable interpretation), the Senate had been constituted to protect minorities in their *political* rights. It gave them a voice in making the laws that might otherwise have gone unheard in a government based on simple universal suffrage. Its obstructive contrivances had been instituted precisely for the thankless task of restraining majoritarian impulses in times of social and economic unrest. Naturally, the more restive the times, the more unappreciated the responsibility. Even among the most widespread calls for change, dissenters could, and did, impose obstructions until the majority abandoned its course, or made an acceptable compromise. In a sense, the floor of the United States Senate was the Thermopylaen Pass on which, until the next election, at least, political minorities had the power to hold an entire nation at bay.

The Explosion of Interests

When Aristotle spoke of such minorities, he generally meant the wealthy few. With few examples of political entities larger than the city-state (besides Persian despotism), it was easy to distinguish the aristocrat from the democrat, and to see in their quarrels over property—the one to maintain it, the other to acquire it—the principal source of political conflict. In the modern nation-state, by contrast, vast geographies and large populations combined with improved arts in industry and economics to splinter the source of conflict in a multitude of different directions. Merchants contended with manufacturers, who contended in turn with the producers of raw materials, while businesses in the same trade were pitted against one another for resources and markets. Labor organizations not only battled their employers, but competed among themselves for membership and supremacy. In the struggle over financial policies, over interest rates and inflation, the retired school teacher with a savings account, odd as it might at first seem, shared a common interest with the banking houses on Wall Street, and their interests directly contradicted those of the debtor classes, which included the faltering interstate corporation no less than the sharecropper with a lien on his mule. Or, as Alexander Hamilton asked more than a generation before the myth of worker solidarity had cast its spell on Western intellectuals, "What greater affinity or relation of interest can be conceived between the carpenter and blacksmith, and the linen manufacturer or stocking-weaver, than between the merchant and either of them?"[29]

Adhering to the classical doctrine of political conflict—rooted in the Aristotelian postulate of struggle between majorities, minorities, and individuals—the framers of the American Constitution certainly understood the insufficiency of that doctrine's traditional applications in modern economy. It was no longer enough to make political distinctions between the masses and the propertied aristocracy in a world where property itself was contested along constantly shifting lines of conflict. As lawyers, planters, and merchants who were thoroughly conversant with the practical aspects of the creation of wealth, the framers knew that political struggle did not arise solely between the "haves" and "have-nots." For one thing, property was not the only source of faction. "So strong is this propensity of mankind to fall into mutual animosities," wrote Madison, "that where no substantial occasion presents itself, the most frivolous and fanciful distinctions have been sufficient to kindle their unfriendly passions and excite their most violent conflicts." But granting that property was the most durable source of political contention, such quarrels arose as often as not over different *kinds* of property, not just different degrees of it. "A landed interest, a manufacturing interest, a mercantile interest, a moneyed interest, with many lesser interests, grow up of necessity in civilized nations," Madison explained, "and divide them into different classes, actuated by different sentiments and views."[30]

The protection of liberty necessitated a constitution that would restrain, not eradicate, these sundry factions to which free people were naturally inclined, but the very fluidity of the battle lines in modern society obviously precluded anything so rigidly inflexible as a balance among hereditary orders. While esteeming the stability, therefore, the founders thus eschewed the actual forms of the "mixed" constitution. Substitutes had to be found for the missing monarchical and aristocratic elements. At the time, the only viable solution to present itself was geography. The states were left to determine their own "natural aristocracy," and so long as they did not admit family distinctions as the basis of political rights (as if there were ever any danger), they were free to adopt and to modify whatever electoral qualifications they saw fit. Their legislatures, representing the collective will of their peoples, were to select the representative hierarchy that restrained the national democracy.

Ironically, the historical explosion of economic diversity in America coincided with the dissolution of representative sophistication in the states, those geographical entities which were to provide the federal aristocracy. Even more ironically, reformers would use the economic and technological complexities which had evolved since the founding era to justify changing the federal system as well, toward purer and simpler democracy. Their motives, in part, stemmed from the fact that, while they uneasily accepted the passing away of the nation's uncomplicated agrarianism, they did not correspondingly relinquish their archaic perception of political and social conflict. Instead, they continued to disparage the old dichotomy of rich and poor, the privileged and the common man.

Hence, when the Senate became obstinate against national proposals which were more or less in favor with the majority of Americans, or with a majority of those who happened to express opinions on such matters, it was said to be protecting "the interests" at the expense of "the people." It had "so legislated and so refrained from legislating," David Graham Phillips vituperatively maintained, "that more than half of all the wealth created by the American people belongs to less than one per cent. of them."[31] The accuracy of his statistics, of course, is not the question, but rather the alleged class-motive of senatorial obstruction. Taking into account the great democratization that had already been achieved before any of the hyperbole against the upper house was ever heard, it is difficult to imagine that many senators did not calculate their actions, or inactions, upon popular appeal. Indeed, the real source of obstruction was that what appealed to a national majority was not always popular in an individual state.

Perhaps no event of the era better underscores this point than the Senate's filibuster against repealing the Sherman Silver Purchase Act. Rightly or wrongly, President Cleveland blamed the purchase bill, which increased Treasury purchases of silver to back a U.S. currency expansion, for causing the Panic of 1893 and the subsequent depression. Having called a special session of Congress to repeal the act, the president managed, not without difficulty, to get the repeal passed in the House, whereupon the entire nation was witness to a battle of attrition in the Senate. For two months, a pro-silver minority engaged in a verbal marathon calculated to prevent a vote and wear the majority into submission, or at any rate, into a more conciliatory mood (Vice President Stevenson, presiding over the debates, ensured that none of the minority lost an opportunity to speak, since he was himself in general agreement with them). The filibuster broke all records for Senate obstruction.[32] Not even an all-night session engineered by the majority could staunch the flow of words, as speeches four days long, quorum calls, and dilatory motions of one sort or another held the nation's fiscal agenda hostage to what one waggish political journal called "government of the silver senators, for the silver senators, and by the silver senators."[33]

Repeal advocates spoke of the "silver interest" in the same invidious language that the Farmer's Alliances used when speaking of the eastern monopolists. After all, senators like Nevada's William Stewart and Colorado's Henry M. Teller represented powerful political machines financed in large part by the regional silver mining industry. As increased production reduced prices, silver miners hoped to sustain profits by selling their surpluses to the Treasury. Yet the aims of the silver industry coincided precisely with those of indebted agrarians clamoring for currency inflation. An entire region, in fact, rallied to the opposition's cause. In the West and much of the South, "the banker, cattleman, miner, farmer and businessman equally felt the shock of depression" and joined the protest against the government's reduction of silver purchases, fearing an even greater tightening of an already scarce supply of money and credit.[34]

Just how closely the interests of the great mining corporations squared with those of grass roots voters was manifest in the early political career of William Jennings Bryan. Bryan, the "Great Commoner," was no more capable of deliberate political deceit than he was of undeceiving himself that the parochial views he espoused were not necessarily the will, the one and only will, of the American people. As a western congressman, Bryan rose to national fame by thundering against the "moneyed interests" which were trying to suppress the silver movement (Although, typical for him, he championed the cause on the grounds that the people were for it, and claimed he would look up the arguments in its favor when he had more time). At the same time, he seems genuinely to have perceived no hypocrisy on his own part in soliciting the mining interests for reelection funds. Nearly a million copies of his speeches, brimful of populist rhetoric, were reprinted and circulated by the silver monopolists.[35]

The fight against repeal, though bitterly protracted, eventually failed for a number of reasons (not the least of which was Cleveland's obstinate refusal to yield the patronage to repeal opponents). Not only was the Sherman Act repealed in 1893, but silver was demonetized altogether a few years later. On the money question, at any rate, it appears that most Americans backed the president, but at the same time, it is equally clear that the silverites were overwhelmingly popular in a number of states. In both branches of the national legislature, the popularly elected House and the legislatively appointed Senate, the vote was split along sectional lines. But in the present discussion, the outcome of the filibuster is not nearly as significant as its origin. The fact that the Senate minority was backed at one and the same time by the money of the mine industry and the suffrage of the farmers ought to have been a sufficient refutation of the simplistic plutocracy versus democracy theories upon which the Seventeenth Amendment has been typically rationalized.

Whether by omission, negating or attempting to negate the so-called "will of the people," or by commission, promoting the "interests" with tariffs and subsidies, the sins of the Senate were mostly on behalf of minorities which in at least one portion of the Union were not minorities. And it was only logical that as the Senate became more directly "responsive" to the will of its respective constituencies, it would become less and less able to treat national affairs as anything more than a bundle of factional issues. Direct expression, as opposed to expression through representative, hierarchical procedures, offered an inherently more subjective and provincial view of the common good.

Yet whatever might be said against the evils of too much power in the hands of Senate minorities needs to be weighed against the opposite evils in the House. In 1890, Speaker Thomas B. Reed of Maine managed to engineer a change in House rules which in effect gave him and subsequent speakers almost autocratic control over which bills would be considered, which committee would handle them, who could speak and for how long, and when debate should end and voting begin. Implemented to bring order to House business and to expedite its legislative affairs, the infamous "Reed Rules" shut the minority party almost completely out of the legislative process. The minority could submit dissenting committee reports, but whether they received attention in floor debate was the prerogative of the Speaker. Adding to the Speaker's power was also the fact that the Republicans, who held the House majority at the time, adhered to a greater degree of party discipline, and showed a greater deference to party leadership, than was probably true before or since. There was little exaggeration, therefore, in the anecdotes about reporters no longer canvassing the House membership when trying to find out the future of a bill; they needed only to ask the "Czar" who sat in the Speaker's chair.

By comparison, the Senate, for all its weakness in preventing minority obstruction, was still the more deliberative body. "The House of Representatives," Kansas Senator William Peffer wrote defensively, "is commonly regarded as being nearer the people and more responsive to the popular will than the Senate is," but under the Reed Rules, it tended "to restrict rather than to enlarge the freedom of speech."[36] Populist Congressman Jerry Simpson claimed he "never had an opportunity before to say anything good about the Senate," but getting in a rare word on the House floor (The Speaker was not presiding that day), he nonetheless conceded it was "the only parliamentary body we have."[37]

Odd as it seemed, the House could pass a mammoth appropriations for internal improvements with very little floor discussion, as it did in the 1900 River and Harbors bill, but the Senate was denounced as the unrepresentative branch of the legislature. It incurred the typical criticisms when it allowed the session to end on a fourteen-hour filibuster by Thomas Carter of Montana, who single-handedly defeated what was obviously a very popular appropriation. One senator, ran the complaints, had managed to obstruct the House, the Senate majority, and quite possibly the president.[38] The bill, however, was nothing more than a $70 million boondoggle sent up from the House with riders thrown in for enough states and districts to ensure passage in the Senate. It was the same sort of pork which was already standard fare in the states, and the truth was that most senators, as Albert Beveridge of Indiana later admitted, "dared not vote against it." Even President McKinley, who could not have failed to see the potential vote-getting appeal of the River and Harbors Bill, was privately relieved that Carter's filibuster saved him from having to veto it, and quietly awarded the senator with an appointment after his term expired.[39]

Clearly, the House could equal, if not excel, the Senate in sheer log-rolling ability, the difference being mainly in the haste with which it served the majority. Senatorial resistance was not always maintained in the spirit of national interest (Carter, as a lame duck senator, could afford to filibuster as a matter of principle). But within the larger scope of constitutional processes, it served as a means of national moderation. Lord Bryce, observing that the Senate attracted the nation's best talent, "so far as that talent flows to politics," believed, on the other hand, that its members were no more attached to the public good than those in the other branches. Yet significantly, Bryce, a British Liberal well aware of the vast changes wrought upon American civilization by capitalism, industrialism and urbanization, continued to use the classical language of political balance to defend the Senate as an authority which corrected and checked "on the one hand the 'democratic recklessness' of the House, on the other, the 'monarchical ambition' of the President. Placed between the two, it is necessarily the rival and often the opponent of both." If the Senate had "achieved less in the way of positive work," it had also to be remembered, as Bryce correctly reasoned, that "the whole scheme of the American Constitution" had placed "stability above activity."[40]

Unquestionably, the American Constitution was meant to sustain the balance, not the speed, responsiveness, or progress of legislative activity. The power which ultimately commanded the government, the voice of the people, was not the General Will, nor as more impiously asserted, the Voice of God. It was a cacophony of private and local concerns, each liable to advance itself at the expense of the others and of the common welfare. In a political sphere the size and scope of the United States, the principal danger of direct democracy lay in sacrificing to the majority sentiment of the hour that "refinement and filtration" process by which all the sundry interests of the people were taken into account.

To a degree not possible between the people and any other agent in the original federal scheme, a state legislator could know the mind of his constituents, and vice versa. In turn, his choice for senators and presidential electors could likewise be made with the competence that only a first-hand acquaintance can provide. A few hundred electors chose the executive, who in concurrence with a few score senators selected the judiciary. From the voters in their constituencies to the justices of the Supreme Court, the majority prevailed in every sphere, yet the size of each sphere remained conducive to deliberation (not mere expression). Lest any branch pursue interests contrary to the general welfare, it was checked by co-equal branches, whose members answered to distinctly different types of constituencies, and were thus less liable to fall under the same influences. And lest, in all these electoral intricacies, the popular will was lost from view, the entire apparatus could be brought to a halt by the House, whose members answered immediately to the people.

In truth, it is hard to see how the popular interests could be more obscured by indirect elections which maintained a high ratio of representation than by direct elections which dissolved the individual voter in a mass constituency. Direct democracy simply multiplied the voices which called upon the government for aid and protection, so that none but the largest or loudest interests could be heard. The states had already shown where this collapse of representative hierarchy would lead. Organization became the paramount necessity. Political machines had to be created to satisfy as many partial interests as it took to attain a mass majority, or even a sufficient plurality, and thereby the means of controlling the government. It was precisely these "combinations" of interests that the federal Constitution was designed to obstruct, and it had proven to be a better bulwark against them inasmuch as it was less democratic. A proposal which became federal law, having survived the diverse meanderings through which the popular will was originally channeled, more probably reflected the interest of all than any policy that was likely to be adopted through the plebiscitary warfare of factional alliances.

Delay and restraint, on the other hand, had never been the watchword of the democrat. From Rousseau and Paine in the eighteenth century, to Bryan and La Follette in the twentieth, the principle of constitutional reform was not to reaffirm the limits of the sovereign, but to minimize the distance and the friction between *vox populi* and the action of government. Whereas classical tradition presumed that conflict and the need for compromise were abiding certainties of politics, proponents of democracy envisioned a millennial conclusion to the struggle between "the people" and "the interests." From the primal, unsullied utterance of the former sprang the fount of political wisdom and social harmony, if only it could be tapped and allowed to flow without hindrance. But the rule of the latter continued as long as the representative labyrinth was permitted to muffle and diffuse the power of the oracle. It mattered not the least that the cries against "the interests" had only grown louder and more militant as the walls of the labyrinth, beginning with state legislatures, were worn away, for neither experience nor logic could vanquish the faith in one-man, one-vote as the nostrum for all afflictions to the body politic. The healing power of the ancient kings had been bestowed upon the popular majority.

Consider, for instance, Robert Owen's 1910 address to the Senate in favor of direct elections. Failure to extend the direct influence of the people in the federal government, maintained the senator from Oklahoma, had cruelly deprived them of the means of obtaining simple justice. "The people," he cried:

> want lower prices on the necessaries of life . . . demand a fair price for their crude products . . . want a systematic development of our national waterways, . . . [not] millions . . . spent on local projects with political prestige . . . [and] universally desire an income tax. . . . The people . . . if they could vote on the question of international peace . . . would heartily be in favor of it. . . . If the people could express themselves, they would immediately vote for good roads, improved waterways, wholesale education, eight hours of labor, improved protection of the public health, lower prices, reasonable control of public utility corporations, reasonable freight rates, reasonable rates by express, telephone and telegraph.[41]

One is almost persuaded by Owen's hymn-like eloquence to believe in the alchemic powers of universal suffrage, and in the Promised Land denied for the want of adequate methods of popular expression. Closer scrutiny, however, exposes the inherently confused and contradictory aims "the people" were trying to articulate. As consumers, for instance, they wanted lower prices on "the necessaries of life," but as producers they wanted higher prices for their "crude products," their milk, their crops, their wool, that is, the necessaries of life for the consumer in the market. Owen also cited the subordination of national waterway development to "local projects with political prestige" as yet another example of governmental defiance against the will of the people. But exactly *who* conferred this political prestige, if not the people, in their capacity as local voters?

Perhaps, as Owen stated, there was a fairly widespread desire for a federal income tax (secured by constitutional amendment two months before the amendment for direct elections). From the very first federal income tax bill in 1913, however, tax rate percentages were made "progressive" in scale, according to the level of individual income, an obvious appeal to the lower and middle classes against the interests of the rich (ninety-nine percent of Americans originally paid no tax at all).[42] As demands on the revenues increased—as they almost invariably do under the egalitarian social ethic—the tax base had to be expanded into lower "brackets." So too expanded the number of Americans demanding exemptions according to their own relative views of equity. With the proliferation of exemptions, those who could afford the best tax lawyers and accountants to find the "loopholes" and the "shelters" would eventually pay the lowest tax rates—an ironic perversion of the "progressive" intent. In any case, if motives may be deduced from results, Americans perhaps did, in Owen's words, "universally desire an income tax," but apparently on the other fellow's income.

"The people," Owen continued, were "heartily [in] favor" of international peace, but although this may have been true as a general rule, there were glaring historical exceptions. After a single term in Congress, Abe Lincoln left office under a storm of constituent anger over his stand against the "manifest destiny" of America's armed expansion at the expense of Mexico.[43] And if, as H. Wayne Morgan believes, President McKinley had made up his own mind to go to war with Spain, he was not exactly countering the force of public opinion, which sought to avenge the suspicious, albeit unexplained, explosion of an American battleship.[44]

As to the rest of the popular agenda that Owen itemized, nearly every American stood for good roads, wholesale education, health improvement and reasonable rates. Where the unanimity broke down was in determining what constituted "good," "education," "improvement" and "reasonable." Every interest, including that supposedly disinterested purveyor of public awareness, the newspaper, had its own definitions, and no doubt identified them as those of "the people." Tens of millions of voters, scattered across the continent, might possibly agree on the ends of national policy, but prescribing the means necessitated some form of representation. As the states had shown, no referendum could resolve any issue without having first been put into voting form by some enterprising, organizing few. How many among the mass of legitimate interests those few actually represented, there was no sure way of telling, but the odds seemed better when various spheres of delegated authority were checked and balanced against one another.

Yet to progressive reformers, delegated authority was the root of all evil in modern politics. "The greatest of all issues," as Owen himself put the case, was the issue "of the government of the people *against* delegated government [emphasis mine]." A truly representative system, claimed the senator, "represents me best" when the elected official "receives my instruction and when I retain the right to instruct him and to recall him and to act independently of him if necessary." This was little short of saying, as Rousseau once said, that in a legitimate government, the citizen obeys no one but himself. The will was intrinsically distorted when not expressed directly, and an authority which had been delegated by a delegated body, as was the case with United States senators, was thus a particularly anomalous counterweight. Twice removed from the pure-intentioned people, complained the senator, "The Senate can block and actually does block every reform the people desire."[45]

There was ample proof, however, in a single but overwhelming example, that the Senate was not at all the obstacle to the popular will that Owen and many others made it out to be. Had it indeed been so adamant, there would have been no amendment for direct elections, or at least not without a popular resort to force. But as Owen's very presence in the chamber testified, senators were more amenable to constitutional reform than perhaps even the people themselves.

Notes

1. G. F. Edmunds, "Shall the People Elect Senators?" *Forum* 18 (November 1894): 278.
2. Congressional Record (61st congress, 2nd Session): 7123.
3. *Ibid.*, pp. 7123, 7121.
4. General Washington to John Jay, August 1, 1786, *The Writings of George Washington*, Worthington Chauncey Ford, ed. (New York: G. P. Putnam's sons, 1891), vol. 11, p. 54.
5. James Madison, Note to the Speech of James Madison on the 7th Day of August (1787), *The Debates in the Federal Convention of 1787* (Buffalo: Prometheus Books, 1987), vol. 2, p. 620.
6. James Madison, *Debates*, vol. l, p. 72,
7. "Power of the Senate," *The Nation*, 76 (February 5, 1903): 104–105.
8. Henry Loomis Nelson, "Overshadowing Senate," *Century* 65 (February 1903): 505.
9. William Dudley Foulke, *Fighting the Spoilsmen* (New York: Knickerbocker Press, 1919), pp. 3–5.
10. John A. Garraty, *The American Nation*, 5th ed. (New York: Harper & Row Publishers, 1983), pp. 517–518; Foulke, p. 212.
11. White quoted in David G. Rothman, *Politics and Power, the United States Senate, 1869–1901* (Cambridge: Harvard University Press, 1966), p. 180; For Senate's role in reform, *see S.133, Congressional Record* (47th Congress, 2nd Session, 1883).
12. Foulke, pp. 211–212; See also, "Report of the Civil Service Commission," November 16, 1908.
13. H. Wayne Morgan, *From Hayes to McKinley, National Party Politics, 1877–1896* (Syracuse: Syracuse University press, 1969), pp. 131–137, 454–458.
14. Madison, vol. 1, p. 203.
15. A. Maurice Low, "The Oligarchy of the Senate," *The North American Review* 174 (February, 1902): 242–243.
16. Alexander Hamilton, John Jay & James Madison, *The Federalist* (New York: Modern Library, 1938), pp. 416–423.
17. "The All Powerful Senate," *The Nation* 72 (January 3, 1901): 4–5; Low, p. 232.
18. Phillips, "Treason of the Senate," *Cosmopolitan*, 40 (April 1906): 634.
19. *Ibid.*, p. 634; Sidney Ratner, *The Tariff in American History*, (New York: D. Van Nostrandt Company, 1972), pp. 13, 23–24.
20. Morgan, pp. 166, 376–377.
21. F. W. Taussig, *The Tariff History of the United States*, 8th ed. (New York: G. P. Putnam's Sons, 1931), p. 452.
22. Kirk H. Porter and Donald H. Johnson, *National Party Platforms 1840–1972*, 5th ed. (Urbana: University of Illinois Press, 1975), p. 90.
23. Morgan, pp. 372–375.
24. Taussig, pp. 373–374.
25. *Ibid.*, pp. 358, 409–410.
26. *Ibid.*, pp. 440–442.
27. *Ibid.*, pp. 411–412.
28. *Ibid.*, pp. 415, 417.

29. *The Federalist*, p. 217.
30. *Ibid.*, p. 56.
31. Phillips, 40 (April 1906): 632.
32. Franklin L. Burdette, *Filibustering in the Senate* (Princeton: Princeton University Press, 1940), p. 59.
33. Morgan, p. 456.
34. *Ibid.*, pp. 343, 454.
35. Richard Hofstadter, *The American Political Tradition & the Men Who Made It* (New York: Vintage Books, 1974), p. 253.
36. William A. Peffer, "The United States Senate, Its Privileges, Powers and Functions, Its Rules and Methods of Doing Business," *North American Review* 167 (July 1898): 190.
37. *Congressional Record* (55th Congress, 2nd Session): 4817.
38. William H. Moody, "Constitutional Powers of the Senate," *The North American Review*, 174 (March 1902): 394; Low, pp. 235, 237.
39. George H. Haynes, *The Senate of the United States, Its History and its Practice*, (Boston: Houghton Mifflin, 1938), vol. 1, p. 400n; Burdette, pp. 69–72.
40. James Bryce, *The American Commonwealth*, 3rd ed. (New York: The Macmillan Company, 1914), vol. 1, pp. 114–116.
41. *Congressional Record* (61st congress, 1st session): 7123–7126.
42. John F. Witte, *The Politics and Development of the Federal Income Tax* (Madison: University of Wisconsin Press, 1985), pp. 77–79.
43. Carl Sandburg, *Abraham Lincoln, The Prairie Years* (New York: Harcourt, Brace & World Inc., 1926), vol. 1, pp. 372–373, 402.
44. H. Wayne Morgan, *America's Road to Empire: The War with Spain and Overseas Expansion* (New York: John Wiley and Sons, Inc., 1965), p. x.
45. *Congressional Record* (61st Congress, 1st Session): 7120, 7126, 7111.

6

Beveling the Congress

The claim that the National Government was but an agency of the States, to be revoked by any one at its will, is departed never to return. But the constitutional principle which requires the most careful preservation of State authority, and the most zealous limitation in the exercise of national power, is sound and salutary and must not be forgotten.
—Senator George F. Hoar

One of the principal questions this study proposed to examine was how the legislatively appointed Senate, corrupted and unresponsive as it was alleged to be, came to endorse a constitutional amendment which placed its elections under direct popular control. Two thirds of the Senate (voting concurrently with two-thirds of the House) and three-fourths of the state legislatures, were required to approve an amendment which supposedly jeopardized their own special interests. The only other method for amending the Constitution was by general convention, which Congress was obliged to call upon the application of two-thirds of the legislatures. Either way, the constituted representatives had to consent to this popular reduction of their authority. To restate one of the introductory contentions, the fact that such an amendment was ever ratified contradicted the very need for the amendment.

The constitutional history of the states revealed no want of enterprising politicians offering to extend the direct role of the people in government affairs. Such reforms inevitably affected the indirect process of federal elections, and as it has been shown, many of the problems attendant upon the election of senators stemmed from its increasing popularization, rather than from the lack of it. On the other hand, it has also been shown that, regardless of the aims and interests of senators in the late nineteenth and early twentieth centuries, they were in the first place thoroughly checked by the other branches, if not by their own colleagues, and in the second place, more than sufficiently amenable to sustained popular opinion. In the light of such evidence, the only plausible explanation for the Seventeenth Amendment is that the original method of Senate elections did not square with the inviolable convictions of democracy.

The notion that every citizen had an equal, and thus direct, voice in commanding the government has been the most consistent and perhaps the strongest force for change in American history. Whether openly expressed, as when the legislatures and state conventions contended over the extension of the suffrage; or whether accomplished by usage and without argument, as in the collapse of the Electoral College; the advance of political egalitarianism has always been considered progress in constitutional history. Not since 1787 had there been a group of statesmen sufficiently capable of persuading the American people otherwise.

By 1913, the argument that any legislative body should represent, not the people, but a natural aristocracy embodied in the states, was so unfamiliar as to be incomprehensible to nearly anyone but constitutional pedants. But even though the original mode of Senate election had been largely undermined by means of the canvass and the primary, the mere formality of indirect elections continued to rub against the grain of democratic consistency. Thus, while the legislative machines were finding new ways of cashing in on the popularity of senators, the movement for a constitutional amendment continued to keep pace. In the early 1870s, a few years after Andrew Johnson's final attempt to obtain the necessary resolution from Congress in 1868, there began a prodigious increase in the number of proposals, memorials, and petitions for direct elections sent from around the country. At roughly the same time, the resolution became a handy and often-used plank in third party platforms. The Prohibition Party had endorsed it intermittently since 1872. An "Anti-Monopolist" Party advocated it in 1884, as did the Union Labor Party in 1888. The proposal was finally brought to the forefront of political discussion in the 1890s during the meteoric rise of the National People's, or Populist, Party, whose 1892 presidential candidate received twenty-two electoral votes, and whose subsequent platforms announced in strong language its intention to secure direct elections.[1]

The House Revolt

Inevitably, this growing demand attracted the sort of political adventurers who promised to deliver the reform. In the Fiftieth Congress (March 4, 1887-March 3, 1889), six proposals were offered by congressman in the

House of Representatives; in the Fifty-first Congress, nine more. In the Fifty-second, there were seventeen submissions by representatives from as many states, plus three resolutions introduced by members of the Senate. From then until the Sixty-second Congress, when the amendment finally passed both houses, members of Congress submitted more than 200 resolutions in its favor.[2] The vast majority of these resolutions were tabled, or met their quietus in one of the committees. Not surprisingly, when the matter was finally taken up for consideration, the House, designed as the more "responsive" body, was the first to do so.

What most characterized the House discussions was the predilection to amend for the sake of amendment. The first House report in 1892 recommended direct elections on the grounds that the press had been "teeming with legislative scandals for years," but that unfortunately, investigating committees and grand juries had been "unwilling or unable to detect the frauds, so skilful have the manipulators of it become."[3] In other words, the lack of tangible evidence only confirmed amendment proponents in their suspicions. Many congressmen, however, were not in the least interested in proving corruption, or even the inefficacy of Senate elections. The fact that "the people" wanted an amendment was a sufficient justification in itself. "It matters not by what course of reasoning we reach that conclusion," Congressman William Jennings Bryan told House colleagues. "Overwhelming sentiment" favored giving the people "the right to elect their Senators by a direct vote." Missouri's David DeArmond likewise abjured the House from delaying the issue with "minute discussion of the supposed abuses which exist in the present method of electing Senators." It sufficed merely to observe that direct elections were necessary in the convictions "of a very large portion of the people."[4]

The minority report made an even greater concession to popular expediency, recommending that direct elections be adopted "when the people of any State shall so desire," but that the people of no state should be compelled to do so, "if they prefer to retain the present method."[5] Submitted by Ralph Bushnell of Wisconsin and Ohio's Robert Doan, the proposal promised to advance the reform "along the lines of least resistance." Flighty as it seemed, it was offered repeatedly during the decade of House debates, and had strong support in Congress. Bryan, for one, thought it the highest expression of trust in the people, who surely were "wise enough to decide for themselves." But realistically, it was simply another instance of constituted authorities offering to abdicate their own judgment in favor of the great numerical opinion.

121

The minority report was just as strong as that of the majority in condemning the legislative election of senators, yet when it came to recommendations, the authors offered nothing more principled than leaving the direct elections remedy to be adopted, repealed, and reenacted, whenever it suited the party in power in any given state. The "lines of least resistance," was simply a euphemism for the ongoing surrender of representative will. "*Vox populi, vox Dei!*" cried Doan enthusiastically.[6]

The House rejected the Bushnell-Doan resolution and others like it on every occasion they managed to reach the floor for consideration. On the other hand, the proposal which the House actually adopted in 1893 was hardly less radical in its implications for Federalism. The majority version, which passed unanimously in 1893, went so far as to make direct elections mandatory in all states, but it left the "times, places and manner" of holding the elections to be prescribed by the states.[7] The clause formerly permitting Congress to regulate federal elections (Article I, Section 4) had been deliberately excluded. There would no longer be any national tribunal to decide on the legality and propriety of Senate elections, since every state was to have its own standards and could change them with impunity. Strangely, the state legislators were charged with being too corrupt to continue electing senators, yet with the change to popular elections it was proposed that they be made the umpires of final appeal. From that standpoint, the House's version of the amendment made no sense at all, but it was perfectly understandable when interpreted as two distinct amendments masking a common purpose: to bend federal authority to the local interests of "the people."

That federal authority had to be made more "responsive" was always the central argument for amendment proponents. The Senate would "more nearly and more surely meet the reasonable expectations of the people" if it were elected by them directly. It availed nothing to point out that it was supposed to represent *states*, not people, that it had in fact been intentionally created to *resist* the popular majority. Amendment advocates simply took it for granted that popular expectations were inherently "reasonable," and they were therefore incapable of thinking in terms of checks and balances. Consequently, their explanation for the original method of Senate elections was that the country had been too large, its inhabitants too remote from one another, to make do without the relaying services of state legislatures. It had "been wise at the time," said Bryan, "because they had poor means of communication and little chance of knowing the character of the men for whom they voted." With the advent of newspapers, telegraphs, and compulsory education, the necessity of delegating power had supposedly passed away.[8]

This was one of the more common misconceptions reformers had about original intent. Since the time of the founders, the remote corners of the continent had been brought into much closer contact, thanks to improvements in communications and transportation. The area over which information could be directly transmitted, and over which in turn the public could directly register its response, was virtually nation-wide. Progressive democracy, insofar as it articulated any coherent constitutional philosophy, premised the annulment of representative institutions wherever direct expression could be substituted. Carried to its ultimate conclusion, the logic presaged a single, mass assembly of the people, if and when it ever became technologically feasible.

Overcoming the obstacles of geography did not, in and of itself, engender a closer harmony of interests. It did not remove the tendency to faction. The information which the new methods of communication were to disseminate, and the "public opinion" they were to return, were as much as ever the subject of partisan struggle. In the most familiar passage of *The Federalist,* James Madison argued that it was precisely the extended sphere of the republic which reduced the probability that "a majority of the whole will have a common motive to invade the rights of other citizens; or if such a common motive exists, it will be more difficult for all who feel it to discover their own strength, and to act in unison." The problem with pure democracy, in which the citizens "assemble and administer the government in person," was that the "communication and concert" of factious designs resulted "from the form of government itself." There was "nothing to check the inducements [of the majority] to sacrifice the weaker party or an obnoxious individual."[9] If, as turn of the century reformers believed, simple popular rule was becoming scientifically feasible, the Federalist line of reasoning pointed to the necessity of preventing it. The advantages lost to the extensive republic would, if anything, have to be compensated for with stronger representative checks *against* direct democracy.

Obviously enough, it was not the Federalists' line of reasoning that prevailed. Factionalism and corruption were treated as systemic problems, rather than inherently human ones, the premise being that "the people," once given complete equality of political expression, would never stray from the common interest. Checks on the people were the problem. More responsiveness by the government was the solution. "Restraint is no longer needed and never was needed in this country," declared Iowa's David Henderson. "The people are the source of all political power and must be trusted," by which he meant that delegated authority needed to be further reduced.[10]

Yet this could not be accomplished without the consent of the very authorities whose interests, it was claimed, were adverse to those of the people. On the one hand, it was argued that the legislators could not be trusted to carry out the people's will in the election of U.S. senators. On the other, it was proposed that they be trusted to carry out the popular will in ratifying an amendment which stripped them of their elective power. During a decade of House debates, or more precisely, declamations, on the necessity of direct elections, amendment proponents advanced these antithetical propositions with no hint of having discerned the irony.

Asked about the dangers of submitting the amendment to boss-ridden legislatures, Henderson's reply unwittingly spoke volumes on the inherent contradiction of the whole movement:

> State legislatures are in close touch with their own people and must respond to them; and there is no body that will respond quicker than a state legislature to the people as a rule. If the people cannot control their legislatures, then of course there is no hope for any reform . . .[11]

No one confronted the congressman with the heretical corollary that a people who could already "control their legislatures" had no need of reducing their authority any further. To be on the safe side, Congressman John Shafroth proposed submitting the amendment to state conventions rather than to the legislatures. It was pointed out, however, that conventions were no more than delegated assemblies. A boss who controlled one might as easily control the other. Moreover, unless any mob was free to call itself a convention, the legislatures would have to prescribe the manner of convening. Shafroth's suggestion was dropped as quickly as it had been raised. There was no getting around the legislatures. As Horace Powers of Vermont asserted, there would be no direct elections "until the people of the States are sufficiently waked up so that their own legislatures will take the initiative measures to secure this amendment."[12] (It was the duty of statesman, apparently, to rouse the people into a reform for which they were already supposed to be clamoring.)

In the meantime, the House would continue to do its part, approving the resolution in one form or another in 1893, 1894, 1898, 1900 and 1902, on the last occasion by unanimous vote for the second time.[13]

Each resolution in its turn was sent to the other wing of the Capitol, only to be shuffled off for burial in a Senate committee. But as always, the Senate would eventually have to relent. The battle cry of direct elections, Congressman Henderson promised an applauding gallery in the House, would not cease "until the thunders of the people make them surrender that Bastille which defies the people on this proposition."[14] Actually, the Senate's capitulation bore less resemblance to the storming of the Bastille than to the infiltration of Troy, for it was not by frontal assault that the citadel was breached, but by the peaceful admission of men who had no intention of defending it.

The Changing of the Guard

Not everyone in the House supported the amendment. The unanimous vote of 1902, for instance, did not record the opinion of abstaining members, and in nearly every session able retorts had been offered on behalf of the *status quo*. Even so, in five out of six congresses, the resolution had been mostly smooth sailing through the House. This was certainly not the case in the Senate, where the resolution was routinely rejected without ever coming to the floor for a vote. But if the proposed amendment generated little sympathy in the chamber, its initial Senate supporters were free to try the direct popular approach for themselves. In June of 1896, Senator John H. Mitchell of Oregon published an article in *Forum* which chronicled the progress of the amendment, pointed out the problems in recent Senate elections, and highlighted his own role in the glorious cause. The latter claims were more than a little disingenuous. Mitchell claimed that his 1890 speech was the first ever to be given by a senator on the subject of direct elections, although, having plainly researched the subject, he could hardly have failed to come across Andrew Johnson's blustering orations some thirty years previously.[15] Mitchell went even further, taking credit for being the first senator even to introduce a direct election resolution, having submitted a proposal as early as December 1887. He may well have been unaware of at least two resolutions submitted by other senators in the mid-1870s, when he was serving his freshman term, but he was present in the chamber when Minnesota Senator William Windom's resolution was referred to committee.[16] While it might be making too hasty a judgment to accuse Mitchell of deliberate fraud in claiming the spotlight for his role in direct elections, it was indeed fraud which eventually ended his political career. In 1905, while serving in the Senate, he was convicted, fined, and jailed for his involvement in a major land swindle—an incident, curiously enough, which the popular press used as proof of the corruption into which legislatively elected senators were prone to fall.[17]

In 1900, the Senate having rejected the House resolutions for the fourth time, Senator William Harris took up his pen for the reform-minded magazine, *Independent*. His main point was that the demand for popular elections had been "growing with cumulative force for more than fifty years." Only the Senate's unresponsiveness stood between the people and their desired reform. To this ad populum rationale, Harris added that the founders had been "comparatively indifferent as to the means or manner of election and very naturally fell into the plan which had largely been in vogue" under the Confederation. This gross misrendering of original intent was typical of amendment proponents, and was argued from sheer ignorance, deceit, or myopic study of the evidence. Having asserted it, Harris was free to state the truth of subsequent history in a more favorable light. Since the founders had been "indifferent," it was easier to justify changes which fit the theories of the hour, changes which on the whole had promoted the unremitting advance of political egalitarianism. "We have gradually enlarged the rights of the people and the extent of their participation in public affairs," attested the senator from Kansas, *restricting or reducing the powers of representative bodies like State legislatures* [emphasis mine]."[18] No Federalist, surveying his dilapidating legacy, could have put the case more accurately.

Notwithstanding this frank acknowledgement that popular power had increased at the expense of delegated authority, Harris, (and this was also common of amendment advocates) blamed the unwelcome consequences on delegated authority, not on the people. One such consequence, naturally, was the "manifest influence of great corporations" in Senate elections, a malady "widespread and deplorable in every direction,"[19]—Kansas elections being a presumable exception. There had already been a good deal of political leveling before any of the smoke and stir was ever raised against plutocracy. Harris had practically admitted as much, but like so many reformers of the day, he was unable or unwilling to make the logical connection. Every corporation was simply one contingency of "the people," practically all of whom had been trying to gain a direct influence over representative decisions. As the intended process of indirect elections gave way to the public canvass and the popular primary, money had quickly become the most critical necessity in waging an election campaign. Given the chronology of this development, it was a complete non sequitur to suppose that direct elections were going to reduce the importance of political finance, but Harris did not have to trouble himself with logical proofs. It was enough to invoke the old specter, the simplistic but popular dichotomy of "the people" and "the interests," and to propose to cure the evils of democracy with more democracy.

It was a cure the senators would themselves administer, once a sufficient number of them had been made to feel, as Harris did, that it was in their own political interest so to do. It has already been observed how, since the Jacksonian Era, the independence of the legislators had steadily crumbled under the weight of direct democracy. In the process of making the laws, innovations such as the initiative, the referendum, and the threat of recall had all but absolved them in many states of having to make difficult and unpopular decisions. Likewise in Senate elections, the senatorial primaries, beginning with Nebraska in 1875, had whittled their responsibility down to a painless formality. The legislator had merely to register the will of the people as expressed in the primary, or more precisely, the will of that powerful coalition of popular interests, his political party. What is obvious enough is that senators who were appointed in this manner, already accustomed to the rough and tumble of mass campaigns for the party nomination, saw no threat in carrying the process to the general elections as well. Suffice it to say, when enough states had instituted the primary, there were enough senators to pass the resolution for direct elections.

The spreading use of the senatorial primary offers yet another important example of the power of democratic ideology over rational political constraints, namely, the excessive influence of the West in national affairs at the outset of the Progressive Era. Although the primary was widely used in the South, and was already making its appearance in a few of the states in the Northeast, in its origin and in its most pronounced development it was a decidedly western phenomenon. A contemporary of the movement, Professor Frederick Jackson Turner, noted that circumstances such as the extreme mobility of the frontier population and the necessity for self-sufficiency in the wilds had produced a region which was "strong in selfishness . . . intolerant of administrative experience and education," and which pressed "individual liberty beyond its proper bounds." Primitive western society, wrote the historian, showed little "intelligent appreciation of the complexity of business interests" and complete "antipathy to control." Accordingly, western constitutions, replete with initiatives, referenda, the recall, and the primaries, were perfect reflections of popular distrust in representative institutions.[20]

That such constitutions were ever adopted, however, reflected as much on the weakening control of the federal government as on the excessive individualism of the frontiers. Congress had the power to regulate the territories, and furthermore, to set the conditions for statehood. In the early republic, many sound objections were raised against the hasty admission of states. In the convention of 1787, in fact, Elbridge Gerry apprehended that western dominance would "oppress commerce" and recommended that the Constitution specify that the number of representatives from new states should not be allowed to exceed the number of the original members of the Union.[21] In 1828, Congressman John Randolph of Roanoke repudiated the egalitarian foolishness of granting statehood to frontier regions that had not yet attained "that degree of constancy and assimilation which is necessary to the formulation of a body politic."[22] Speaking against the 1812 admission of Louisiana, which had been acquired from the French only nine years previously, Josiah Quincy of Massachusetts upbraided his House colleagues for attempting to throw "the rights and the property of this people into 'hotch-potch' with the wild men on the Missouri." John Quincy Adams repeatedly urged that the territories be safeguarded as a national asset, to be settled gradually, if at all. The alternative was an orgy of land speculation and jockeying among the parties to control the Senate, since each new state would have equal representation with its forbearers.[23]

Congress was no more capable of restraining expansion in the nineteenth century than Parliament had been in the eighteenth. Perhaps the unstaunchable flow of humanity bore the markings of "Providence," as Edmund Burke once told the House of Commons,[24] and certainly, historians cannot be wholly skeptical of the twin principles of self-sufficiency and self-determination which inspired the vast majority of westward migrants. Nevertheless, the Congress, in capitulating to the squatters' cry for a voice in federal affairs, summarily carved out "states" from the map with an almost geometric precision, elevating their barely settled populations to the ranks of the older commonwealths. This concession to a democratic demand actually achieved a very undemocratic outcome, for as the census of 1900 revealed, it had become possible to amend the Constitution by a combination of states whose populations amounted to well under half of the nation's total.[25] While no such catastrophe occurred, the rampant creation of states resulted in a gross inflation of western representation in the national councils, especially in the upper house, where the "free-coinage of Senators"—President Benjamin Harrison's unflattering term for the statehood process[26]—had suffused that body with the elements of radicalism against which it had formerly been insulated. Entering the Union with the senatorial primary, or adopting it shortly thereafter, the states created since the last quarter of the nineteenth century had all but guaranteed the popular election of senators.

This is not to say that the primary always attained a popular outcome. Deadlocked legislatures and the primaries went almost hand in hand. In states where the primaries were merely local, but senatorial preferences were part of the legislative candidate's platform, state legislatures were sometimes irrevocably divided over the multiplicity of popular mandates. In states which had the direct senatorial nomination, victories were usually obtained by pluralities, and as was often the case, a legislative majority might only be united for the purpose of opposing the leading candidate. Many states adopted laws declaring a plurality holder the winner of the primary nomination, thus placing the political obligation on legislators in the same party to give him their votes. But there was still the irritating possibility that a candidate who had garnered a bare plurality of primary votes in one party would win the Senate seat over a much more popular candidate whose party was not in the legislative majority.

Typically, when solutions were sought, reformers never looked back to the original but little used idea of electing legislators who could be trusted to negotiate the choice of senator on their state's behalf. Quite the contrary, progress was always seen in terms of further curtailing the legislator's authority. In the "laboratories of democracy," as the states have been called (usually by way of compliment), one experiment failed after another until Oregon, the trailblazer in plebiscitary government, finally hit upon a foolproof method for dictating the outcome of Senate elections on the basis of direct popular opinion. In 1904 the state passed an initiative establishing a general election runoff between the primary nominees of the two major parties. It was completely unofficial, but funded by the state. Candidates for the legislature were then "permitted" to include in their platform one of two statements regarding their views on the election of senators. "Statement #1" assured the voters that a candidate would, regardless of party affiliation, abide by the results of the general election. "Statement #2" declared the candidate's intention to vote according to his personal discretion, and no doubt to his own political peril. Needless to say, this crude piece of popular extortion proved quite effective. Thenceforth, there was little deviating from the decree of popular numbers in the state of Oregon.[27]

The "Oregon System," with various adaptations, was quickly imitated throughout the states. The Nebraska legislature, with the backing of William Jennings Bryan, mandated that after each candidate's name on the legislative primary ballot would follow the words "Promises to vote for people's choice for United States Senator" or "Will not promise to vote for people's choice for United States Senator." A North Dakota law required would-be legislative candidates to take an oath promising to vote for the party's choice for senator as determined by the popular primary. Although the state Supreme Court overturned the specific clause in the legislation which would have added "another oath, declaration and test, as a qualification for office," it yet upheld the remaining provisions, permitting "the electors to designate their choice of a candidate for the United States Senate."[28] By "electors," of course, the court meant the people directly, not the legislators.

In one-party states, such as existed in the South, primary nominations virtually assured election by the legislature, but even so, there were still a few vestiges of free agency for reformers to wrest from constituted authority. In 1906, the Alabama Democratic Executive Committee ordered primary elections for nominating two Senate alternates, whom the governor was supposed to appoint, in descending order by the number of popular votes that each received, in the event of a Senate vacancy ("If vacancies happen by Resignation, or otherwise, during the Recess of the Legislature of any State, the Executive thereof may make temporary Appointments until the next meeting of the Legislature, which shall then fill such Vacancies." Article I, Section 3). No matter how slim the popular plurality turned out to be in nominating these alternates, candidates for gubernatorial nominations were faced with the same choice as the legislators as to whether or not to endorse a public statement promising to defer their own judgment to that expressed in the party primary. Amid all the clangor about state machines, there were few instances which matched this amazing display of arbitrary party power, of the ability of a small circle of political brokers outside the formal representative structure to coerce not only the legislators, but also the state's chief executive, in the conduct of their constitutional duties.[29] And it was coercion of the most successful kind, since it was advanced under the aegis of popular rights.

It must be remembered, however, that the constituted authorities did not simply acquiesce, but often took the lead in diminishing their own responsibilities. Although the "Oregon System" was instituted via the popular initiative (no doubt with the endorsement of many legislators), the Nebraska and North Dakota laws were not even referred to the people. They were ordinary legislative enactments. Similarly around the United States, the elected lawmakers were introducing and endorsing legislation which established the direct senatorial primary. Again, this was the Achilles' heel of the American system of checks and balances. The idea that representatives of the states would, or could, preserve the Union from democracy seems in retrospect a perfect contradiction of the political experience. It was state democracy, after all, which the founders had been trying to restrain when they barred the doors and closed the windows to deliberate in Philadelphia.

The most compelling proof of this contradiction lies in the movement among the states themselves to change the manner of Senate elections, if not by the ordinary amendment process than by constitutional convention. With the exception of armed revolt, no remedy for the nation's political ills could be more drastic than the convention. The American people have had only one to date: When that august assemblage of 1787 convened for the purpose of making a few alterations in the Articles of Confederation. The radically new document they produced was an obvious improvement, but while subsequent attempts would likely be no less revolutionary, there is utterly no guarantee that the results would be as fortunate. State conventions had historically delivered a long and steady hammering to the principles of representative government, and of those national proposals that gained a significant following in the Progressive Era, few, if any, did not aim with equal force at the foundations of the federal edifice. The American National Prohibitionist Party wanted to abolish the Electoral College. The Socialist Labor Party issued its "demand" for getting rid of the president, the vice-president, the Senate and all upper houses in the states. The Socialists urged the initiative and the referendum at the national level, as did the National Party. The Progressive Party declared it imperative to find a "more easy and expeditious method of amending the Federal Constitution."[30]

These and certainly many other lawless ideas were bound to have representatives in a national convention. They already had their advocates in the Congress. In 1912, seven senators from the Judiciary Committee endorsed a resolution to make the Constitution amenable to the popular initiative. Another group of senators proposed a provision for the recall of lower court judges.[31] By 1908, there were one hundred and ten members of the House of Representatives pledged to support an "advisory" referendum and initiative on most of the divisive issues of the time.[32] The 1912 platform of the Progressive Party, which received more popular votes in the presidential race that year than the Republican incumbent, and eleven times as many electoral votes, called for national referenda to overturn unpopular court decisions.[33] Meanwhile, the Constitution made no provisions for the manner of selecting and apportioning delegates, nor yet for the place of holding a convention, for the rules of its proceedings or for the scope of its authority. The mere calling of a convention, in other words, might possibly have been the subject of intense partisanship in itself, without even entering into the great questions of fundamental law that it would supposedly settle.

Yet the majority of states were willing to risk opening Pandora's Box for the sake of securing the popular election of senators. California was the first to make its "application" to Congress in 1893.[34] Texas followed suit in 1899, joined by Pennsylvania, Michigan, Colorado, Oregon, and Tennessee two years later. Kentucky applied in 1902; Arkansas, Washington, and Illinois in 1903.[35] In 1906 Governor Albert Cummins, *at the request of the Iowa legislature,* called a meeting of delegates from the several states to discuss strategies for getting the Congress to call a federal convention, resulting in the formation of a national lobby organization dedicated specifically for the purpose. The resolution agreed upon at the "Des Moines Conference" showed a clear preference to pass upon the direct elections amendment "as a single question,"[36] but once a convention was actually called, there was no way of confining its deliberations. The entire Constitution could be treated as if it were tabula rasa. Even so, by 1908, under the impetus of the Des Moines resolution, Delaware, Indiana, Iowa, Kansas, Louisiana, Missouri, Montana, Nevada, New Jersey, North Carolina, Idaho, Oklahoma, South Dakota, Utah, and Wisconsin had all joined the convention movement.[37] The pointed irony was that state legislatures were trying to popularize the federal Constitution during the nadir of their own popularity. It was the heyday of the muckrakers, the Des Moines Conference meeting in the same year that David Graham Phillips was gaining celebrity status with articles on the "treason" of the senators and the legislatures that elected them.

State by state, the legislators were demanding that their power be remitted to the people, even at the cost of having to rewrite the entire federal compact. By 1910, twenty-seven of the thirty-one legislatures then required to call a convention had made their formal petitions to Congress. The number was twenty-eight, counting Delaware, whose call for a convention to abolish polygamy was nevertheless a call for a convention. The territories of Arizona and New Mexico, with the typically plebiscitary constitutions of the West, were on the threshold of statehood (1912), and would almost certainly have endorsed a scheme which promised to bring the federal system closer to the level of their own. Alabama and Wyoming submitted resolutions reflecting their support for a convention without expressly calling for one.[38] That could be easily rectified. Senator Weldon Heyburn, a shrewd, if overly legalistic constitutionalist, pointed out that the precise wording of some resolutions, coupled with the fact that certain legislatures had changed majorities without the new party in power expressing itself on the subject, reduced the legitimate number of convention applicants to only seventeen.[39] But there have not been many instances of democratic reformers suspending their plans in the face of constitutional technicalities. After all, a simple majority in both houses of Congress sufficed to determine what constituted a legitimate "application." Was it too far-fetched to suppose that among that generation of ambitious popularizers at least a bare majority of them would not have hesitated, upon adequate pretexts, to inscribe their names upon a fresh new tablet of fundamental laws?

The lesser of two evils prevailed. The direct primary had done its work before the convention became necessary. Twenty-nine states had instituted the direct senatorial primary, most of them tightening the reign on legislative discretion with enactments similar to those of the "Oregon System." At least eight more states had popular preference votes in the legislative primaries. Before the legislatures which were to elect senators in 1911 had even convened, the *Boston Herald* could boast that "Fourteen out of the thirty Senators who take the oath of office at the beginning of the next Congress, have already been designated by popular vote."[40] And this did not include the senators elected in similar fashion from the two preceding Congresses. Meanwhile, the Democratic minority, suffering the worst political drought in the party's national history, adopted a direct elections plank in 1900, and continued to support it in succeeding national campaigns.[41] The combination of Democrats and direct primary nominees was large enough to tilt the balance in the Senate by the opening of the Sixty-first Congress in March of 1909. A new generation of senators would thus take up the standard of reform. Like the muckrakers, congressman, and legislators before them, these Senate reformers would now sound the battle cry against the bosses and the moneyed interests. But if the majority of both congressional houses, and the majority of the legislatures, had come to agree with the public's adverse opinion of the political system, exactly where were all the bosses and the corrupting influences to be found?

The Progressive Bosses

The personal background of the Senate's progressive element, the "insurgents," as some of them called themselves, offers an elementary but generally overlooked truth about the Seventeenth Amendment. Proportionally, the fifty-four senators who supported it on the first Senate vote in February 1911 were as representative of the great capitalist interests as the thirty-three senators who voted against it. Oregon's Jonathan Bourne, a devout believer in direct elections, presidential primaries, direct legislation, and the general inerrancy of the mass electorate, had prospered as an attorney for the Southern Pacific Railroad, developed interests in mining, big business agriculture, and cotton manufacturing, and was the head of several corporations by the time he reached the U.S. Senate.[42] Oklahoma's Robert L. Owen, whose ultra-progressivism has already been introduced, was the founder of the Muscogee National Bank, and was also an active speculator in mining, oil production and the sale of public lands.[43] Another direct elections proponent, Isaac Stephenson, was—like his senatorial predecessor, Philetus Sawyer—one of Wisconsin's foremost lumber magnates, but unlike Sawyer, who was a product of the old legislative caucus, Stephenson enjoyed the luxury of spending more than a hundred thousand dollars of his personal fortune to sound his own trumpet in the senatorial primary.[44] Simon Guggenheim, who also supported the amendment, came to the Senate from one of the largest ore smelting and refining houses in the country. Ellison "Cotton Ed" Smith of South Carolina was an unabashedly partisan representative of the South's largest industry. California's multi-millionaire, George Perkins, was associated with virtually every profit making venture on the West coast. Listing the financial holdings of Delaware's Henry DuPont, former president of the Wilmington & Northern Railroad, would require a separate volume.[45]

In other words, the struggle for direct elections was not, as it has been so often characterized, a contest between the henchman of plutocracy and the defenders of pious labor. Nor was it always easy to distinguish the Progressives from the Bosses when it came to the exercise of senatorial power. Owen, for example, used his influence to lift congressional restriction on the sale of Indian territories which he and other Oklahoma businessmen sought to acquire for themselves. He also managed to get a law passed permitting the Federal Claims Court to adjudicate a case in which he had deep financial interests. As a Democrat, Owen naturally stood for tariff reductions, unless there was talk of lowering the duties on imported oil, which would have threatened the profits of one of Oklahoma's leading industries.[46]

Albert Beveridge, Owen's progressive colleague, can not be accused of such self-serving use of his high office, but he was no less a servant of the interests that put him in power. The senator referred to those interests, probably in all sincerity, as "the people," although his original constituency consisted almost solely of Indianapolis' substantial bankers, manufacturers and merchants. Under the leadership of David M. Parry, president of the Manufacturers Association of Indiana and vice president of the National Association of Manufacturers, the city's leading capitalists established the "Businessmen's Association for Beveridge" to raise funds and lobby the legislature on his behalf.[47] Beveridge's strong advocacy of imperial expansion and tariff reduction were squarely in accord with producers ready to compete in overseas markets.

It was one thing to have the support of influential private citizens, but Beveridge also needed to win over a majority of the party professionals, which his campaign managers did in the election of 1898 by brilliantly exploiting a rift among the state's Republican chieftains. Having slipped through a narrow window of opportunity, the newly elected senator had to consolidate his winnings through the federal patronage.[48] In an intense, seesaw battle with Senator Fairbanks for control of the Indiana Republican machinery, federal judges, revenue collectors, port surveyors, postmasters, U.S. marshals, and pension agents were promoted by Beveridge from the ranks of the politically loyal or the camps of the politically useful. *The Nation* considered him a progressive, albeit with "a pretty taste in spoils."[49] No doubt, it was all necessary to advance the rule of the people, which postulated the end of such distasteful practices.

Beveridge's maneuvering was a dull affair when compared to the exploits of Robert La Follette, Sr., the archbishop of Progressivism himself, whose reign over Wisconsin's electoral apparatus would have been the envy of old-time bosses in the Gilded Age. La Follette's victory in the gubernatorial race of 1900 stemmed from his shrewd organization of interests disaffected with the old Sawyer machine, mostly Milwaukee businessmen, the dairy industry, and farmers from the Norwegian districts, where the great reformer had spent much of his youth. In spite of his given political adroitness, he would never have reached the governor's mansion without the considerable financial support of Isaac Stephenson, the discontented millionaire who had been passed over for a U.S. Senate seat after years of generously contributing to the Republican party. Cutting his ties to the old party leadership, Stephenson literally threw his fortunes in with La Follette's insurgents, spending more than half a million dollars in support of La Follette and his allies on the Republican ticket. He also founded the *Milwaukee Free Press,* which touted the La Follette line on every major issue.[50] Having further assisted the insurgent cause in two more gubernatorial campaigns, and in La Follette's 1906 bid for the Senate, Stephenson was awarded the object he had long coveted, joining La Follette in the Senate in 1909, and, incidentally, adding another vote to the pro-amendment forces.

Once in power, Governor La Follette, like any other machine politician had to do, set about the task of rewarding the faithful and damning the opposition through ruthless use of the spoils system. His old pals from the Norwegian districts figured prominently in his campaign victory, and were well represented in the new administration. The proliferation of regulatory agencies under the new regime, whatever else it might have accomplished, offered a fresh source of patronage which the governor did not hesitate to use for partisan appointments. He expanded the utility and oil inspectorships to accommodate the rank and file. His most notorious accomplishment, however, was the conversion of the game wardens department into a vast encampment for the toilers of his own political vineyards. After a wholesale purge of his predecessor's appointees, these game warden battalions played a crucial role in La Follette's subsequent elections. His enemies joked bitterly about the wardens "hunting for men who will vote for La Follette at the next state convention." The payroll of the department significantly increased, and its expenditures more than tripled, during La Follette's administration, and noticeably receded when he left the governor's mansion to take his seat in the Senate, where bigger and better spoils were at his disposal, and from whose Olympian heights he continued to sway the fortunes of Wisconsin politicians for years to come.[51]

Certainly, La Follette stood for social and economic change, but like previous rulers of state machines, perhaps even more than most, he also stood for his friends, and "demanded complete loyalty from his supporters." He may have been a reformer, but he was unquestionably a "reform boss."[52] His example, as those of Beveridge and Owen, hardly supported the contention that direct elections would make wholesale improvements in senatorial conduct. Granted, many amendment opponents had little room for pointing fingers, but then, they were not publicly grandstanding about the evils of the political system. Yet despite the sometimes glaring disparity between the promise and the practice of Progressivism, it is not contended that the era's constitutional reformers were simply demagogues who cynically pulled the strings for popular effect. In all fairness, they seem actually to have believed in their own rhetoric, failing to see that mass democracy, rather than the lack of it, was the real culprit behind the organization of professional electioneering machinery and the party enlistment of "moneyed interests." These undemocratic results they proposed to cure with more democracy, although in order to do so they had to gain power through much the same methods as the old bosses they replaced. Even their own experiences could not shake their conviction that a more direct form of popular expression would, ipso facto, purify the nation's politics.

Opposed to them was a dwindling coterie of men who believed in the essential synonymity of "the interests" and "the people." Direct expression they suspected of partiality and local prejudice. They regarded the popular impulse as a force to be restrained and refined, not unleashed and encouraged. The dispute over the Seventeenth Amendment, in their view, was a class struggle only in the minds of the progressives. Yet it is the legacy of the victors under which traditional understanding of the contest falters. In reality, the Senate's debate (here greatly abridged and paraphrased), reveals a quite different conflict, having its origins not in the nation's socio-economic transformations, but in the two sets of principles which had been contending since the eighteenth century. At long last, after scores of victories in the states, proponents of the General Will were ready to take on the defenders of checks and balances for control of the federal Constitution and, perhaps, for mastery of the American political soul.

Notes

1. Kirk H. Porter and Donald H. Johnson, *National Party Platforms 1840–1972*, 5th ed. (Urbana: University of Illinois Press, 1975), pp. 46, 64, 84, 106.
2. Herman V. Ames, *The Proposed Amendments to the Constitution of the United States during the First Century of its Existence* (New York: B. Franklin, 1970), pp. 24, 60–63; George H. Haynes, *The Senate of the United States, Its History and Practices* (Houghton Mifflin Company, 1938), vol. 1, p. 96n.

3. *H.Rep. 368* (52nd Congress, 1st Session): 3.
4. *Congressional Record* (53rd Congress, 2nd Session): 7775, 7724.
5. *H.Rep. 368*, pt 2, p. 1.
6. *Congressional Record* (52nd Congress, 1st Session): 6071, 6069.
7. *Ibid.*, (52nd Congress, 2nd Session): 617.
8. *Ibid.*, (53rd Congress, 2nd Session): 7724, 7775.
9. Alexander Hamilton, John Jay & James Madison, *The Federalist* (New York: The Modern Library, 1937), pp. 61, 58.
10. *Congressional Record* (55th Congress, 2nd Session): 4815.
11. *Ibid.*
12. *Ibid.*, pp. 4818, 4819, 4814.
13. Haynes, vol. 1, p. 97 n.
14. *Congressional Record* (55th Congress, 2nd Session): 4814.
15. John H. Mitchell, "Election of Senators by Popular Vote," *Forum* 21 (June 1896): 394; *Congressional Globe* (35th Congress, 1st Session): 3044; (36th Congress, 2nd Session): 1654; (36th Congress, 1st Session): 82–83.
16. Mitchell, p. 394; *Congressional Record*, (50th Congress, 1st Session): 163; (43rd Congress, 1st Session): 3, 1580; (44th Congress, 1st Session): 756.
17. Jerry A. O'Callahan, "Senator John H. Mitchell and the Oregon Land Frauds, 1905," *Pacific Historical Review*, 21 (August 1952): 255–261; "The Senate's Roll Call of Dishonor," *The Nation*, 81 (December 7, 1905): 456.
18. William A. Harris, "The Election of Senators by the People," *Independent* 52 (May 31, 1900): 1291.
19. *Ibid.*
20. Frederick Jackson Turner, *The Frontier in American History* (New York: Henry Holt and Company, 1920), pp. 30–32; Dana Lee Thomas, *The Story of American Statehood* (New York: Wilfred Funk, Inc., 1961), pp. 209–210.
21. James Madison, *Notes of Debates in the Federal Convention of 1787*, Gaillard Hunt and James Brown Scott, ed. (Buffalo: Prometheus Press, 1987), vol. 2, p. 251.
22. Powhatan Bouldin, Home Reminiscences of John Randolph of Roanoke (Danville, Va.: Clemmett & Jones Printers, 1876), pp. 277.
23. Turner, pp. 208, 26.
24. Burke quoted in Turner, p. 34.
25. Sylvester Baxter, "The Representative Inequality of Senators," *The North American Review*, 177 (December 1903): 897.
26. Harrison quoted in H. Wayne Morgan, *From Hayes to McKinley, National Party Politics 1877–1896* (Syracuse: Syracuse University Press, 1969), p. 343.
27. George A. Thatcher, "Significance of the Oregon Experiment," *Outlook*, 83 (July 14, 1906): 612–613.
28. Haynes, vol. 1, pp. 103–104.
29. Emmett O'Neal, "Election of United States Senators by the People," *The North American Review*, 188 (November 1908): 703–704.
30. Porter and Johnson, pp. 64, 96, 176.
31. *S.Rep. 147* (63rd congress, 2nd session), Pt 2, pp. 1–3.
32. Margaret A. Schaffner, "The Initiative, The Referendum, and the Recall," *American Political Science Review*, 2 (November 1907): 39.
33. Porter And Johnson, p. 176.
34. *Congressional Record* (61st Congress, 3rd Session): 2770.

35. Walter K. Tuller, "A Convention to Amend the Constitution—Why Needed, How It May be Obtained," *North American Review*, 193 (March 1911): 369–371.

36. "The Des Moines Conference," *Outlook*, 84 (December 15, 1906): 902.

37. Tuller, p. 370.

38. *Congressional Record* (61st Congress, 1st Session): 7113–7120; Tuller, p. 373.

39. *Congressional Record* (61st Congress, 3rd Session): 2770.

40. Quoted in Hayes, vol. 1, p. 104.

41. Porter and Johnson, p. 115.

42. Leonard Schlup, "Republican Insurgent: Jonathan Bourne and the Politics of Progressivism, 1908–1912," *Oregon Historical Quarterly*, 87 (Fall 1986): 229–230.

43. Kenny L. Brown, "A Progressive from Oklahoma, Senator Robert Latham Owen, Jr." *Chronicles of Oklahoma* 62 (Fall 1984): 236.

44. Haynes, vol. 1, p. 136n.

45. *Biographical Directory of the United States Congress 1774–1989* (Washington, D.C.: United States Government Printing Office, 1989), pp. 1103, 1827, 1633, 939.

46. Brown, pp. 238, 241, 244.

47. John Braeman, "The Rise of Albert J. Beveridge to the United States Senate," *Indiana Magazine of History*, 53 (December 1957): 367; Claude G. Bowers, *Beveridge and the Progressive Era* (New York: The Literary Guild, 1932), pp. 270, 275.

48. Braeman, pp. 379–380.

49. "The President and the Bosses," *The Nation*, 82 (January 18, 1906): 47.

50. Robert S. Maxwell, "La Follette and the Progressive Machine of Wisconsin," *Indiana Magazine of History*, 48 (March, 1952): 56, 61–62.

51. *Ibid.*, pp. 59–60, 63, 67.

52. *Ibid.*, p. 57.

7

The Deliberation to End All Deliberations

As Ulysses required his followers to bind him to the mast
that he might not yield to the song of the siren as he sailed by, so
the American democracy has bound itself to the great rules of right
conduct, which are essential to the protection of liberty and justice
and property and order, and made it practically impossible that the
impulse, the prejudice, the excitement, the frenzy of the moment
shall carry our democracy into those excesses which have wrecked
all our prototypes in history.
—Senator Elihu Root

It had been six years since the House had passed a resolution for direct senatorial elections, but the dormancy was deceptive. The primaries and the applications of the legislatures were undeniably metamorphasizing the upper chamber. With various members endorsing not only direct elections, but direct legislation at the national level, the federal recall, even popular referenda on Supreme Court decisions, the Senate had already become what the Seventeenth Amendment proposed to make of it. A more "responsive" body, it would actually lead the fight in bringing about its own surrender from an unpopular position.

May 21, 1908, Senator Owen introduced a direct elections resolution which, when ratified, would "prevent the corruption of legislatures," "prevent men [from] using money improperly to obtain a seat in the Senate," and "compel the selection of the best-fitted men, and so forth," not to mention that it would "make the Senate more responsive to the will of the people of the States." At this early stage, his resolution was defeated by a simple flanking movement, consigned to the committee on Privileges and Elections, whose "Old Guard" leadership was still considering the issue when the Congress expired. On July 7, 1909, Owen submitted another resolution, but it showed every indication of meeting the same fate. After ten months in committee, there had been no word of any impending report.[1]

As the "insurgents" persisted, however, and as their numbers grew, their opponents were less successful at this sort of procedural juggling. If the progressives were to be stopped, it would have to be done on the open field of debate, which was not the most favorable terrain for many of the Senate's traditional "oligarchy." Nelson Aldrich, the most vilified senator of the age, was not noted for speaking, and confined his involvement to making a point of order over one of Owen's typical parliamentary blunders. Otherwise, he took no part in the debate, and never cast a vote on the subject. Boies Penrose, the consummate manipulator of Pennsylvania politics, made a feeble effort at tripping up Owen by adding an amendment to his resolution which would have made a directly elected Senate proportionally representative of state population. Who knows? Coming from one of the more populous states, perhaps Penrose would have voted for such a resolution, but since Article V of the Constitution provided that no state could be deprived of its equal representation in the Senate without its consent, the senator's real motive was obviously obstruction. None of his colleagues gave it a second thought, and Penrose was reduced to silence for the remainder of the debate.[2] From that point forward, the amendment's opposition had to be shouldered by men who could wage their resistance solely on the basis of logical and historical argument.

Perhaps that was because the parliamentary tables had been turned during the Sixty-first Congress. Stronger in numbers, and wiser in the ways of the Senate, the insurgents managed to maneuver subsequent amendment resolutions to the more sympathetic Committee on the Judiciary. The committee chairman, William E. Borah of Idaho, had been defeated in his first bid for the Senate at the hands of a state legislative caucus, but succeeded on his next attempt in 1907, after Idaho had established the direct senatorial primary. Admitting he could never have come to power without the popular intervention, Borah was a natural champion of the amendment. With the resolution safely in his hands,[3] it was guaranteed to come to the floor for a vote before the close of Congress.

Meanwhile, debate had begun even before this new proposal had been committed. On May 31, 1909, when Owen moved that the Privileges and Elections committee render a report on his earlier resolution, both he and Beveridge used the occasion to lecture the Senate on the necessity of amending the Constitution. There has already been occasion to quote at length from Owen, the gist of whose argument was that the Senate was an obstacle to desired change; that directly elected, it would accede to the popular demand for tariff reduction, an income tax, banking reform, postal improvements, a better system of roads and canals, higher wages, lower prices, shorter working hours, and world peace.

The fulfillment of all these wants and needs, so the logic went, was simply a matter of letting the people express themselves. The political struggle at hand, as he put it, was the struggle of the people "against delegated government." Thus, to the senator from Oklahoma, the direct elections amendment was but the "gateway to other needed reforms." Next would come the national initiative and referendum, then the recall, perhaps even the election of local federal administrators. To keep the people apprised of all the national issues they would have to decide, Owen proposed a federally funded "publicity pamphlet," his assumption being that the government would be inherently neutral in such matters. These innovations, Owen promised, would lay the foundations for "an absolute government by the people." But typical of so many egalitarians, there were undertones of the most intolerant exclusiveness when it came to the actual establishment of the utopia. The senator insisted, for instance, that conservatives "must not be allowed to change a word of these laws that does not stand the approval of the friends of the rule of the people [that is, himself and others of like mind]." Politicians who did not "support cordially the legislative programme of the people's rule [the program outlined by Owen] deserve to be defeated."[4]

The reference to "absolute government," the idea that there should be no agency of legislative restraint upon the sovereign majority, and the implicit belief in perfect and impartial solutions which could only be derived by direct and universal expression—a belief strongly reminiscent of the General Will—could not have contrasted more strikingly with the founding principles. Understandably, Owen made no attempt at all to justify the amendment in terms of preserving or restoring the structure wrought by the founding fathers. Instead, he left the trick of pulling the progressive rabbit from the hat of original intent to Senator Beveridge, who took the floor immediately after him.

For a lawyer who prided himself on cutting to the constitutionality of every case he argued, and as a self-made historian who would one day write the biography of Chief Justice John Marshall, one of the premier Federalists, Beveridge showed a remarkably shallow appreciation for the genesis of the federal system. A decade previously, Senator William

Harris had argued that the founders had been "comparatively indifferent" as to how the Senate was elected. Beveridge went even further, claiming that "the great majority of those whose names are now household words for constructive statesmanship" were actually opposed to election by the legislatures. Confusing the rancorous division over senatorial apportionment with the more civil deliberations over the manner of senatorial appointment, the senator from Indiana maintained that "the plan that was adopted ultimately was forced by the insistence of the smaller States." Otherwise, the Senate would have been elected directly, a proposal which "had its origin in the wisest minds that formulated the Constitution, who were overruled only by a compromise forced upon them."[5]

Although far wide of the mark in explaining the origins of indirect elections, Beveridge was clearly on target in stating that the practices of his own day were a distant cry from the senatorial appointment procedures agreed upon in 1787. "The theory was that the legislature of the State should look all over the State, bound by no consideration of party, restrained by no obligation of any kind except the duty of selecting the wisest, the bravest, and the purest man for Senator." Then came the convention system, which, since Andrew Jackson's time had "radically changed in its practical operations much of our Constitution." The same was true for the College of Electors, who were created to "sweep the whole Republic" for the best man. Here again, the party system had "nullified that phase of the Constitution." Original intent, said the senator from Indiana, simply did not contemplate the "unforeseen development of the political party."[6]

The senator had inadvertently painted himself into a corner, intimating that the development of mass political parties had become a substitute for finding "the wisest, the bravest, and the purest man for Senator." Jacob Gallinger, the senator from New Hampshire, could not resist a little playful parrying on this point. "The Senator from Indiana suggests, and I presume correctly," Gallinger interjected, that the Constitution's framers intended "the selection of Senators without reference to political or party consideration." Beveridge assented. "I was just wondering," Gallinger continued, "whether the Senator's mind was running along the same channel as the minds of the great men to whom he alluded, that the States should select their best men irrespective of any consideration except purity of character and ability."[7]

How could Beveridge have objected? Yet to answer in the affirmative meant repudiating the party system, which had been developed in response to the popular attempts to control, among other things, the senatorial choice of the legislatures. It would have been tantamount to admitting that the popularization of the nominating process had vitiated the freedom of the legislator to select the fittest candidates in accordance with his own conscience. Beveridge evaded an outright answer, and when Gallinger persisted, concluded that further discussion would have to wait until the Senate was "not so much pressed for time."[8]

This recourse to lack of time was a recurring peculiarity among amendment proponents. As they saw it, the people had been discussing it for years. Their minds were made up. The Senate had only to comply. When Senator Borah at last brought the direct elections resolution to the floor on January 13, 1911, the Senate was already overladen with pending business, and only six weeks remained before the expiration of the Sixty-first Congress. Waiting to be discussed were yet an ocean mails bill, a bill to revise and codify over thirty years of accumulated laws affecting the judiciary, a number of proposals for tariff reform, and a host of other legislative matters, much of it unfinished business from previous sessions. Compromises and amendments would have to made before such measures came to a vote, and any legislation that was approved had to be sent to the House, where differences would arise that had to be resolved before the third of March. It was the sort of business which, according to Owen, the Senate was perennially obstructing, yet it was now apparently going to be held up further in the rush to alter the fundamental law—ironically, for the purpose of making the Senate more responsive. Borah expressed his sympathy for colleagues like Gallinger, Eugene Hale of Maine, and his fellow Idahoan, Weldon Heyburn, who had all worked for years on various reform bills, and waited months after reporting them for Senate consideration. All the same, he demanded that direct elections be given the right of way. In order to attend to the Senate's other remaining affairs, he hoped to close off debate within ten working days. In fact, if he could get the Senate's consent to have a date guaranteed on the calendar, he was even willing to confine the deliberations, the submission of amendments, and the actual voting to a single day.[9]

As the junior senator from Idaho saw it, the movement for direct elections had already received the nation's mature consideration. Recounting its history since the first congressional proposal in 1826, Borah declared "the sober second thought of the people" was strongly in its favor, notwithstanding the fact that the constituted means of

145

determining such "sober second thought" were supposed to include the deliberations of the Senate.

That Borah's resolution was not immediately adopted, however, was hardly the fault of direct election opponents. The necessary votes already existed in the Sixty-first Congress, but the committee's resolution, as in the original resolutions passed by the House, had placed the times, places and manner of the direct elections in the hands of state legislatures. Immediately after the secretary finished reading the committee resolution, George Sutherland of Utah tossed in an amendment to retain federal control.[10] For the remainder of the session, and for three months into the succeeding Congress, until the resolution was finally approved, the direct elections movement was stalled by a fissure in its own ranks. Faction had insinuated itself among those who proposed to end the rule of faction, each side accusing the other of secretly siding with the anti-amendment forces, and of trying to sabotage direct elections by insisting on conditions which would not be approved by "the people."

Nationalists strongly objected to the attempt to submit two resolutions under the guise of one, providing for direct elections while stripping the federal government of any power to ensure the validity of the outcome. Supporters of the committee's version ingeniously retorted that without this addition the federal authority would be extended to where it had not formerly existed, from merely overseeing the Senate elections by the legislatures to overseeing the people directly at the polls. It was the "Sutherland Amendment," they said, which altered the scope of federal power by leaving the language unchanged with respect to the regulatory control of elections. To southerners, the question of who controlled Senate elections was of greater concern than whether or not they were determined by popular vote. States' rights senators who ardently supported the committee resolution would not endorse the Sutherland proposal, and warned fellow amendment advocates "not to load it down with propositions that mean its death."[11]

New York's Chauncey Depew attempted to do precisely that when he submitted an amendment providing that voting qualifications for both House and Senate elections "shall be uniform in all the States," and that Congress be empowered to provide appropriate legislation to ensure the registration of all citizens entitled to vote, and to oversee all congressional elections (He was not concerned with state elections).[12] Although Depew was opposed to popular Senate elections on any account, and was not above trying to defeat the proposal by offering an amendment unacceptable to the South, there was no affectation in his desire to retain the federal control of the Congress. He had started his career in politics as a Republican legislator half a century previously, at the outset of the Civil War in 1861, and considered himself an heir of the original antislavery principles of the Republican party.[13] No senator was more blunt in denouncing this not-too-subtle attempt to usurp the voting rights established in the Fifteenth Amendment by attaching this "race-rider," as one colleague referred to it, to the direct elections resolution.

For years the southern states had been effectively eroding those rights through various contrivances, especially literacy tests, deliberately intended to exclude the black man from the polls. In 1890, southerners had launched the most impassioned filibuster in Senate history over a federal elections bill, which provided that a bipartisan elections board would be permitted to investigate voting irregularities, not only in the South, but in every ward and borough in the country, upon the petition of a sufficient number of registered voters. Whatever decision the board reached could have been appealed in circuit court. The author of the legislation, then Congressman Henry Cabot Lodge, stated that there was nothing in it preventing the states "from excluding ignorance from the suffrage," a principle in which he strongly believed, and which had long been practiced in his own state of Massachusetts, but any educational test had to be fairly applied. Nevertheless, southern senators dubbed it the "Force Bill," and to a constituency still mortified by the turpitudes of Reconstruction and the humiliating memories of an occupying army, it was not difficult to raise the fearsome spectre of federal bayonets ensuring Republican victory at every voting booth in Dixie.[14] Having thus defeated the congressional attempt to enforce the Fifteenth Amendment, states' rights partisans saw an opportunity in the Borah resolution to annul it entirely with respect to the election of senators. Its supporters, and in fact Borah, himself, had hopes it would lead to an amendment for state control of House elections as well.[15]

It was Depew's conviction that "under the guise of giving the power directly to the people," the proposed amendment was being used to permit "unlimited restrictions upon the people's right to vote." Southern newspapers, he observed, were denouncing the Sutherland amendment as an obstruction to direct elections without even informing their readers what the amendment said. "The whole trend of their comment is that unless the repeal of this section of the Constitution [Article I, Section 4, authorizing Congress to regulate its own elections] which has existed for 122 years is coupled with the resolution for a popular vote," the southern states were opposed to direct elections. "In other words, we are informed that the underlying purpose of this movement is to take away from Congress all power over disfranchisement by State laws and remit to the States unlimited authority to limit the suffrage."[16]

Depew did not want to allow what he considered the racial majoritarianism of certain states to encroach upon the federally guaranteed rights of individuals, but he objected just as strenuously to the remaining provisions of the amendment, claiming they were a gross encroachment upon the federal system of checks and balances. As one of the more prominent villains associated with Senate plutocracy, Depew's opposition to popular elections was typically ascribed to economic self-interest. The real Depew was more complex. Well educated and an extremely good orator, he was also a shrewd and resourceful man of affairs, but not necessarily dishonest. David Graham Phillips portrayed him as the partner-in-crime of his former New York colleague, Senator Thomas Platt, which as rumor begot rumor, implicated Depew in the latter's alleged sale of insurance legislation, though nothing concrete was ever brought against him. In fact, Depew had consistently opposed the Platt machine's control of the New York Republicans.[17] Traveling through Europe in 1902, he refused to release his "pair"—an agreement not to vote between two senators whose votes would cancel each other out—with Platt, who was in league with Matthew Quay of Pennsylvania to rush through an "omnibus" statehood bill for the admission of Arizona, Oklahoma, and New Mexico. Even though the bill probably would have added more members to the ranks of the Republican senators, Depew was convinced that Senator Quay was more concerned with furthering his western railroad and mining interests than with giving federal representation to the western peoples.[18]

As for his own interest in the railroads, Depew pointed out that, as president of the New York Central, he represented the interests of a great multitude of men in the railway service. It was an insult to them, he said, to claim that no railway man could "serve the public as well as a farmer." The progressive ranting against the interests was simply a "vast amount of humbug." Constitutional reformers held out the ridiculous promise that "no representative of the interests can be Senator," then broadly defined the interests "as every man who in his personal business or in any employment he may have is interested in legislation." No one directly or indirectly affected by the tariff, no one serving as counsel for those affected by the tariff, no stockholders, no bondholders, or counsel for corporations, no labor union members were, in the progressive quest for political purity, supposed to hold a position of public trust. "They reduce the opportunities for choice by process of elimination," joked the senior senator from New York, "until, if they ultimately succeed, the United States Senate will be composed entirely of undertakers whose profits are in the increasing number of those who die."[19]

To Depew, it was impossible to represent "people" without representing "interests." There was no "will of the people" in the sense that his opponents often used the term, that is, a universally recognizable political answer, inherently transcendent of selfish and local concerns, which could be instinctively expressed en masse at the voting booth. It was not instinct, but second thought and compromise, that represented the true will of the people. Checks and balances had been intended to create a necessary delay. Charged with "distrusting the people," Depew responded that every form of representative government in a certain sense reflected such distrust. "Wherever a measure must take its chances first with the lower House and then with the upper House, and then again in running the gauntlet must escape the club of the veto of the Executive, every step is a distrust of popular government." But it was not distrust in the ultimate deliberations of the people, only in their reflexive responses. No one man should be trusted who acted solely on impulse. Why was it any different with men in the aggregate? The whole course of Western political evolution, claimed Depew, had been "to escape on one side, from the arbitrary power of the autocrat," but on the other, "to devise processes by which the passions of the hour shall not crystallize into legislation without plenty of time for deliberation and calm judgment."[20]

The premise underlying the proposed amendment, however, flatly contradicted this evolutionary development. "It was all very well when there were no railroads, no telegraphs, and no telephones, or morning and evening papers, to have a Senate to hold in check the House until the people could be heard from;" said the senator, mocking the arguments of his adversaries, "but now, with all these means of instantaneous and intelligent information, the people are informed every day, and can reach their immediate representatives every hour, and they need no protection by a conservative and critical body elected for a longer term and with securer hold of office."[21]

Depew had been the first senator to make a fully prepared speech against the resolution of the judiciary committee. It was not well received in progressive quarters. Most amendment proponents admired the old senator's eloquence and strength of convictions, but thought him too out of touch with the changing times to appreciate the need for constitutional reform. Jeff Davis of Arkansas, however, would not even credit him with that much. Depew was anathema, a lame duck senator who had been ignominiously renounced by the people in the last election (the election was still in a stalemate between the Sheehan supporters and the "insurgent" faction led by Franklin Roosevelt, with Depew's Republicans sitting quietly on the sidelines as the minority party). In a speech delivered on January 30, Davis advised Depew to "betake himself to the courts of the Old World, there to bask in the sunshine and smiles of the crowned heads and bow down in obeisance at the shrine of royalty. This will be a fitting close to the career of the senior Senator from New York."[22]

When not personally insulting Depew, Davis was positively fulminating class resentment. The interests, he said, had made the cost of living so high that the poor man, "with his meager wage," could "scarcely drive the wolf from the door." The Payne-Aldrich tariff of 1909 was the result of a deliberate political conspiracy to make "the rich richer and the poor poorer." Great economic inequities, declared the senator from Arkansas, had been secretly engineered by a body of men who did not feel their obligation to the people. Direct elections would naturally bring about a change in the Senate's allegiances.[23]

It would also eliminate fraudulent elections. With the people in control, said Davis, Lorimer would not have been sitting across the aisle, voting away the bread of those who had labored for it. Although some progressives sided with the unfortunate senator from Illinois, including most of those who had served on the investigating subcommittee, Lorimer had become something of a rallying symbol for Senate radicals, standing proof that "Legislatures can be corrupted." As Depew pointed out with the recent exposure of the practices of Adams County, Ohio, so could the people, but the point was utterly lost on Senator Davis, who could only think of "the people" in their abstract perfection.[24]

Wandering from one topic to the next, there was little consistency in anything Davis said. In a discussion purportedly about the direct election of senators, he fell to berating Theodore Roosevelt, warning that "he had become more dangerous than Napoleon to the free spirit of the times," He had seen the former president "ride at the head of a multitude, each clamoring almost for the privilege of touching his garment." Yet after expressing in no uncertain terms his despair that the people had gone whoring after demagogues, he drifted back to the subject at hand. The Senate must permit the people "to exercise their freedom of choice which is so essential to the proper selection of their servants"[25]—even if they chose, one wonders, a Roosevelt or a Napoleon?

When Davis was at all comprehensible, he had little to say, as he himself admitted, "that would not be subject to the charge of repetition." This was especially true of his call for prompt senatorial action on direct elections. The people, he charged, would "brook no delay in the passage of this resolution." Like every other advocate of the amendment, Davis reasoned that the people had given the subject their mature deliberation, and in essence had decided they wanted a Senate which would make reflexlike responses to their demands.[26]

This had been Borah's argument since the day he reported the resolution out of committee. On February 1, two days after Davis' unparliamentary invective, Borah again attempted to get the unanimous consent of his colleagues (there were as yet no rules for cloture in Senate debate) to commit itself to a date on which to vote, although they had not yet been given full opportunity to discuss the subject or propose amendments—a highly irregular request in those days. Nevertheless, this great question of fundamental law needed to be "disposed of." Borah was already a week past the date on which he originally had hoped to vote, and adding to his irritation, Senators Lodge and Root desired another week to prepare their speeches. Borah suspected dilatory tactics were afoot, and moved that the resolution be voted on no later than the ninth of February, eight days hence. He demanded to set down for the *Record* the "real purpose" any senator would need more time than that.

"I think I shall desire to speak" upon the question, Weldon Heyburn interrupted, "as late as about the 4th day of March," proposing, in other words, to annul the entire resolution with the expiration of Congress.[27] Heyburn, as will be seen further, was never one to be intimidated with having to set his reasons down for the record.

In any event, in less than a week Lodge was prepared for his speech. A skilled politician who knew how to use the patronage and who was thoroughly familiar with the promises, bargains, and compromises which kept a senator in office, Henry Cabot Lodge was, nevertheless, more often associated in the public mind with statesmanship than with the senatorial villains of muckraking lore (although he did receive dishonorable mention in "The Treason of the Senate"). The scion of ancient wealth and New England aristocracy, Lodge had been a scholar not a businessman, before entering politics. Although he had invested his inheritance in various successful enterprises, he was by no stretch of the imagination a "servant of the corporations." As a gentleman of the old breed, he despised the coarseness of modern millionaires and denounced their rapaciousness with all the invective of a socialist. But notwithstanding its abuses, he believed in the overall benefits of the corporation, and thought the essential structure of capitalism worth preserving. As at least one biographer reasons, it was out of this sense of conservatism that he supported much of the reform legislation of the Progressive Era.[28]

What in the way of practical reform, Lodge began, had not been, or could not be, enacted under the present method of electing senators? Citing the recent history of federal legislation, the antimonopoly statutes, railway bills, and consumer protection laws, the senator from Massachusetts wanted to know how the Congress, divided as it was between the representatives of the people and the representatives of the states, had failed to address the public problems of the hour. "All this has been accomplished, all the legislation regulating trusts and transportation and food production has been carried to enactment under the Constitution as it is." There was still more work to do; there would always be more work to do if the rule of law were to keep pace with a diverse and inventive people. Particularly pressing were the questions of child labor and the protection of natural resources from "reckless and destructive consumption for the sake of immediate personal profit." Nevertheless, the Constitution had "shown itself capable of adaptation to the new demands, as it has adapted itself to those of the past." Under its present forms of representation, it had successfully weathered the secession crisis and the moral dilemma of human slavery, far more alarming issues, Lodge believed, than anything which faced his own generation.[29]

"But new prophets have arisen who are not content with the reforms which have been and which will be effected by law and they demand that the Constitution itself shall be changed. Its success in the past," lamented the senator, "which has commanded the admiration of the world, is not to be considered as any plea in its behalf." Reformers claimed to be restoring popular government, but Lodge contended that what they really advocated was not a restoration, but a "retrogression" to those sad times when representative bodies were but "a convenient machine for the registration of someone else's edicts."[30]

It was no longer a monarch who issued the edicts, but the phenomenon was just as threatening.

The whole thrust of the amendment, as urged by its advocates, was to make the Senate more "responsive" to the popular sovereign. It did not occur to the founders, said Lodge, "that they were destroying the popular quality of their work by ordaining that Presidents should be chosen by electoral colleges or Senators by legislatures." Besides the fact that they hoped such methods would secure the best representatives, they felt much more deeply that the built-in inertia of the separate modes of election would provide governmental restraint, the principle "upon which political freedom and personal liberty absolutely depended." Lodge made essentially the same point that Depew had made earlier, insisting that the whole point of the electoral system as it was designed was that there should be "opportunity for reflection, a space for second thought, and no rash haste in reaching important decisions upon which the welfare of millions might depend."[31]

After Lodge had finished, the Senate spent most of the next four days wrangling over the disposition of the Lorimer case. There were brief interludes for regular business, and for a short response to Lodge's speech by Senator Joseph Bristow of Kansas on February 9. He, too, was of the opinion that the subject had been considered long enough, and did not "hope to add anything new to the discussion." He felt compelled, however, to say that while he joined with the senator from Massachusetts in paying "high tribute to the great wisdom and patriotism" of the founders, there were nevertheless "wide differences between the conditions that prevailed in this country at the time the Constitution was adopted and those that prevail today." On the one hand, there was more democracy than under the early republic. The people had shown "intelligence and patriotism" thus far, and there was no reason not to give them "greater power and more direct responsibility for the administration of the Government." On the other hand, there were now more sinister influences at work within the political system. Bristow noted that over the past forty years, there had been fifteen cases where corruption was charged in the election of senators, "while during the preceding 84 years of our history there had been but one such case." Taken together, the premise that there was more democracy and more corruption did not make much of a case for further democratic reforms, but the senator concluded that the growing corruption stemmed from "the radical changes" in American industrial and commercial life. He did not say how; he only said that in answer to those changes, the people should exercise more power directly.[32]

The following day, Elihu Root made precisely the opposite argument. "Strangely," said the junior senator from New York, "this movement comes at the very time when the development of our country in its business and social and political life makes it all the more necessary that we should depend upon representative government." It was now far from the realm of possibility to run the country along the lines of the old New England town meeting. "I doubt if some of the Senators coming from States of small population realize how far we have gone in the great industrial communities of the East and the Middle West from that condition in which direct democratic government is possible." Yet the direct elections resolution was endeavoring to bring about such a reversal, reflecting a profound aversion to the representative ideal. In this, said Root, the resolution did not stand alone:

> It is a part of the great movement which has been going on now in these recent years throughout the country and in which our people have been drifting away from their trust in representative government. These modern constitutions which are filled with specific provisions, limiting and directing the legislature in every direction, furnishing such startling contrasts to the simplicity of the Constitution of the United States, are an expression of distrust in representative government. The initiative is an expression of distrust in representative government. The referendum is an expression of distrust in representative government.

The proposed amendment was likewise "an expression of the same sentiment."[33]

Root grasped the amendment in its full historical significance. Depew and Lodge maintained that human nature was a constant the founders thoroughly understood, and that economic and social changes did not alter the validity of the fundamental laws which they devised. It was a sound argument as far as it went, but Root saw with a chilling perceptivity that the movement for direct elections had not arisen in a vacuum. It had begun in the states with the gradual sapping of legislative strength. It rode the crest of the same wave which brought the initiative and the referendum, the recall, and the insufferable limitations upon delegated government in general. It was part of America's recurring attempt at what he later described as "rehabilitating one of the most impracticable of Rousseau's theories," that the people could rule directly simply by voting.[34]

The undermining of representative effectiveness in the states, moreover, had not gone without serious consequences to the Union. Root insisted that modern civilization had made America's far-flung individuals permanently and increasingly "interdependent" upon one another, that government therefore necessarily had to play a greater role in regulating the myriad institutions which industrialized society had made indispensable, and that the task was likewise beyond the scope of what individuals could accomplish independently, without representative government. In many of the problems now confronting society, it was no longer a question of whether or not government should extend its regulatory function, but of which government should do so.[35]

"If the State government is abandoned, if we recognize the fact that we cannot have honest legislatures, sir, the tide that now sets toward the Federal Government will swell in volume and power."[36] Coming from a man who considered himself a "convinced and uncompromising nationalist of the school of Alexander Hamilton,"[37] this was a highly noteworthy observation. "I fear the breaking down of the Government of the United States through the gradual weakening of the State governments," said Root, "by the accumulation of demands upon it through the failure of the State governments to keep pace with the continually increasing demands of our social and business life."[38] Already, the senator reflected:

> Our executive officers are overburdened. The business of this Congress is conducted with less and less knowledge on the part of members of the body in general as to what the committees have been doing. We are forced session by session to more complete reliance upon the reports of committees, with less and less consideration from the Members of the Congress at large. Our judicial force is being overburdened and our calendars clogged, and we are looking about for ways to relieve this court and that from too heavy a burden and to prevent the law's delays.[39]

The leader of Root's adversaries, William Borah, had repeatedly criticized this bureaucratization of American politics. Unlike many progressives, he did not share the era's faith in technocratic management. "We are fast becoming a government by commission," Borah complained. Thousands of government agents and representatives "deal with matters of almost daily concern to the people who are beyond their selection or dismissal and are fast becoming beyond their reach. With startling and almost mad celerity we are rushing in that direction."[40] Borah's answer, naturally, was to put politics back in the hands of the people with more democracy.

If Root was correct in his fears, such a solution would only drag the people deeper into the bureaucratic quagmire. If state legislatures could not be trusted to exercise their powers, said Root, the federal government would inevitably fill the void. With its constituted authorities already laden with more responsibilities than they could carry, more power would have to be handed over to an ever growing army of unelected bureaucrats. "The time will come when the Government of the United States will be driven to the exercise of more arbitrary and unconsidered power, will be driven to greater concentration, will be driven to extend its functions into the internal affairs of the States." In the stead of competent states which governed their own affairs, "we shall go through the cycle of concentration of power at the center while the States dwindle into insignificance, and ultimately the breaking up of the great Republic upon new lines of separation."[41]

It reflected the degree of tilt in the constitutional balance that Root, a disciple of Hamiltonian nationalism, was now echoing the warnings of George Mason, the old Anti-Federalist. Mason, it will be recalled, had considered the legislative appointment of senators an essential obstacle to national concentration. Likewise, the states' rights champion, John Randolph of Roanoke, had prophesied in Virginia's 1830 convention that the weakening of checks and balances in the states would invite the intrusions of a federal leviathan. Root argued from a different perspective, but his fears were the same: Efficient, responsible use of federal power was not possible without the states taking up their fair share of the deliberative burden. While he was utterly opposed to the scheme of robbing the national legislature of the power to superintend the election of senators—who were accountable for the national welfare—he was not deaf to the southerners' concerns over growing, federal usurpations. Only the phenomenon of which they complained was not usurpation so much as an abdication on the part of the states. As he had previously told a joint session of the legislature which elected him, those who made the most noise about states' rights were very apt to be "the most desirous to have the national government step in and usurp the functions of a State when there is an appropriation carried with the usurpation."[42] If senators were truly concerned for the sovereignty of their states, there was but one way for them to preserve it, and that was "by repudiating absolutely and forever the fundamental doctrine upon which this resolution proceeds," the doctrine that the states were incapable of exercising delegated authority.[43]

Aside from these grave, but mostly philosophical implications, which must have taxed the concentrative powers of Root's opponents and allies alike, the senator also had more palpable objections to the proposed amendment. The founders had intended the two houses of Congress to be as dissimilar in character as republican principles would allow. The Representatives were expected to be men of energy, full of fight, restless and innovative. The Senate, by contrast, was to consist of elder statesmen, men who in life and experience had "attained the respect of their fellow citizens," and were "willing to undertake the burdens of public office," but were "unwilling to seek it," who would "accept the burden as a patriotic duty," but would "never subject themselves to the disagreeable incidents, the labor, the strife, the personalities of a political campaign."[44]

Modesty prevented Root from saying so, but he obviously included himself among those elder statesmen. He preferred the bar to politics. Certainly, it provided his family with a better livelihood, and he was not subjected to "the abuse of the press" and public "controversies about performance of duty."[45] But he was serious about "duty." Although he never intended to become a "politician," he joined the local Republicans as a young man, espoused the virtues of party "regularity," but was never afraid to speak out on matters of principle against New York's ruling "Platt machine." A successful lawyer in private practice, he did his stint reluctantly but conscientiously as a district attorney. He spoke on occasion as a campaign orator for candidates he knew and trusted, such as Theodore Roosevelt when the latter ran for the governorship. By 1894, he had earned enough credibility among the political leaders of New York that he was entrusted to serve as the floor manager of the proceedings of the state's constitutional convention.[46] From his earliest days of service, both to the party and to the public, he turned heads for his sagacity and moral integrity—and selflessness. Elihu Root never sought an office in his entire life.

In 1899, when President McKinley, upon the recommendation of a New York politician, asked Root, who was enjoying the full fruits of private practice, to be his Secretary of War, Root turned the offer down on the grounds that he knew nothing about war or the army. McKinley replied that what he wanted was a capable lawyer to direct the government of the occupied territories acquired in the recent war with Spain. As Root later reminisced, "I took the United States for my client," (and made no complaints that this new client paid only about five percent of his former ones). The nation's inexperience with colonialism, the pathetic economic conditions of the Spanish islands, and America's initiation into the barbarism of guerrilla warfare in the Philippines, belied the miracle of Root's modest achievements in administering the territories. His overhaul of a corrupt and inefficient army, however, and his creation of the General Staff, were nothing short of revolutionary, and drew the admiration of the governments of Europe.

President Roosevelt made Root his Secretary of State in 1905, drawing on his experience in international law. Root's ability to draft legislation, and his handling of the Senate with the same diplomacy he used with foreign governments, enabled him to succeed where his brilliant but more stubborn predecessor, John Hay, had often failed. Of the more than one hundred treaties he signed, only three failed to obtain ratification in the Senate.[47] In 1912, the senator was to be awarded the Nobel Prize for Peace.

In short, Elihu Root was exactly the sort of statesman whom the indirect elections process was supposed to promote, one who had given "the strongest proofs" of his attachment to his country.[48] Roosevelt wanted to name *him*, not Taft, as his presidential successor, but Root declined and could not be dissuaded. For one thing, he knew that the press, especially the papers of Hearst—who attributed his own defeat for the governor's race against Charles Evans Hughes to Root's stinging campaign speeches against the menace of yellow journalists—would not hesitate to use the former lawyer's corporate connections against him. He did not care to spend the better part of his campaign refuting irresponsible charges, and for that matter, had absolutely no stomach for the sort of self-promotion that mass campaigning required. Perhaps, if the Electoral College had been what it used to be, Root would have accepted. Roosevelt was gravely disappointed that the man he called "without question the greatest living statesman" had not the slightest chance of serving the people in the exalted office he so clearly merited.[49]

The Senate was the one elective office to which Root could still aspire. But again, the office sought the man, rather than vice-versa. Unbeknownst to himself, his candidacy was advanced in the autumn of 1908 by friends in the New York legislature, and within two days of giving them his assent the state's party chairman informed him that a majority of the Republicans, who controlled the legislature, were solidly behind him. Without making a single speech on his own behalf, spending a single campaign dollar, or making a single promise as to what he would do if elected, Root was unanimously nominated by the party's legislative caucus, and subsequently elected on the first ballot.[50] Granted, this was no longer the way most Senate contests were conducted, but Root's election proved that the ideal was still attainable through the intermediate agency of the legislatures.

Popular elections, Root continued, were not only likely to reduce the role of such elder statesmen in the national legislature, but would also diminish the candor of the upper house in general. As it was, senators could still explain concessions and compromises of the state's immediate interests to politicians who were "familiar with the incidents and the difficulties of legislation," and who understood how impossible it was that "any one man, or any one locality, or any one State can have all of its own way." Direct elections would do away with "the fair and open-minded yielding to the argument" of fellow senators. "This will cease to be a deliberative body," the senator from New York remonstrated, "if every Senator has to convince, to explain to the great body of the people of his State every act he performs and every concession he makes."[51]

And particularly now was the time for candor. The Senate was created occasionally to rebuke, never to flatter, the sovereign people. "Here, if anywhere, the truth ought to be told," said Root. "Here, if anywhere, should be found men with the courage to say to their constituents: 'The trouble in the election of senators of the United States is not in the Constitution; it is with you; it is because you are not doing your duty.'" For years the people had been stripping their legislatures of dignity and authority, and now were surprised at the sort of men they attracted. "You can never develop competent and trusted bodies of public servants by expressing distrust of them, by taking power away from them, by holding them up to the world as being unworthy of confidence." The people complained of legislative deadlocks and corrupt elections, but they, too, had allowed "personal favoritism to supplant their desire to select the best public servants," that is, when they even bothered to vote. They, too, had been "bought to cast their franchises, as the people of Adams County, Ohio, were bought." Rather than "curing themselves and performing their duty in the election of their State legislatures," they were now trying to "cure neglect of duty by changing the form." The logic was that voters "who can not elect honest men from their own neighbors can elect honest men to the Senate of the United States." Instead of concerning themselves with choosing the best representatives available in their counties and districts, they directed their attention to state-wide candidates about whom most of them knew very little or nothing, "except what they get from the newspapers."[52]

Root thus pleaded with the Senate not to give its assent to this evasion of popular responsibility. If the people did their duty as required by the existing Constitution, it needed no amendment. Otherwise, "you can amend the Constitution a thousand times without any utility." If the Senate, of all places, could not muster the scruples and the fortitude to bring home these truths to the American people, "then we are caucusing over idle words when we talk of an amendment to the Constitution."[53]

Root was followed on the same day by Albert Beveridge, who "listened with pleasure to the engaging remarks of the Senator from New York," but dismissed everything he had to say as coming from "a certain type of mind, perfectly sincere, no doubt," which inherently saw danger in every great "advance." In what was probably meant as a compliment, Beveridge said there was no one in the Senate, indeed, in the entire nation, "who more ably and artfully could gather together these forebodings of disaster and paint in somber colors upon that melancholy background a more grewsome picture to make us afraid than that distinguished Senator to whom we have just listened." But he, Beveridge, had managed to detach himself from the "spell" of Root's oratory long enough to note some inconsistencies which would "paint with a silver lining the cloud which he has cast over us." The senator from Indiana assured his colleagues that the people were reading the news and knew as much about the issues and about Senate candidates as their legislators. They understood their own best interests and had the right to decide whether or not their senators were serving them. If they were apathetic in local elections, it was because they were usually offered a choice of men who could not be trusted.[54] Point for point, in other words, Beveridge argued from an entirely different set of premises, and the only thing he really proved was that, no matter what Root or any other senator had to say, it would not convince him to change his mind.

And this was essentially true for everyone else who took part in the debate. While numerous speeches of varying eloquence were still to come, there was little to add on either side. Jonathan Bourne of Oregon, like Root, saw the direct elections resolution as part of the great extension of state democracy, along with direct legislation and the recall, only it was a movement he strongly favored. What made Bourne's analysis unique was his recognition of the dichotomy in eighteenth century political thought. He did not delude himself about which philosophy the proposed amendment embraced. The Constitution, he said, was "against the spirit of democracy." He conceded that *"conditions were not then ripe for Rousseauism, in the application of popular sovereignty, on a national scale* [emphasis mine]," but with advanced technology, of course, all that had changed. Bourne had invented his own hybrid of Madisonianism and Rousseauism in what he called "The Composite Citizen." Like Madison, he believed that human beings were individually capable of error and selfishness, but like Rousseau, he thought perfect equality of political expression would reflect the General Will. "The composite citizen is made up of millions of individuals, each dominated in most cases by selfish interest," claimed the senator from Oregon:

> But because of the difference in the personal equations of the individual units making up the composite citizen, there is a corresponding difference in the interests dominating said units, and while composite action is taking place, friction is developed, attrition results, selfishness is worn away, and general welfare is substituted before action is accomplished.[55]

Although Bourne was certainly an easy target, he was not attacked by the sole remaining member to speak for the opposition, Weldon Heyburn. The senior senator from Idaho, the most reactionary opponent of direct democracy, did not lack that most desirable of senatorial qualities—candor—though many would have said it was a virtue he carried to a fault. No man in the chamber, probably in all of American politics, was more indifferent to the pressures of popular opinion than Weldon Brinton Heyburn. He came to the Senate, he once said, "to represent the interests, not the views of the people of the United States."[56] He told members of a popular convention that had nominated him for reelection in 1909 that he did not recognize their action, that their only duty was to elect a Republican legislature, "and let me take my chances." He publicly denounced the senatorial primary as a form of burglary. Furthermore, he told the legislators who elected him that if they wanted popular elections they had better vote for a different man, and when the succeeding legislature from his state petitioned Congress for an amendment, he dismissed the petition as "a piece of political impertinence." Colleagues who reminded him of how widely the states were making this request received a blunt reproof: "A man who is afraid of his legislature, whose vote is affected at all by what his legislature may do, is not fit to be here." When told that the reform had widespread support among the people at large, his response was, "I am not a poll-taker."[57]

161

At the core of this abrasive obstinacy and seeming callousness was a profound respect, indeed, reverence, for the constitutional proprieties. It was not that he opposed all change. Long involved in state politics, Heyburn had recommended the repeal of Idaho's navigation laws, which awarded "corporate greed" (words he did not use lightly) with franchises to levy tolls on private citizens. In tandem with his denunciation of regulating railroad rates, he argued that the competition from free navigation on the rivers would of itself force down the cost of rail transportation. But he was not a *laissez faire* absolutist. He was among the first in Idaho to call for government protection of the nation's forests. And as chairman of the Senate Committee on Manufactures, he had urged the Pure Food and Drug Act upon reluctant colleagues. In short, he was not impervious to the need to adjust the rule of law to the industrial revolution. But as a firm believer in the "divinity of the Constitution," he recognized no expression of popular will outside its ordained representative processes.[58]

He was singularly unimpressed by the fact that numerous legislatures and party platforms were calling for an amendment. The Senate was the constituted authority, and only the Senate's deliberations should determine the matter. The Constitution said nothing about having to submit an amendment at the instigation of states. They had only the authority to call for a convention, nothing less, and until they called for one in the numbers required by the Constitution, two-thirds, they were still in the minority so far as the senator from Idaho was concerned. His associates had the right to submit a resolution for an amendment, but they could not claim that they were doing so in response to the wishes of the people, not when the people had failed to express themselves as a constitutional majority. The provision for an amendment did not say "that if some man or a million men stand up and clamor for it we shall submit it to the legislatures." The constitutional majority was the only one which mattered. Otherwise, any malcontent with "half a dozen friends under a lamp post" could legitimately call themselves "the people," and make demands upon the government.[59] In Heyburn's view, to submit to judgments made outside the constituted process was the very essence of lawlessness.

Hence, if senators wanted his vote to amend the Constitution, they were going to have to give a better reason than popular demand. Deadlocks and corrupt elections were likewise insufficient. They did not occur nearly as frequently as the newspapers insinuated. The sensationalism surrounding deadlocks belied the fact, said Heyburn, that in the vast majority of elections the legislatures appointed a senator within the first two or three days of the session. The statistics on corruption were hardly more convincing. Of the 1,180 senators elected from 1789 to 1909, only fifteen were contested due to allegations of corruption, not always on the part of the senator. Only seven were denied their seats. "That is a pretty good record," Heyburn observed in a rare display of understatement. Deadlocked and corrupt elections also failed to make the case for reform for another reason. The premise was that legislatures were too incompetent and unworthy to elect senators. How, then, were they any better qualified to pass upon a constitutional amendment? "To submit this question to the very tribunals we are seeking to discredit would be a most singular performance." It also implied something about the senators themselves which they should have been ashamed to admit. "I should like to see some Senator rise in his seat and say that the legislature of his state which elected him was not competent, was not fit, was not honest enough to be trusted," said Heyburn. "Then I should be interested to see him go back and say 'I am a candidate for reelection.'"[60]

"I am looking for a reason, in this hour and this moment for entering upon the change," announced the senator from Idaho:

> and I have not heard any reason given. Is it ambition that some one should want to be known hereafter as the man who changed the Constitution of the United States or amended it? Is it ambition that some man or some men have failed under the system that has stood the test of a century to obtain that which he wanted and, failing to get it, seeks to brush away the barrier that stood between him and his ambition? Is that it?[61]

Without some answers, Heyburn was going to assume that the proposition came from that "coterie of men who stand on the street corner and acclaim themselves 'The people.'" It was yet another scheme advanced by those who were "looking rather how to change the law than how to obey it," seeking to dissolve the bonds of constituted authority by transferring the high function of Senate elections "to the ward politics down along the river." In place of the "selected and picked men from the state who comprise the legislature," it proposed to substitute "the ward heeler, precinct politics, and all that goes with them as a more reliable and trustworthy medium between the people and their Government."[62]

These dark portrayals seem more alarmist today than they probably were at the time, due in large part to the success of the amendment's opponents in maintaining federal control over Senate elections. The votes already existed for direct elections in one form or another the day that Borah reported the resolution out of committee, and with no one persuaded to change his mind after more than a month of debate, the only real question remaining was who should control the elections. Premising, on the one hand, incompetent legislatures, yet on the other conferring upon them the final authority over who shall participate in popular elections, and in what manner, it is difficult to construe the committee resolution as anything less than what Heyburn pronounced it—an amendment "intended to enable juggling over a seat in this body to be made more easy or more convenient." His grounds for cynicism were increasingly born out in the attitude of certain Senators from the South, who were demonstrably more irritated as debate dragged on. Isidore Rayner of Maryland put it most bluntly. "You do not want, Senators, if you could, to interfere with [the] right of suffrage and the supremacy of the white race in the South."[63]

Heyburn did not consider himself a dilatory man. In eight years of Senate service, he contended, "I have been content . . . with verdicts against me, judgments of the courts against me, votes in this body against measures that I deemed of great importance." As for amending the Constitution, he felt "more strongly upon this question than upon any question that I have ever participated in since the days of my responsibility as a citizen of the United States." It now seemed obvious he would lose on the prospect of direct elections, but he was determined to support the Sutherland amendment, "just as I would reach out and grab the last of an escaping treasure." While filibustering went against his nature, he warned his colleagues that if the Sutherland proposal was not adopted, "there will not be much progress in what is left of the amendment."[64]

Certainly, the vote of the Sixty-first Congress went to Heyburn's complete satisfaction. On February 24, a week before the Congress dissolved, the Sutherland proposal carried by a total of fifty to thirty-seven, with four abstentions. Half of the southerners bolted the amendment forces on the spot (half did not), Senator Bacon of Georgia declaring on their behalf, "We will not take it at this price." They could afford to wait. "The time is near at hand when this amendment can be so framed as to relieve it of this objectionable feature." On February 28, the amendment received fifty-four yeas against thirty-three nays, thus failing to pass by the necessary two-thirds vote.[65] An unlikely alliance of states' rights progressives and old guard nationalists had defeated the popular election of senators in yet another Congress.

Two things were assured when the new Congress assembled the following week. One was the expulsion of Lorimer by men who had pledged to do so before they had even read the evidence. The other was passage of the resolution for a constitutional amendment. But on whose terms? The resolution which the Senate took up for debate in April of 1911 had been initiated in the House and had there received the necessary two-thirds vote, a condition strongly in its favor. It was almost word for word the proposition of the Senate judiciary committee from the previous Congress. Originally, the resolution went to the privileges and elections committee, but on May 1, Borah managed to get it transferred to the judiciary and reported it back favorably half an hour later. His committee had already determined the matter at a meeting held before the new Congress had even authorized it to take control.[66] Senator Bristow of Kansas, who had voted against the Sutherland proposal in the previous Congress, reversed himself by submitting an amendment to retain the federal regulatory power.[67] The fact that the debates were stalled throughout the spring had utterly nothing to do with the obstructions of the old guard. The hostilities were waged between two camps with differing views as to what "the people" were demanding.

As far as the direct elections question was concerned, Senator Root declared that he had already said all he was going to say. It was in the *Record.* He submitted a resolution for a Senate election law designed to address the problem of deadlocks, and announced his position: *for* the Bristow amendment, and then *against* the entire joint resolution, whether the Bristow amendment passed or not.[68] The same was true for all the opponents of direct elections. It is interesting to contemplate that, in the widely accepted wisdom of the era, these opponents of "progress," these "enemies of the people's rule," were primarily concerned with retaining control of their regional political dominions. This was hardly congruous with their unanimous support for the amendments offered by Sutherland and then Bristow. In both votes, every senator who opposed the direct elections resolution, regardless of its wording, also opposed transferring the control of the elections to the state legislatures, that is, to the very machines which allegedly did their bidding.

In the Sixty-second Congress, only Senator Heyburn continued to speak out at any length against popular elections, but that was mostly incidental to his unflagging attempt to retain federal control. To him, the proposal to have the legislatures abdicate as electors, and that which would wrest the regulatory power from Congress, were separate but inextricably related phenomena, arising from the "same spirit" of rebellion against constituted authority. But even Heyburn had had enough of words. On June 7, with the fate of the regulatory power still in the air, he declared, "Mr. President, the next time I speak upon this question it will be to the people of the United States."[69]

No one could have been more relieved to hear that than Senator Borah, who had been trying for months to end discussion and rush the resolution to a vote. The reason for Borah's haste was understandable. He had secured, or so he thought, enough votes to defeat the Bristow resolution, and more debate might break up a fragile coalition. Hearts must have stopped in every corner of the chamber, however, when, on June 12, the vote on the Bristow amendment resulted in a forty-four to forty-four tie.[70] As a certainty, some version of the amendment was going to be submitted to the states. There were enough senators pledged to support popular elections, "in one form or another," that they would give their support to whatever resolution the chamber adopted. For one brief instant, nobody knew just how far the balance of representative federalism was going to be tilted—except Vice-President James S. Sherman, on whom all eyes were assuredly fixed.

"On this vote the yeas are 44 and the nays are 44," the vice president announced. "The Chair votes in the affirmative." Thus, against the judgment of the leading progressives, Borah, La Follette, and Owen, the Bristow Amendment carried, sustaining Congress' power to oversee and regulate Senate elections. An infuriated freshman senator from Missouri, James Reed, rose to object to Sherman's having cast the deciding vote, but the latter was well within his rights.[71] Senator Bacon of Georgia then pointed out that the matter of electoral control had been decided in Committee of the Whole. Although the full Senate had participated in the debate, it was, technically speaking, a committee decision yet to be ratified in the Senate. Whether Bacon was attempting to overturn the close vote on the Bristow resolution, or was simply a stickler for parliamentary procedure, the measure had to be voted on again, the result being that one defector and one previously absent senator carried the Bristow resolution without the need of the vice president to break the tie.[72] The only question remaining was whether enough of the losers on the regulatory provision would support the final version of the direct elections resolution.

Wyoming's Senator Francis Warren spoke briefly before the vote to remind his colleagues of their duty to submit an amendment in some form or another to the American people for ratification. It was a pathetic appeal, offered by a statesman who felt that the constitutional amendment proposed, "in effect, to deprive the Republic of a Senate," but he would vote for it anyway:

> I believe that this Senate is convinced that election of the Senate by direct vote would not be for the best interests of the people of the United States or tend to perpetuate the tried institutions of our Government.
>
> But, on the other hand, the Senate, I believe, does not arrogate to itself omniscience. Higher than its own views it holds the right of the people to express their views upon all questions affecting their welfare.[73]

At the federal level, at least, this was a most revolutionary argument. It disregarded the fact that the voice of the United States senator *was* the voice of the people, refined and filtered through indirect elections, and articulated via the constitutional processes. In surrendering his own judgment, Warren was essentially throwing the power of government to that shapeless mass of contending interests that reformers vaguely referred to as "the people."

He was not the only one. In a speech made earlier that day, Senator Porter McCumber from North Dakota equated the principle of the amendment with that of the lynch mob. Both premised that the people never erred, and needed no restraint. He warned, moreover, that in removing the inducements to bribe legislators, reformers would find themselves on a field "of equally insidious danger and broader opportunities for the corruptionist." Direct bribery might cease or be diminished, but new evils would arise in the battle for "controlling the source of public political instruction and thereby [the means of] molding public sentiment." The direct primary had already opened up wonderful opportunities for the millionaire and the demagogue. Senators should not blind themselves, said McCumber, to the fact "that with the primary-election system has grown the practice on the part of candidates of establishing and purchasing papers by wholesale and retail, with no loftier motive in view than that of destroying their opponents by political libel and falsehoods." Money would inevitably have more, not less, influence on elections, "first in the ability of a candidate possessing means . . . to secure . . . advocates for his cause, both on the platform and in the closer communication with the public; second, in the ability to own or subsidize a goodly portion of the press." Say what they may about a corrupt practices act, McCumber told amendment advocates, such laws would only hurt the honest candidates. "The rogue will work himself through its meshes."[74]

And yet McCumber voted to approve the resolution. The people had a right to judge for themselves, and had been clamoring to exercise that right for decades. Like Warren and many other senators, he felt that the obligation to honor the instructions of his legislature and the petitions of constituents outweighed his own sense of the national interest. Although the ancient wisdom held that lawlessness ensued when the constituted magistrates announced "the people ought to decide," such was the motive on which the Senate passed the resolution, sixty-four to twenty-four.[75]

Of course, the solemn question was not actually going before the people, but to those discredited and incompetent bodies—the state legislatures. And what sort of indictment did this fact hold for the entire process? Perhaps Root had summed it up most aptly a few months earlier, in rewording the proposition according to what he deemed its true principle:

> Whereas the people of the several States have proved incompetent to select honest and faithful legislators in their own States:
>
> *Resolved,* That the Constitution of the United States be so amended as to relieve the people from the consequences of their incompetency by taking from the State legislatures the power to choose Senators of the United States and vesting that power in the same incompetent hands.[76]

That was precisely the sort of senatorial candor which direct elections were destined not to promote.

Notes

1. *Congressional Record,* (60th Congress, 1st Session): 6803; (61st Congress, 2nd Session): 7109.
2. *Ibid.,* (60th Congress, 1st Session): 6803, 6806.
3. *Ibid.,* (61st Congress, 3rd Session): 2774.
4. *Ibid.,* (61st Congress, 2nd Session): 7120, 7121, 7125.
5. *Ibid.,* pp. 7126–7127.
6. *Ibid.,* p. 7127.
7. *Ibid.*
8. *Ibid.*
9. *Ibid.,* (61st Congress, 3rd Session): 847, 927–928.
10. *Ibid.,* pp. 1103, 847.
11. *Ibid.,* p. 1164.
12. *Ibid.,* p. 1336.

13. *Biographical Directory of the United States Congress 1774–1989* (Washington, D.C.: United States Government Printing Office, 1989), p. 899.
14. John A. Garraty, *Henry Cabot Lodge, A Biography* (New York: Alfred A. Knopf, 1953), p. 119.
15. *Congressional Record* (61st Congress, 3rd Session): 851.
16. *Ibid.*, p. 1335.
17. David Graham Phillips, "The Treason of the Senate," *Cosmopolitan,* 40 (March 1906): 488–491; Philip C. Jessup, *Elihu Root* (New York: Dodd, Mead & Company, 1938), vol. 1, p. 171.
18. Claude G. Bowers, *Beveridge and the Progressive Era* (New York: The Literary Guild, 1932), pp. 182–184.
19. *Congressional Record* (61st Congress, 3rd Session): 1337.
20. *Ibid.*
21. *Ibid.*
22. *Ibid.*, p. 1635.
23. *Ibid.*
24. *Ibid.*, pp. 1635–1636, 1337.
25. *Ibid.*, p. 1636.
26. *Ibid.*, pp. 1634, 1636.
27. *Ibid.*, p. 1768.
28. Garraty, pp. 225–227.
29. *Congressional Record* (61st Congress, 3rd Session): 1979, 1976–1977.
30. *Ibid.*, pp. 1976, 1978–1979.
31. *Ibid.*, p. 1979.
32. *Ibid.*, pp. 2178–2180.
33. *Ibid.*, p. 2243.
34. Elihu Root, *Addresses on Government and Citizenship,* collected and ed. by Robert Bacon and James Brown Scott (Cambridge: Harvard University Press, 1916), vol. 1, p. 93.
35. *Congressional Record* (61st congress, 3rd Session): 2243.
36. *Ibid.*
37. Root, p. 251.
38. *Congressional Record* (61st Congress, 3rd Session): 2243.
39. Ibid.
40. *Ibid.*, p. 1107.
41. *Ibid.*, p. 2243.
42. Root, p. 252.
43. *Congressional Record* (61st Congress, 3rd Session): 2243.
44. *Ibid.*, p. 2244.
45. *Ibid.*
46. Jessup, vol. 1, pp. 162, 134, 136, 174, 200.
47. *Ibid.*, pp. 215, 221–222, 240–241, 452.
48. Jonathan Elliot. *Debates In the Several State Conventions on the Adoption of the Federal Constitution as Recommended by the General Convention at Philadelphia in 1787 Together wyth the Journal of the Federal Convention . . .* (Philadelphia: J.B. Lippincott, 1836), vol. 4, p. 40.
49. Jessup, vol. 2, pp. 113–120, 125.
50. *Ibid.*, pp. 139–144.
51. *Congressional Record* (61st congress, 3rd Session): 2244.

52. *Ibid.*, p. 2243.
53. *Ibid.*
54. *Ibid.*, pp. 2251, 2257–2258.
55. *Ibid.*, pp. 2494–2495, 3553.
56. R. G. Cook, "Pioneer Portraits: Weldon Brinton Heyburn," *Idaho Days,* 10 (Spring 1966): 22.
57. *Congressional Record* (61st Congress, 3rd Session): 2774; (62nd Congress, 1st Session): 7112, 1540, 1543; (61st Congress, 3rd Session): 2769, 2772.
58. Cook, pp. 26, 22.
59. *Congressional Record* (62nd Congress, 1st Session): 1540–1541.
60. *Ibid.*, (61st Congress, 3rd Session): 2771; (62nd Congress, 1st Session): 1540, 1743.
61. *Ibid.*, (61st Congress, 3rd Session): 2952.
62. *Ibid.*, (62nd Congress, 1st Session): 1539, 1543; (61st Congress, 3rd Session): 2771.
63. *Ibid.*, pp. 2951, 2762.
64. *Ibid.*, pp. 2774, 2775.
65. *Ibid.*, pp. 3307, 3536, 3639.
66. Haynes, vol. 1, p. 112, 112n.
67. Larry J. Easterling, "Senator Bristow and the Seventeenth Amendment," *Kansas Historical Quarterly,* 41 (Winter 1975): 499; *Congressional Record* (62nd Congress, 1st Session): 1205.
68. *Ibid.*, p. 1485.
69. *Ibid.*, (61st Congress, 3rd Session): 2771; (62nd Congress, 1st Session): 1743.
70. *Ibid.*, p. 1923.
71. *Ibid.*, pp. 1923, 1924.
72. *Ibid.*, p. 1924.
73. *Ibid.*, p. 1923.
74. *Ibid.*, pp. 1883, 1881.
75. *Ibid.*, p. 1925.
76. *Ibid.*, (61st Congress, 3rd Session): 2242–2243.

Epilogue

Some Sober Second Thoughts

The fine theory of a republic insensibly vanished.
—Edward Gibbon

Although the resolution for the amendment passed the Senate, at last, on June 12, 1911, it was not the same version that had already been approved by the House. Thus, a deadlock ensued in which the two chambers wrangled for eleven months over whether the states or the Congress should have the regulatory power over the popular election of senators. Despite the narrow passage of the Bristow resolution, the Senate resisted the temptation to reverse itself for the sake of obtaining the amendment, and eventually wearied the House into submission on May 13, 1912. The resolution for the Seventeenth Amendment as it now reads in the Constitution was submitted to the states for ratification.[1]

Had the premise of reformers been correct, the state "machines" would never have endorsed a constitutional change which proposed to strip them of power, but few amendments have been more quickly ratified. In less than a year, it had received the necessary consent of three-fourths of the state legislatures. Fifteen states passed the proposal by unanimous vote in both houses. Seventeen others endorsed it with margins of more than nine to one. The only states formally to reject the resolution were Delaware and Utah, a strange oasis of constitutional conservatism in the great West. Vermont, with a 62 percent vote in favor, and Connecticut, with 66, were the only other states to show any signs of an opposition. When the Connecticut Senate ratified the resolution on April 8, 1913, the requisite number of states had been secured. A little over a month later, on May 31, William Jennings Bryan, as secretary of state, officially signed the Seventeenth Amendment into the fundamental laws of the United States.[2]

In the great enthusiasm for this advance of popular rule, no one seemed to notice that those same political bodies that had been charged with representing special interests had themselves engineered the change. Not surprisingly, there was no substantial overthrow of the "Bosses" when the first direct elections were held in 1914. Indeed, with the exception of two candidates defeated for renomination, all of the twenty-five senators running for reelection were returned to their seats.[3] One of the few machine politicians who bore any resemblance to the muckraking caricature, Boies Penrose of Pennsylvania, had voted against the Seventeenth Amendment at every turn, but his landslide victory apparently engendered a change of heart about the virtues of popular elections. "Give me the people every time," he is reported to have remarked.[4] Elihu Root, on the other hand, did not seek renomination when his term expired. Weldon Heyburn died in the autumn of 1912,[5] spared the sight of what he considered America's constitutional suicide, and it is questionable whether either of them would have had a chance in a mass election. The field now opened to the ambitions of a Huey Long or a Joseph McCarthy left little room for men who refused to flatter their sovereign constituents.

As has been consistently maintained, the Seventeenth Amendment offered more democracy to cure the evils of democracy. Hence, the changes it brought about have generally exacerbated the problems they were intended to solve. The most obvious example is the importance of money. Compared to the ten or so millionaires of the early 1900s, over half the Senate members are millionaires today.[6] An inflationary century might make this a relative comparison, but it does not change the fact that the Senate after direct elections is as much a rich man's club as it has ever been.

There is nothing intrinsically wrong with senators belonging to the wealthier classes. More disconcerting is how influential, if not indispensable, money has become to win an election. In the century since the Seventeenth Amendment went into effect, the cost of winning a Senate seat has risen to an average of more than $10 million nationwide.[7] An increasing proportion of campaign contributions comes from nationally organized interests outside the state a senator actually represents, the difficulties of uniting factions in a large republic having been apparently overcome by mass communications. Whereas such interests, in attempting to influence the Senate, had once presumably needed to buy a majority of the legislators in a majority of states, they now attempt their purchase more directly. It is the legislative "machine" all over again, but on a national level.

As was true when the state legislatures still elected senators, corporate donors prefer to give to incumbents, no matter what their ideological persuasion. Challengers often have to wait until after the primaries, or even until late in the campaigns, in short, until they look like a more certain bet for the money.[8] It is not too unusual to see two opposing candidates obtaining funds from the same contributor. In saying that the Senate is hostage to "special interests," however, it would be a mistake to think of it as the servant of the few exclusively. A great diversity of competing constituencies are represented in the lobby, and Congress must endeavor to please them all.[9]

Not that the institution has gained the popular trust since it became more "responsive" to popular demands. Opinion polls consistently reveal that the vast majority of Americans think members of Congress are "dishonest" and "favor special interests over the needs of the average citizen."[10] As one late-twentieth century liberal senator observed, Congress's popularity is at about "the level of a used car salesman."[11] Interestingly enough, the same majority thinks their own congressmen and senators are doing a fine job. The latter apparently represent "the people." Lawmakers from other constituencies are catering to special interests.

But the sad truth is that the average citizen is apt to know far less about the character and conduct of his senator than he did before direct elections. This is probably the single greatest irony of the whole direct democracy movement. It was predicated in large part on the ability of the modern media to inform the public, and yet the amount of voter attention to what their politicians have said and done has been inversely proportional to the immediacy with which it was possible to report it. A hundred years ago, entire speeches from Senate proceedings were quoted verbatim in the daily newspapers. Today, senators vie with each other for as few as five-second sound bites on the evening news. Some of them go to extreme lengths, however, to keep up appearances. Full-time staffs are retained for the sole purpose of keeping in touch with the Folks Back Home. A wide variety of form letters, generated by "constituent-minded computers," are available to any senator wanting to assure all inquirers that he is in complete agreement with them— whatever the issue. For good measure, Senate staffers are equipped with the latest office technology, such as automatic pens that add the boss's personal signature to the correspondence churned out in mass-mailing campaigns.[12]

During election season, when Senate candidates are turned loose to meet the public, voters are rarely brought any further out of the dark as to who is asking for their endorsement. The vast majority of campaign money is spent on advertising, increasingly on thirty- or even fifteen-second appeals on television. Large commissions are paid out to successful public relations firms, armed with the latest marketing data, to yield the highest emotional response to any issue. Media consultants rehearse with candidates to enhance the personality that comes across the airwaves.[13] It would seem that as much as ever, if not more so, Senate elections still hinge on decisions made in the smoke-filled room.

In sum, the Seventeenth Amendment has failed to drive the influence of money, special interests, and backstage manipulators from the election of United States senators. On the other hand, as intended, it succeeded in making the Senate more responsive, by definition less deliberative. Its role in restraining federal expenditures, for example, has gone the way of indirect elections. While it is true that electing senators by state legislatures was intended to protect the states from federal encroachments, it is conversely true that it was also designed to insulate senators against popular pressures to sacrifice the national interest to regional ones. In the decade before the direct election of US senators, monetary grants to states and localities amounted to less than 1 percent of all federal expenditures and provided less than 1 percent of all state and local revenues. A century afterwards, the federal government now supplies one out of three dollars in state and local revenues.[14]

This proportional shift reflects how far the balance of the original "partly federal, partly national" republic has tilted in the direction of mass democracy. To recall, observers as widely divergent in their political views as Elihu Root, James Bryce, and Herbert Croly understood the direct democracy movement of the Progressive Era to be a surrender of the representative authority and responsibility of state legislatures. The ability to represent the interests of a state had been difficult enough in the early republic, when elections were annual and legislators were expected not to deviate from constituent instructions. When they complied with popular wishes, the ensuing carnival of expenditures resulted in constitutional amendments restricting what legislatures were permitted to deliberate. Matters ably addressed by ordinary statute had to be written into state constitutions to keep them beyond the reach of the special interests that state legislatures were said to represent, while a history of tax revolts, particularly in states with some form of the plebiscite, reduced the means of raising revenues locally.[15]

Even though it was justified in part to redress pork-barrel spending in Washington, the Seventeenth Amendment did not abate the appetite of constituencies for government services. On the contrary, coming as it did less than two months after the Sixteenth Amendment, also known as the Income Tax Amendment, it provided popular access to a far larger pool of revenue than the states could ever have summoned individually. In other words, the democracy that undermined the representative capacity of state legislatures, that brought about direct legislation, the direct election of senators, and the all-but-direct election of presidents also brought the direct taxation on personal income by the federal government and thus, over time, the distribution of federal resources directly to the people. Accordingly, federal expenditures on constituents now go well beyond state and local budgets, subsidizing massive programs of direct entitlements.

This system of wealth redistribution has been in place for so long and is so ingrained in American political and economic life that to object to its constitutionality at this point is to lock the barn door after the proverbial horse has escaped. As a phenomenon of mass democracy, however, it is noteworthy that such extraordinary outlays are categorized as "mandatory," in contrast to the mere third of federal budgeting that Congress considers to be "discretionary." Confiscating all taxable corporate income, as well as the adjusted gross income of every taxpayer earning more than sixty-six thousand dollars a year, could not fund these programs without increasing the already astronomical public debt,[16] yet it is virtually impermissible for Congress to deliberate upon the costs. The concept of mandatory funding is, of course, a contrivance intended to portray these entitlements as the inviolable rights of the people, above the sordid reach of self-interested politicians. When economic reality ultimately trumps wishful thinking, it will prove as meaningless and revocable as debt ceilings and automatic sequestrations, the congressional contrivances for demonstrating fiscal accountability and resolve. In actuality, they are all examples of the longstanding American tradition of legislators exculpating themselves from having to deliberate the contingencies of legislation.

As Senator Root predicted, without strong representative institutions in the states, Congress would get weighed down by the minutiae of legislative and administrative burdens that should rather be borne locally. As it turned out, without statesmen in the national legislature willing to withstand constituent pressures—statesmen whom state legislatures no longer had responsibility for promoting—Congress would buckle under the tonnage of special interest legislation that members in both houses have had to vote upon, largely without reading. All that seems to matter is that constituents and sponsors are taken care of and that the party justifications sound grandiose enough for mass consumption.

The scale of politically driven redistribution being attempted in the United States does not bode well for basic accountability. While the United States has never been more democratic in its political participation, it has never been more plutocratic in its political rewards. The government that is reluctant to require even basic proof of citizenship as a qualification to vote is the same government that loans hundreds of billions of dollars on exceedingly generous terms to politically connected enterprises deemed too big to fail, regardless of their prior mismanagement or morally hazardous risk taking with other people's money. It is tempting to suggest that the minimal property qualifications of the past preserved a better distribution of wealth than has been accomplished through universal suffrage. At the very least it can be asserted that the mass democracy that doles out mobile phones and breast pumps to needy constituents is by no means inconsonant with the insider government that hands over monstrous bailouts and subsidies to crony capitalists.

By comparison, the Kingdom of Sweden, that imagined paragon of socialist democracy, only disburses government entitlements among a population smaller than that of North Carolina. With respect to that nation's notoriously heavy taxes on wages and salaries, the greater portion of such revenues are collected and distributed by municipalities and county governments, with only the wealthiest citizens paying the national income tax.[17] By contrast, the percentage of payroll taxes raised and disbursed by Washington is a marvel of imperial tribute. To put the Scandinavian kingdom under a comparable scheme would require Swedes to hand over at least a quarter of their paychecks directly to the European Union government in Brussels.

A 300 million–member nation state cannot be well governed without a recognition of the limits of political egalitarianism. Strong representative institutions capable of deliberating the national interest are by definition inegalitarian, to the extent that it is only the representatives who may participate in the making of the laws. Strong state and local governments are likewise inegalitarian, inasmuch as they place a ceiling on all but the few issues that merit consideration at the national level. But the passion for equality overwhelms these intermediaries and favors centralized decision making. With the demise of representative

176

hierarchy and the virtual surrender of the smaller platoons of government signified by this demise, Congress has had to resort to an executive bureaucracy to sort out the details of all its unread enactments. It is no wonder that after two hundred years of democratic advance, the president is popularly expected to be the giver of laws, the declarer of wars, and the overall arbiter of resources.

Henry Jones Ford observed that when the House of Representative was the only branch elected directly by the people, it was the engine of the federal republic, the initiator of legislation, the keeper of the purse, and the branch of government that enjoyed the popular trust above all others. That was before the presidency became a popular institution. In choosing George Washington, presidential electors had been unanimous, and appointing the chief executive was a dull but solemn affair. Alas, party faction over the presidency ensued ever after. By Andrew Jackson's time, the idea of electors having wills of their own had gone the way of indirect elections, and the House had lost its luster in the popular eye. The president, after all, was elected by a much larger constituency.[18]

This was the nascency of America's mass democracy. Effecting popular elections for the highest office in the land required permanent party machinery at the national level, machinery that would require funding and sources of funding that would expect political consideration in return. At the scale of the continental nation state, demagoguery is an intrinsically expensive proposition. Even local elections become tainted with party money in a regime so engrossed in the mass election of its highest officers that prospective congressmen and state legislators have to hire advertising strategists to get the attention of their community's electorate.[19]

Meanwhile, the president has become a global celebrity, traveling the world in opulent comfort, accompanied by a princely entourage and a Praetorian Guard. He is expected to make a speech of condolence or concern or apology after every misfortune and to have a plan for the relief of every aggrieved constituency. It could be argued that the job of being hero of the people impinges on his ability to execute the laws, exercise discretion in treating with foreign powers, and command the respect of the armed forces, but as the one officeholder elected by all the people in the land, he carries the burden of delivering all that politics is expected to deliver, which is almost everything. Accordingly, he enforces only the laws he agrees with, makes his own proclamations where there is no law, and regularly commits impeachable offenses, with rarely an objection from those constitutionally empowered to stop him, at least not from those in his party.

The egalitarian finds gratification in everyone having an equal vote in the appointment of "the most powerful person in the world." It concerns him little that the individual voter has statistically zero influence over the outcome of mass decisions, and even less that this enormous power in which he imagines himself to be participating was born out of the corruption of the representative hierarchy, without which checks and balances are doomed and federalism is a dead letter. The story of this corruption begins at the very founding of the republic, in the heady days when the colonies declared their independence from an abusive monarchy only to engage in the abuses of democracy when exercising their power as sovereign states. The Constitution created a stronger union while attempting also to restore the classical balance of the one and the few against the many, using separate, indirect systems of election to promote the president and Senate. But the rationale for indirect elections and for the classical balance of power they were intended to sustain was no match for the Enlightenment era notion of citizens obeying no one but themselves, a notion which was ultimately at odds with representative government.

If the collapse of the College of Electors in the 1820s represented the first wave of mass democracy to strike against the edifice of original intent, then 1913 was the year in which the waters finally rose above the federal level, having steadily submerged the system of representative checks and balances for more than a century in the states. The states were supposed to be the fail-safe dikes against the national democracy, but given their own democratic proclivities, they could not indefinitely uphold the original mode of federal elections against the egalitarian tide. Structurally weakened, the state legislatures finally gave in with the direct election of United States senators. While the amendment did not dissolve every constraint on popular sovereignty, it certainly helped to set in motion a government over hundreds of million of souls that could be "managed merely by decrees." What repercussions those decrees would have upon the national interest and the preservation of liberty the few remaining constitutionalists of 1913 were hardly equipped to forecast, but to their reasoning the jubilation over the Seventeenth Amendment was proof enough that the American polity was already out of kilter.

And to this sobering reflection was cruelly added the next Progressive amendment, which constitutionally denied them the solace of drink.

Notes

1. *Congressional Record* (62nd Congress, 2nd Session): 3366–3367.
2. *Senate Document 240* (71st Congress, 3rd Session):12; *Guide to U.S. Elections* (Washington, D.C.: Congressional Quarterly, Inc., 1975), p. 450.
3. *Ibid.*, p. 451.
4. Leona and Robert Rienow, *Of Snuff, Sin and The Senate* (Chicago: Follette Publishing Company, 1965), p. 304.
5. *Biographical Directory of the American Congress, 1774–1989* (Washington, D.C., Government Printing Office, 1989), pp. 1741, 1181.
6. Eric Lipton, "Half of Congress Members Are Millionaires, Report Says." *New York Times* (January 10, 2014): A13, http://goo.gl/FJrALV.
7. Paul Steinhauser and Robert Yoon, "Cost to Win Congressional Election Skyrockets." CNN, July 11, 2013, http://goo.gl/YmUhcV.
8. "Give Early, Give Often." *The Economist* 298 (March 1, 1986): 26; Frederick H. Katayama, "Pragmatic PACs Prefer Incumbents." *Fortune*, 118 (November 7, 1988): 12; Ed Garvey, "It's Money That Matters." *The Progressive* 53 (March 1989): 18.
9. Robert J. Samuelson, "The Campaign Reform Fraud." *Newsweek*, 110 (July 13, 1987): 43.
10. "Majority in Poll Criticizes Congress." *Washington Post*, May 26, 1989, p. A8.
11. *Congressional Record* (101st Congress, 2nd Session): S11468.
12. James A. Miller, *Running in Place: Inside the Senate* (New York: Simon & Schuster, 1986), pp. 110–111, 178–179.
13. Paula Dwyer and Douglas Harbrecht. "Congress: It Doesn't Work. Let's Fix It." *Business Week* 16 (1990): 57; Garvey, p. 17.
14. Tom Miller, "Return of the Pork Barrel Congress." *Wall Street Journal* (September 11, 1987), p.26; George E. Hale and Marion Lief Palley, *The Politics of Federal Grants* (Washington, DC: Quarterly Press, 1981), pp. 8, 12–13; Vivien Brownstein, "Why State Budgets are a Mess." *Fortune* 123 (June 3, 1991): 21; "Federal Grants as Share of States' Budgets Decline After Hitting Historic High." The Pew Charitable Trusts, March 7, 2014, http://goo.gl/aZ3i6a.
15. Larry Reynolds, "Fed to States: Do More with Less." *Management Review.* 81 (August 1992): 20.
16. Chris Cox and Bill Archer, "Why $16 Trillion Only Hints at the True U.S. Debt," *The Wall Street Journal*, November 28, 2012, http://goo.gl/Pp2FIw.
17. *Taxes in Sweden: An English Summary of Tax Statistical Yearbook of Sweden.* S.l.: Swedish Tax Agency, 2012, p. 46.
18. Henry Jones Ford, *The Rise and Growth of American Politics: A Sketch of Constitutional Development* (New York: Macmillan Company, 1898), 188–196.
19. C. H. Hoebeke, "The Futility of Campaign Finance Reform," *The World & I* 12 (August 1997): 316–329.

Bibliography

Adams, John. *The Works of John Adams*. Edited by Charles Francis, Adams. Boston: Little, Brown, 1850–1856.

Alexander, De Alva S. *History and Procedure of the House of Representatives*. Boston: Houghton Mifflin, 1916.

"The All Powerful Senate." *The Nation* 72 (January 3, 1901): 4–5.

Allen, Phillip L. "Toward a Pure Democracy." *Outlook* 84 (September 15, 1906): 120–125.

"Amending the Constitution." *The Nation* 92 (January 19, 1911): 52.

Ames, H. V. *The Proposed Amendments to the Constitution during the First Century of Its History*. 2nd ed. New York: Burt Franklin, 1970.

Aristotle. *Politics*. Translated by Ernest Barker. New York: Oxford University Press, 1958.

"Arrogance in the Senate." *Outlook* 73 (February 7, 1903): 270–271.

Babbitt, Irving. *Democracy and Leadership*. Boston: Houghton Mifflin, 1924.

Baker, Lewis. *The Percys of Mississippi: Politics and Literature in the New South*. Baton Rouge: Louisiana State University Press, 1983.

Barnes, Fred. "The Snit Brothers." *The New Republic* 195 (November 10, 1986): 13–15.

Baxter, Sylvester. "The Representative Inequality of Senators." *North American Review* 177 (December 1903): 877–898.

Beard, Charles A. *An Economic Interpretation of the Constitution of the United States*. 2nd ed. New York: Macmillan Company, 1935.

Becker, Jo, and Scott Shane. "Secret 'Kill List' Proves a Test of Obama's Principles and Will." *The New York Times*. May 29, 2012, http://goo.gl/dlBzbb.

Biographical Directory of the United States Congress, 1774–1989. Washington, DC: United States Government Printing Office, 1989.

Bouldin, Powhatan. *Home Reminiscences of John Randolph of Roanoke*. Danville, VA: Clemmett & Jones Printers, 1876.

Bowers, Claude G. *Beveridge and the Progressive Era*. New York: Literary Guild, 1932.

Braeman, John. "The Rise of Albert J. Beveridge to the United States Senate." *Indiana Magazine of History* 53 (December 1957): 355–382.

Brown, Kenny L. "A Progressive from Oklahoma, Senator Robert Latham Owen, Jr." *Chronicles of Oklahoma* 62 (Fall 1984): 232–265.

Brownstein, Vivian. "Why State Budgets Are a Mess." *Fortune* 123 (June 3, 1991): 21–24.

Bryan, William Jennings. "The People's Law: Address Delivered at Columbus, Ohio, March 12, 1912, Upon Invitation of the Constitutional Convention." *Senate Document 523*. 63rd Congress. 3rd Session, 1912.

Bryce, James. *The American Commonwealth*. 3rd ed. New York: Macmillan Company, 1914.

Burdette, Franklin L. *Filibustering in the Senate*. Princeton: Princeton University Press, 1940.

Burke, E. *Reflections on the Revolution in France: And on the Proceedings in Certain Societies in London Relative to That Event. In a Letter Intended to Have Been Sent to a Gentleman in Paris*. 8th ed. London: J. Dodsley, 1791.

Butler, Nicholas Murray. "Why Should We Change Our Form of Government?" *Senate Document* 238. 62nd Congress, 2nd Session, 1912.

Butler, Smedley D. *War Is a Racket: The Antiwar Classic by America's Most Decorated Soldier*. Skyhorse Publishing Company, 2013.

Calhoun, John C. *A Disquisition on Government*. Edited by Richard K. Crallé. New York: Peter Smith, 1943.

Carey, George. "The Separation of Powers." *Founding Principles of American Government: Two Hundred Years of Democracy on Trial*, edited by George J. Graham and Scarlett G. Graham. Bloomington, IN: Indiana University Press, 1977.

Carter, Thomas. "New and Dangerous Proposition." *Independent* 70 (February 9, 1911): 291–294.

Chandler, William E. "Election of Senators by Popular Vote." *Independent* 52 (May 31, 1900): 1292–1294.

Childs, Richard S. "The Short Ballot." *American State Government*, edited by Paul S. Reinsch. New York: Ginn & Co., 1911.

Chinard, Gilbert. "Polybius and the American Constitution." *Journal of the History of Ideas* 1, no. 1 (1940): 38–58.

Congressional Quarterly Almanac. Vol. 46. Washington, DC: Congressional Quarterly, 1990.

Congressional Quarterly Weekly Report 48 (May 26, 1990): 1624–1625.

Cook, R. G. "Pioneer Portraits: Weldon Brinton Heyburn." *Idaho Days* 10 (Spring 1966): 22–26.

Cooper, James Fenimore. *The American Democrat, or Hints on the Social and Civic Relations of the United States of America*. New York: Alfred A. Knopf, 1931.

Crawford, Coe I. "Direct Election of Senators." *Independent* 70 (June 22, 1911): 1367–1368.

Creel, George. "Carnival of Corruption in Mississippi." *Cosmopolitan* 51 (November 1911): 725–735.

Croly, Herbert D. *The Promise of American Life*. Indianapolis: Bobbs-Merrill, 1965.

Dealey, James Quayle. *Growth of American State Constitutions, from 1776 to the End of the Year 1914*. New York: Ginn & Co., 1915.

"The Democratic Blunder in New York." *Independent* 70 (July 9, 1911): 527–529.

"The Des Moines Conference." *Outlook* 84 (December 15, 1906): 902.

"Direct Election." *Independent* 64 (August 23, 1906): 643–644.

"Direct Election of Senators." *Independent* 56 (June 4, 1903): 1311–1312.

"Direct Election of Senators." *Outlook* 98 (June 24, 1911): 370.

"Direct Primaries in New Jersey." *Outlook* 85 (January 19, 1906): 101.

Dishman, Robert B. *State Constitutions: The Shape of the Document.* New York: National Municipal League, 1960.

Dodd, Walter F. *State Government.* New York: The Century Company, 1922.

Dostoyevsky, Fyodor. *The Brothers Karamazov.* Translated by Constance Garnett. Edited by Max Bollinger. London: World Classics, 2012.

Dwyer, Paula, and Douglas Harbrecht. "Congress: It Doesn't Work. Let's Fix It." *Business Week* 16 (1990): 57.

Easterling, Larry J. "Senator Bristow and the Seventeenth Amendment." *Kansas Historical Quarterly* 41 (Winter 1975): 488–511.

Eaton, Allen H. *The Oregon System: The Story of Direct Legislation in Oregon: A Presentation of the Methods and Results of the Initiative and Referendum and Recall in Oregon, with Studies of the Measures Accepted or Rejected, and Special Chapters on the Direct Primary, Popular Election of Senators, Advantages, Defects and Dangers of the System.* Chicago: A.C. McClurg & Co., 1912.

Eaton, Clement, ed. *The Leaven of Democracy: The Growth of the Democratic Spirit in the Time of Jackson.* Newark: George Braziller, 1963.

Edmunds, G. F. "Shall the People Elect Senators?" *Forum* 18 (November 1894): 270–278.

"Election of Senators by Popular Vote." *Independent* 54 (July 10, 1902): 1672–1674.

Elliot, Jonathan. *The Debates in the Several State Conventions on the Adoption of the Federal Constitution: As Recommended by the General Convention at Philadelphia, in 1787: Together with the Journal of the Federal Convention, Luther Martin's Letter, Yate's Minutes, Congressional Opinions, Virginia and Kentucky Resolutions of '98–'99, and Other Illustrations of the Constitution.* Philadelphia: J.B. Lippincott, 1836.

"The End of the Lorimer Case." *Outlook* 97 (March 11, 1911): 521–522.

"Everlasting Negro." *Independent* 70 (February 23, 1911): 417–418.

Farnam, Henry W. *Chapters in the History of Social Legislation in the United States to 1860.* Washington, DC: Carnegie Institution of Washington, 1938.

Farrand, Max, ed. *The Records of the Federal Convention of 1787.* New Haven: Yale University Press, 1966.

"Federal Spending: Where Does the Money Go?" *National Priorities Project.* Accessed December 9, 2013. http://goo.gl/76iPL1.

Flock, Elizabeth. "Education Department Agents Raids California Home." *Washington Post.* June 13, 2011, http://goo.gl/4xe1tf.

Ford, Henry Jones. *The Rise and Growth of American Politics: A Sketch of Constitutional Development.* New York: Macmillan, 1889.

Foulke, William Dudley. *Fighting the Spoilsmen: Reminiscences of the Civil Service Reform Movement.* New York: Knickerbocker Press, 1919.

Fox, Charles J. "Popular Election of United States Senators." *Arena* 27 (May 1902): 456–457.

Franklin, Benjamin. *The Papers of Benjamin Franklin.* Edited by William B. Willcox, et. al. New Haven: Yale University Press, 1959.

Garraty, John A. *The American Nation: A History of the United States.* 5th ed. New York: Harper & Row, 1983.

———. *Henry Cabot Lodge: A Biography.* New York: Alfred A. Knopf, 1953.

Garvey, Ed. "It's Money That Matters." *The Progressive* 53 (March 1989): 17–21.

"Give Early, Give Often." *The Economist* 298 (March 1, 1986): 26.

Globalising Torture: CIA Secret Detention and Extraordinary Rendition. Open Society Justice Initiative (February 2013), http://goo.gl/CtjrHn.

Goodrich, Carter. *Government Promotion of American Canals and Railroads. 1800–1890.* Westport, CT: Greenwood Press, 1960.

Greenwald, Glenn. "Three Myths about the Detention Bill." *Salon* (December 16, 2011):, http://goo.gl/Ttv2mj.

Guide to US Elections. Washington, DC: Congressional Quarterly, 1975.

Gwyn, W.B. *The Meaning of the Separation of Powers: An Analysis of the Doctrine from Its Origin to the Adoption of the United States Constitution.* New Orleans: Tulane University Press, 1965.

Hale, George E., and Marian Lief Palley. *The Politics of Federal Grants.* Washington, DC: Congressional Quarterly Press, 1981.

Hamilton, Alexander, James Madison, and John Jay. *The Federalist.* New York: Modern Library, 1937.

Harris, Fred R. *Deadlock or Decision: The U.S. Senate and the Rise of National Politics.* New York: Oxford University Press, 1993.

Harris, William A. "The Election of Senators by the People." *Independent* 52 (May 31, 1900): 1291–1292.

Haynes, George H. *The Senate of the United States: Its History and Practice.* Boston: Houghton Mifflin Company, 1938.

Hicks, John D., George E. Mowry, and Robert E. Burke. *The Federal Union: A History of the United States to 1877.* 5th ed. Boston: Houghton Mifflin, 1970.

Hoar, George F. *Autobiography of Seventy Years.* New York: Charles Scribner's Sons, 1903.

———. "Has the Senate Degenerated?" *Forum* 23 (April 1898): 144.

Hoebeke, C.H. "The Futility of Campaign Finance Reform," *The World & I* 12 (August 1997): 316–329.

Hofstadter, Richard. *The American Political Tradition and the Men Who Made It.* New York: Vintage Books, 1974.

Hoogenboom, Ari. "The Spoils System." *The Gilded Age: A Reappraisal,* edited by H. Wayne Morgan. Syracuse, NY: Syracuse University Press, 1963.

"How We Elect Senators." *Outlook* 97 (February 25, 1911): 389–392.

Howard, John R. "Shall the People Elect Senators." *Outlook* 97 (March 4, 1911): 518.

"Initiative and Referendum Measures, 1902–1953." In *Oregon Blue Book.* Salem, OR: Secretary of State's Office, 1954.

"Internet Voting Systems Too Insecure, Researcher Warns." *Computerworld.* (March 1, 2012) http://goo.gl/QZClsJ.

Jefferson, Thomas. *Notes on the State of Virginia.* Edited by William Peden. Chapel Hill: University of North Carolina Press, 1955.

——. *The Papers of Thomas Jefferson*. Edited by Julian P. Boyd, et. al. Princeton: Princeton University Press, 1950.

Jessup, Philip C. *Elihu Root*. New York: Dodd, Mead & Company, 1938.

Kales, Albert M. *Unpopular Government in the United States*. Chicago: University of Chicago Press, 1914.

Katayama, Frederick H. "Pragmatic PACS Prefer Incumbents." *Fortune* 18 (November 7, 1988): 12.

Kelly, Alfred H., and Winfred A. Harbison. *The American Constitution; Its Origins and Development*. 4th ed. New York: W.W. Norton, 1969.

Kolko, Gabriel. *The Triumph of Conservatism: A Reinterpretation of American History, 1900–1916*. London: Free Press of Glencoe, 1963.

"Legislatures Deadlocked and Disgraced." *Outlook* 73 (January 31, 1903): 234–235.

Lippmann, Walter. *Public Opinion*. New York: Free Press, 1965.

Lobingier, Charles S. "Popular Election of Senators." *The Nation* 80 (June 1, 1905): 435.

Low, Maurice A. "The Oligarchy of the Senate." *The North American Review* 174 (February 1902): 231–244.

Madison, James. *The Debates in the Federal Convention of 1787: Which Framed the Constitution of the United States of America*. Edited by Gaillard Hunt and James Brown Scott. Buffalo, NY: Prometheus Books, 1987.

——. *The Papers of James Madison*. Edited by Robert Rutland, et al. Chicago: University of Chicago Press, 1962.

——. *The Writings of James Madison, Comprising His Public Papers and His Private Correspondence, including Numerous Letters and Documents Now for the First Time Printed*. Edited by Gaillard Hunt. New York: G.P. Putnam's Sons, 1900.

Main, Jackson Turner. *The Upper House in Revolutionary America, 1763–1788*. Madison: University of Wisconsin Press, 1967.

"Majority in Poll Criticizes Congress." *The Washington Post*, May 26, 1989, p. A9.

Martineau, Harriet. *Retrospect of Western Travel*. New York: Greenwood Press, 1969.

Maxwell, Robert S. "La Follette and the Progressive Machine in Wisconsin." *Indiana Magazine of History* 48 (March 1952): 55–70.

McCormick, Richard P. *The Second American Party System: Party Formation in the Jacksonian Era*. Chapel Hill: University of North Carolina Press, 1966.

McDonald, Forrest. *Novus Ordo Seclorum: The Intellectual Origins of the Constitution*. Lawrence, KS.: University Press of Kansas, 1985.

McGreal, Chris. "Military given Go-ahead to Detain US Terrorist Suspects without Trial." *The Guardian* (December 16, 2011): http://goo.gl/LFUOE9.

Meredith, Ellis. "The Senatorial Election in Colorado." *Arena* 38 (October 1907): 353–360.

Merriam, C. Edward. *Primary Elections: A Study of the History and Tendencies of Primary Election Legislation*. Chicago: University of Chicago Press, 1908.

Miller, James A. *Running in Place: Inside the Senate*. New York: Simon and Schuster, 1986.

Miller, Tom. "Return of the Pork Barrel Congress." *Wall Street Journal,* September 11, 1987.

Mitchell, John H. "Election of Senators by Popular Vote." *Forum* 21 (June 1896): 385–397.

"Money and Senatorship." *The Nation* 70 (April 1900): 295.

Montesquieu, Baron De (Charles De Secondat). *The Spirit of The Laws.* Translated by Thomas Nugent. Edited by Robert M. Hutchins. Great Books of the Western World, Vol. 38. Chicago: Encyclopedia Britannica, 1952.

Moody, William H. "Constitutional Powers of the Senate." *The North American Review* 174 (March 1902): 386–394.

Morgan, H. Wayne. *America's Road to Empire: The War with Spain and Overseas Expansion.* New York: John Wiley & Sons, 1965.

———. *From Hayes to McKinley: National Party Politics, 1877–1896.* Syracuse, NY: Syracuse University Press, 1969.

Nelson, Henry Loomis. "Overshadowing Senate." *Century* 65 (February 1903): 505.

O'Callahan, Jerry A. "Senator Mitchell and the Oregon Land Frauds, 1905." *Pacific Historical Review* 21 (August, 1952): 255–261.

O'Neal, Emmet. "Election of United States Senators by the People." *The North American Review* 188 (November 1908): 700–715.

Paine, R. T. "Popular Election of Senators." *Outlook* 79 (April 8, 1905): 911.

Paine, Thomas. *Common Sense.* New York: Penguin, 1968.

A Pamphlet Containing a Copy of All Measures "Referred to the People by the Legislative Assembly," "Referendum Ordered by Petition of the People," and "Proposed by Initiative Petition," to Be Submitted to the Legal Voters of the State of Oregon at the Regular General Election to Be Held the First Day of June, 1908, Together with the Arguments Filed, Favoring and Opposing Certain Said Measures. Salem, OR: Willis S. Duniway, State Printer, 1908.

Peffer, William A. "The United States Senate, Its Privileges, Powers and Functions, Its Rules and Methods of Doing Business." *The North American Review* 167 (July 1898): 48–63; (August 1898): 176–190.

Peters, Ronald M. "The Written Constitution." *Founding Principles of American Government: Two Hundred Years of Democracy on Trial,* edited by George J. Graham and Scarlett G. Graham. Bloomington, IN: Indiana University Press, 1977.

Peterson, Merrill D. *The Great Triumvirate: Webster, Clay, and Calhoun.* New York: Oxford University Press, 1987.

Phillips, David Graham. *The Treason of the Senate.* Chicago: Quadrangle Books, 1964.

Polybius. *The Rise of the Roman Empire.* Translated by Ian Scott-Kilvert. *The Histories.* New York: Penguin Books, 1986.

"Popular Election of Senators." *Outlook* 97 (March 11, 1911): 521–522.

Porter, Kirk H., and Donald B. Johnson, comps. *National Party Platforms, 1840–1972.* 5th ed. Urbana: University of Illinois Press, 1975.

"Power of the Senate." *The Nation* 76 (February 5, 1903): 104–105.

"The President and the Bosses." *The Nation* 82 (January 18, 1906): 46–47.

Proceedings and Debates of the Convention of Louisiana which Assembled at the City of New Orleans January 14, 1844. New Orleans: Besancon, Ferguson & Co., 1845.

Proceedings and Debates of the Virginia State Convention of 1829–1830: To Which Are Subjoined, the New Constitution of Virginia, and the Votes of the People. Richmond: Printed by Samuel Shepherd & Co., for Ritchie & Cook, 1830.

"Proven Failure." *Outlook* 86 (May 4, 1907): 17–19.

Ratner, Sidney. *The Tariff in American History*. New York: D. Van Nostrand Co., 1972.

Reports of the Proceedings and Debates of the New York Constitutional Convention 1821: Assembled for the Purpose of Amending the Constitution of the State of New-York: Containing All the Official Documents, Relating to the Subject, and Other Valuable Matter. Edited by Carter, N. H., W. L. Stone, and M. T. C. Gould. Albany: Hosford, 1821.

Reynolds, Larry. "Fed to States: Do More with Less." *Management Review*. 81, no. 8 (August 1992): 20–21.

"Rich Men in the Senate." *The Nation* 50 (January 16, 1890): 44.

Rienow, Robert, and Leona Train Rienow. *Of Snuff, Sin, and the Senate*. Chicago: Follett Publishing Co., 1965.

Riker, William H. *The Development of American Federalism*. Boston: Kluwer Academic Publishers, 1987.

Rothman, David J. *Politics and Power; the United States Senate, 1869–1901*. Cambridge, MA: Harvard University Press, 1966.

Rousseau, Jean Jacques. *Discourse on the Origins and Foundations of Inequality among Men*. Translated by Maurice Cranston. New York: Penguin Books, 1984.

———. *The Social Contract*. Translated by Maurice Cranston. New York: Penguin Books, 1968.

Ryn, Claes G. *America the Virtuous: The Crisis of Democracy and the Quest for Empire*. New Brunswick: Transaction Publishers, 2003.

Salvian, the Presbyter. *The Writings of Salvian, the Presbyter*. Translated by Jeremiah F. O'Sullivan. Fathers of the Church Vol. 3. Washington, DC: Catholic University of America Press, 2008.

Samuelson, Robert J. "The Campaign Reform Fraud." *Newsweek* 110 (July 13, 1987): 43.

Sandburg, Carl. *Abraham Lincoln: The Prairie Years*. New York: Harcourt, Brace & World, 1926.

Schaffner, Margaret A. "The Initiative, the Referendum, and the Recall." *American Political Science Review* 2 (November 1907): 32–42.

Scheer, Robert. "Indefensible Spending." Latimes.com. June 1, 2008. http://goo.gl/VzqAl6.

Schlup, Leonard. "Republican Insurgent: Jonathan Bourne and the Politics of Progressivism, 1908–1912." *Oregon Historical Quarterly* 87 (Fall 1986): 229–244.

"The Senate's Roll Call of Dishonor." *The Nation* 81 (December 7, 1905): 456.

"Senator Lorimer." *Independent* 70 (March 9, 1911): 525–526.

"The Senatorial Primary." *The Nation* 80 (March 2, 1905): 166–167.

Simpson, John A. "Weldon Heyburn and the Image of the Bloody Shirt." *Idaho Yesterdays* 24 (Winter 1981): 20–28.

Sowell, Thomas. *A Conflict of Visions: Ideological Origins of Political Struggle.* New York: Quill Publishers, 1987.

Tarr, Joel A. *A Study in Boss Politics: William Lorimer of Chicago.* Urbana: University of Illinois Press, 1971.

Taussig, F. W. *The Tariff History of the United States.* 8th ed. New York: G. P. Putnam's Sons, 1931.

Taxes in Sweden: An English Summary of Tax Statistical Yearbook of Sweden. S.l.: Swedish Tax Agency, 2012, http://goo.gl/noJy2b.

Taylor, George Rogers. *The Transportation Revolution, 1815–1860.* New York: Holt, Rinehart and Winston, 1951.

Thatcher, George A. "Significance of the Oregon Experiment." *Outlook* 83 (July 14, 1906): 612–613.

Thomas, Dana Lee. *The Story of American Statehood.* New York: Wilfred Funk, Inc., 1961.

Thorpe, Francis Newton, ed. *The Federal and State Constitutions, Colonial Charters, and Other Organic Laws of the States, Territories, and Colonies Now or Heretofore Forming the United States of America.* Washington, DC: Government Printing Office, 1909.

Tocqueville, Alexis De. *Democracy in America.* Translated and edited by Henry Reeve. New York: Vintage Books, 1945.

Tuller, Walter K. "A Convention to Amend the Constitution — Why Needed, How It May Be Obtained." *The North American Review* 193 (March 1911): 369–387.

Turner, Frederick Jackson. *The Frontier in American History.* New York: Henry Holt and Co., 1920.

Unger, Irwin. *These United States: The Questions of Our past.* 2nd ed. Boston: Little, Brown, 1982.

US Congress. *Congressional Globe.*

———. S. Rep. 22, 19th Congress, 1st Session, 1826.

US Congress. *Congressional Record.*

———. H.R. 368. 52nd Congress, 1st Session, 1892.

———. S.R. 942. 61st Congress, 2nd Session, 1911.

———. S.R. 147. 63rd Congress, 2nd Session, 1914.

———. S Doc. 240, 61st Congress, 3rd Session, 1931.

———. H.R. 3076, 107th Congress, 1st Session, 2001, http://goo.gl/NbNhI4.

Vile, M. J. C. *Constitutionalism and the Separation of Powers.* Oxford, UK: Clarendon Press, 1967.

Washington, George. *The Writings of George Washington.* Edited by Worthington Chauncey Ford. New York: Putnam's Sons, 1891.

West, Henry L. "The Place of the Senate in Our Government." *Forum* 31 (June 1901): 430.

White, William Allen. *The Old Order Changeth: A View of American Democracy.* New York: Macmillan Company, 1910.

Witte, John F. *The Politics and Development of the Federal Income Tax.* Madison: University of Wisconsin Press, 1985.

Wood, Gordon S. *The Creation of the American Republic 1776–1787.* New York: W.W. Norton & Co., 1969.

Zywicki, Todd J. Review of *The Road to Mass Democracy. The Independent Review: A Journal of Political Economy* 1 (Winter 1997): http://goo.gl/FTEJSN.

Index